Living Logos

Living Logos

The Fiction of Michael D. O'Brien

⥥

GREG MAILLET

☙PICKWICK *Publications* · Eugene, Oregon

LIVING LOGOS
The Fiction of Michael D. O'Brien

Copyright © 2025 Greg Maillet. All rights reserved. Except for brief quotations in critical publications or reviews, no part of this book may be reproduced in any manner without prior written permission from the publisher. Write: Permissions, Wipf and Stock Publishers, 199 W. 8th Ave., Suite 3, Eugene, OR 97401.

Pickwick Publications
An Imprint of Wipf and Stock Publishers
199 W. 8th Ave., Suite 3
Eugene, OR 97401

www.wipfandstock.com

PAPERBACK ISBN: 979-8-3852-3708-1
HARDCOVER ISBN: 979-8-3852-3709-8
EBOOK ISBN: 979-8-3852-3710-4

Cataloguing-in-Publication data:

Names: Maillet, Greg [author].

Title: Living logos : the fiction of Michael D. O'Brien / Greg Maillet.

Description: Eugene, OR: Pickwick Publications, 2025 | Includes bibliographical references.

Identifiers: ISBN 979-8-3852-3708-1 (paperback) | ISBN 979-8-3852-3709-8 (hardcover) | ISBN 979-8-3852-3710-4 (ebook)

Subjects: LCSH: O'Brien, Michael D. (Michael David), 1948– | Catholic Church—In literature. | Catholic fiction—History and criticism. | Catholics in literature. | Canadian fiction—Catholic authors—History and criticism. | Christian fiction—History and criticism. | Fiction—Religious aspects—Christianity. | Spiritual life in literature. | Christianity and literature.

Classification: PS153.C3 M355 2025 (print) | PS153.C3 (ebook)

The author gratefully acknowledges permission from Michael D. O'Brien to reprint O'Brien's visual art and from Ignatius Press to reprint excerpts from O'Brien's novels. Italics in O'Brien quotations have been preserved from the originals.

Scripture quotations have been retranslated by the author with reference to the King James or Authorized Version.

For Sheila O'Brien

Contents

Introduction: "O Lord Most High": *By the Rivers of Babylon* 1

"The Victory of Christ": *Father Elijah* 13

"Places of True Home": *Strangers and Sojourners* 39

"Father at Night": *Plague Journal* 61

"Seeing the Form": *Eclipse of the Sun* 81

"Words-without-Words": *A Cry of Stone* 107

"Love?" *Sophia House* 139

"God Is Master of Time": *Elijah in Jerusalem* 171

Conclusion: "To Shift the Balance of the World": *Letter to the Future* 191

Bibliography 207

"The Guardian" from *By the Rivers of Babylon*

INTRODUCTION

"O Lord Most High": *By the Rivers of Babylon*

> What service can I offer you, O Lord Most High, I who am so poor in holiness, who can offer no sacrifice, who have so little learning, who am a ragged remnant of your Temple here in this desolation!
> —Ezekiel, in O'Brien, *By the Rivers of Babylon*, 391

ALTHOUGH THE FICTION OF Michael O'Brien has now been translated into twelve different languages, and is clearly a major inspiration for the "Catholic literary renaissance" that critics such as Joseph Pearce have found in twenty-first-century American literature,[1] O'Brien's art remains very much on the margins of contemporary culture. Yet literary critic David Lyle Jeffrey praises O'Brien's "penetrating spiritual insight,"[2] while philosopher Peter Kreeft has deemed O'Brien "the greatest living Catholic novelist."[3] In an important sense, however, positive or negative comments from human critics of his work are irrelevant for, as Tolkien learned from Hopkins, "the only just literary critic is Christ."[4] Or, as O'Brien puts it in *Letter to the Future*, his most recent novel, "the truth must be spoken, even if no one listens, no one hears."[5]

It is, in fact, an important part of the faithfulness of O'Brien's art that he is well outside the mainstream of contemporary culture. In the words of the character just quoted, "our civilization was slowly mutating into anti-civilization," but, "when you're *inside* the belly of the beast you

---

1. Pearce, "New Catholic Literary Revival?"
2. David Lyle Jeffrey, back cover endorsement of O'Brien, *Eclipse of the Sun*.
3. Peter Kreeft, back cover endorsement of Cavallin, *On the Edge of Infinity*.
4. Tolkien, *Letters*, 183, letter 113.
5. O'Brien, *Letter to the Future*, 275.

can't see where you are. You have to be spit *outside* the beast in order to recognize it."[6] Defenders of our literary establishment could cite the critical appreciation of a twentieth-century Catholic novelist such as Graham Greene, but such a case could also contribute to my argument; Greene's aesthetic achievements, such as *The End of the Affair*, are often celebrated due to their unorthodoxy, influenced in no small part by Greene's own heresies later in life. For many literary critics today, the only good Catholic is a bad Catholic, and to be a good writer of any stripe is to rebel against traditions that Catholicism, par excellence, evidently embodies.

Such a rebel O'Brien certainly is not, and so the very orthodoxy of his work has prevented thorough attention to his aesthetic. This is a loss not only for Catholic or Christian culture, but for literary studies in general. O'Brien is among the most prolific and original writers of our time, and any humane reader will be rewarded by reading O'Brien's work. For those interested in understanding Catholicism today, O'Brien's novels are essential reading. Of course, it must be admitted that part of the reason that O'Brien's novels have not been more widely read is their length, especially by today's standards. One cannot avoid the fact that to read O'Brien's work, let alone comprehend it, one must find time for reading, preferably in a silence also attentive to the Holy Spirit.

What kind of literary criticism is appropriate to O'Brien's work?

Because there is now a quality biography of O'Brien,[7] and biographical hints are so easy to see in the work of a relatively unknown yet still living author, biographical criticism is an obvious approach. O'Brien was a working journalist, and has published a number of insightful books of nonfiction. My text here normally eschews reference to such texts, or to the personal information that I have been fortunate to acquire through brief acquaintance with O'Brien himself, for the following reason. Whereas biographical criticism attempts to confirm the meaning and significance of art through the authority of the author himself, I am interested in the significance of O'Brien's work on a much broader, more universal level. Rather than the topical and historical insight that might be gleaned from O'Brien's work—and harvesters in that field will bring

---

6. O'Brien, *Letter to the Future*, 274.
7. Cavallin, *On the Edge of Infinity*.

forth good fruit—I aim rather to explore the potentially universal significance of O'Brien's work.

Rather than biographical criticism, my work follows the approach pioneered by Catholic theologian Hans Urs von Balthasar, an approach that has become popular in the twenty-first-century academy: theological aesthetics. Both theology and aesthetics are clearly crucial to O'Brien's work, but, moreover, one must always be aware of the "extratextual" intention of his words. Such intention is a key feature of theological aesthetics; as David Jeffrey and I put it in a guide to Christian literature in English,

> The core of Christian theological aesthetics is the religious experience of reestablished communion with God, mediated in this case by aesthetic structures which create, facilitate or sometimes even require a triune meeting between the work of literary art, the spiritually awakened human person, and the divine life of God revealed by faith and reason.[8]

Theological aesthetics can seem far too sublime for fiction and literary criticism, texts that our world often regards as trivial and secular, but O'Brien's words often remind us of the Word who would speak to our hearts. Yet, we should not expect mere information or knowledge to allow us to hear this Word. A complete critical analysis of any one of O'Brien's long novels could easily be a long book, and even if such length were possible, it is not desirable; any competent work of criticism runs the risk of being substituted for the primary text, but in this instance that would be especially tragic. O'Brien's novels contain far more riches than I have room to discuss, and his narratives are ordered in a spiritually intentional way that is not possible for criticism to reproduce or emulate, but rather merely notice. Readers of this introduction should thus not expect detailed interpretative or evaluative argument; instead, my aim is a radical, spiritual openness to the holy, sacred world that O'Brien's novels convey.

A crucial and unusual feature of O'Brien's work as a novelist is that throughout his career he has been an equally prolific painter of sacred art. O'Brien personally selects one of these paintings to act as an iconographic introduction to his narrator. Thus, with each of O'Brien's novels, before readers begin with a single word from the page, their soul sees and silently hears a nonverbal word, the Word conveyed through a painting that O'Brien has chosen for the cover of his novel. Invariably, the painting

---

8. Jeffrey and Maillet, *Christianity and Literature*, 87.

acts as an icon that, like much sacred art, conveys not just a "message," not just information, but rather an initiation into mystery, in the specifically religious or theological sense of the word: the mystery of divine being that must by definition be beyond the capacity of any human being to know through their senses. Because sacred art, like all art, must appeal directly to the senses, there is an inherent paradox in any icon; a religious icon transcends its physical qualities, but the mystery of its meaning must evade verbal explication, reaching beyond cognitive formulation and, in silence, stretching towards the soul of the viewer, seeking to unite the human being with the infinite being of the eternal God.

My own title alludes to two crucial concepts in O'Brien's literary and visual art. O'Brien's conception of *logos*, usually translated into English as "the Word," largely follows St. John the Divine, whose famous Prologue imaged Jesus as "the Word" spoken by the Father before all creation (John 1:1), but O'Brien's work often reminds us that each individual human being is a "word" spoken by our Father-God. Becoming a "child of God" is not a return to innocence but a grand adventure in which our Father teaches us to more fully understand our identity, so that we become ready to live in the creative harmony of heaven. O'Brien often alludes to Tolkien, whose great poem "Mythopoeia" sees human art as something continuing even in heaven.

So far from a solely intellectual understanding of "word" or *logos* according to the Greek philosophical tradition, O'Brien's theological aesthetic seems much closer to the beloved disciple's fully developed conception of the relationship between Father and Word. In the farewell discourses to the apostles in the Gospel of John, Jesus stresses, "As the Father has loved Me, so I have loved you," and promises that this love will later send the Holy Spirit to allow believers full interior communion with the divine: "The glory which thou gavest them; that they may be one, even as we are one: I in them, and thou in me, that they may be made perfect in one" (John 17:22–23). As O'Brien puts it at the end of *Letter to the Future*, his interest is not mainly "the writing of literature," nor "philosophical arguments," but rather our own deepest heart-soul words—living *logos*."[9]

The first word in my title, "living," naturally precedes *logos* because the triune reality articulated by John the disciple always has and always will be the source of life. The cover painting for this book, *Creation of the*

---

9. O'Brien, *Letter to the Future*, 407.

Birds, vividly portrays divine creativity. Awakening us to this basic truth is key to all of O'Brien's art. Both the divine *Logos* and human words created by the divine awaken believers and prepare them to commune with the divine in eternity. In *Father Elijah*, O'Brien's first and still most famous novel, there are three crucial instances in which the spiritual implications of being "awake" are strongly suggested. First, there is the epigraph from the book of Revelation: "Awake, and strengthen what remains, and is on the point of death" (Rev 3:2). In the middle of the novel, we twice hear how a holy man named Pawel Tarnowski rides a train towards Auschwitz but is able to write: "I go down at last to sleep, but my heart is awake."[10] Finally, at the novel's end, as archaeologist Father Elijah discovers the miracle of Mary's assumption, she, through a supernatural medium from heaven sends a similar message: "I sleep but my heart is awake."[11]

Becoming spiritually "awake" is a key part of the rationale for my critical approach. My words on O'Brien's words are not intended merely to convey information, as could one day be found upon the O'Brien Wikipedia page that already exists. Rather, as Christ models for Christian literary art through his parables, O'Brien's fiction seeks to awaken the eyes and ears of our inner spirit, allowing us to awaken to awareness of divine reality. Transcendent art of this kind does not seek to replace religion, but rather to point towards the living God.

When my approach succeeds, it introduces a writer whose art yields extraordinary fruit. Although O'Brien is best known for *Father Elijah*, his most popular novel was written as part of a *Children of the Last Days* series that includes six other novels. Released at the same time as the *Left Behind* series, and near the end of the second millennium of Christian history, both the popularity and critical dismissal of O'Brien's work were easy to understand. "End-time" speculation, to use the *lingua anglais* common at the time, in the light of Canada's monetary system, brought in the loonies and allowed many to dismiss O'Brien as loony. Both responses miss much of the value of his work, for *Father Elijah*, especially, is not a speculative stab at political prophesy, but rather a reflection on the strength of the sacred to have the final say in any story, personal or political.

Father Elijah became popular only after O'Brien and his large family had spent more than twenty years in poverty, and he had already written

---

10. O'Brien, *Father Elijah*, 251, 368.
11. O'Brien, *Father Elijah*, 558.

earlier parts of the series. Considered chronologically, the *Children of the Last Days* series begins with *Strangers and Sojourners*, a novel set in British Columbia, on the West Coast of Canada, and initially concerned with the spiritual struggles created for Catholic Christians by theosophy and other cultish practices common in the early twentieth century; as the novel progresses, though, it becomes the story of an extraordinary marriage. *Plague Journal* continues to follow the family introduced in the first novel, but personalizes and politicizes the story by focusing upon a father's struggle with the rise of a totalitarian state in Canada. *Eclipse of the Sun*, surely O'Brien's darkest novel, follows this story to its ominously logical conclusion, particularly critiquing the impotence of the ecclesiastical establishment to prevent Canada's spiritual decline. However, a key clerical figure from this novel, Father Andrei, does act as a bridge to connect the story to the more international concerns of *Father Elijah*. Father Andrei also appears in the far more local *A Cry of Stone*, which reveals the Holy Spirit at work among native Canadians, a community whom O'Brien knows well, as the Canadian government and ecclesiastical establishment caused so much long-lasting damage through the abuses of the residential school system. *Sophia House* returns to the international stage, serving as a prequel to *Father Elijah* by showing how David Schäfer, later to become Father Elijah, was spiritually prepared for his divine mission through the Polish Holocaust in World War II.

My focus here, in part necessitated by space, is this *Children of the Last Days* series. Novels completed after this series further suggest, however, the range of O'Brien's creativity. *Theophilos*, to my mind O'Brien's most significant theological work, imagines that the mysterious title figure, to whom St. Luke addresses his writing at the start of the Acts of the Apostles, was a "stepfather" of the apostle. As a learned physician, the title character in *Theophilos* enacts the universal agon facing humanity in any age: Why should one believe that Jesus Christ was divine and performed the miracles reported in the New Testament? Very different and in many ways more painful issues are faced in *Island of the World*, which O'Brien himself regards as his best book. This novel follows a heroic figure, Josip Lasta, through the tumultuous twentieth-century history of Croatia, both in its time as part of Communist Yugoslavia and through its later struggles with Serbia. O'Brien's interest in Eastern Europe, especially Russia, is most fully shown in *A Father's Tale*, his longest novel, which details a father's search for a son lost to a religious cult. Travelling even further abroad is *Voyage to Alpha Centauri*, O'Brien's attempt at science fiction; much like Lewis's space trilogy, however, the extraterrestrial setting is less important than the recurrence of theological concerns faced by all of the Creator's creatures. Back to earth comes *The Fool of New York City*, perhaps O'Brien's most unusual novel, one that shows God at work in an "odd couple" friendship facing the urban challenges of post-9/11 New York.

Given such diverse texts, it is by intention rather than necessity that O'Brien finally wrote the last novel discussed here, a sequel to *Father Elijah* entitled *Elijah in Jerusalem*. A less spiritually serious writer might have used this sequel as an opportunity to "cash in" on the popularity of *Father Elijah* by depicting heroic events in which the apocalyptic prophecies possible to interpret in *Father Elijah*, and in the book of Revelation, are fulfilled by present-day political events. Instead O'Brien makes *Elijah in Jerusalem* a warning against spiritual pride and false prophecy, reminding readers that providence always remains in God's hand, not the human will, and surely not in the hand of any artist, however skilled.

In the decade or so since *Elijah in Jerusalem*, O'Brien's creativity again took very different settings, with *The Lighthouse* set on the wild coasts of Nova Scotia and *The Sabbatical* among the aristocracy of the Romanian mountains. Both novels explored deeply the nature of Catholic humanism, but O'Brien's theological relevance to the twenty-first century is perhaps best shown by his two most recent novels. Both novels explored deeply the nature of Catholic Humanism and both show how O'Brien has mastered the short form of the symbolic novel; *The Lighthouse* is being made into a short film by the creative duo of Eric Groth and Andrew Hyatt, who gave us the brilliant "Wildcat" starring Maya Hawke as Flannery O'Connor. O'Brien's theological relevance to the twenty-first century is perhaps best shown by his two most recent novels.

By the Rivers of Babylon retells the life of Old Testament prophet Ezekiel, and is as biblically and historically realistic as *Theopholos*. Yet as is common in the genre of historical fiction, it both objectifies and magnifies an issue of obvious relevance for twenty first-century Catholics: the multifaceted crisis caused by sexual and doctrinal scandal within Roman Catholicism. Narrated by Ezekiel himself, *By the Rivers of Babylon* never makes this explicit, but the phrase that scripturally follows the title, "I sat down and wept," strongly suggests O'Brien's own narrative voice, and the Scripture with this verse, Ps 137, is the novel's epigraph.

Allegory is not intended, but the application that Tolkien approved of in historical fiction is plausible. The Babylonian captivity of Israel was precipitated by general loss of faith in the Most High, especially among the priests who should directly defend the holy presence of God in the holy of holies. Before the Babylonian captivity, both historically and in O'Brien's novel, altars to pagan idols multiplied, with hideous sacrifices offered. In representing this apostasy, O'Brien asks all the questions that so trouble twenty first-century Catholics scandalized by the Pachamama at the Vatican in 2019, abusive priests, and apostate cardinals such as McCarrick: "Does the *evil* behaviour of our most exalted ones" ensure the destruction of our civilization?";[12] "Is it possible to revolt against [the most High God] while still believing in him?"[13] Are the problems of the post–Vatican II Catholic Church caused by "relying on man rather than on God"?[14]

Yet in asking such questions, O'Brien never makes himself the "most high" who can ultimately judge others' sins. Rather, O'Brien's Ezekiel seems to lament how such scandal adds to his own sinfulness:

> I find it difficult to look at the face of each and every priest and not wonder if he is faithful in his heart as well as in his role, or if he is a secret betrayer. I am distressed by this new habit of suspicion that is growing in me. So much easier it would be to ignore the problem. I ponder and grieve, yet I am unable to do anything about it.[15]

O'Brien's Ezekiel does do much, however, to remind us also that though "those who serve" God "are not always so . . . the presence of the Lord is ever holy."[16] From his childhood on, this prophet (like Daniel, Jeremiah, Isaiah, and David, all of whom the novel also references) is visited spiritually by a "man of light" who embodies holiness and eternal hope. Christ's holiness is "the center of the world; it is the measureless, invisible light of the Most High shining upon the whole earth."[17]

Yet no one should dismiss O'Brien's ancient Israel as, at best, Catholic appropriation. It is of the essence of Christianity that Christ is part of the triune God before the beginning of our world, and is often glimpsed in the Old Testament. For the most part, *By the Rivers of Babylon* is realistic

---

12. O'Brien, *By the Rivers of Babylon*, 81.
13. O'Brien, *By the Rivers of Babylon*, 59.
14. O'Brien, *By the Rivers of Babylon*, 93.
15. O'Brien, *By the Rivers of Babylon*, 85.
16. O'Brien, *By the Rivers of Babylon*, 96.
17. O'Brien, *By the Rivers of Babylon*, 55.

historically, though O'Brien does draw on the long tradition, Jewish and Christian (including many literary writers), of connecting characters typologically with scriptural figures who are historically distant. O'Brien's Ezekiel lives in the time of the Babylonian captivity, but in addition to the many prophets whom he would have known from recent history (Isaiah, Elijah, Jeremiah), the novel has other characters whose names are both scripturally typological and, within a Jewish context, realistically named.

The most important example of this is the wife of O'Brien's Ezekiel, named Leah and the daughter of Ruth. Of course O'Brien knows these women in Scripture, but his Ezekiel knows them typologically, saying, "For me there is no cunning Laban, and my Leah is as cherished as Jacob's Rachel."[18] The point here is much more than aesthetic, though, because O'Brien also draws on the strong biblical evidence that Ezekiel and his wife had no offspring; O'Brien dramatically shows the pain this must have caused them, but also eloquently and succinctly shows the joy of divinely forged marriage. Perhaps most importantly, O'Brien presents this affliction as prelude to the extraordinary blessing famously given to the biblical Ezekiel. From "the same light" the novel's Leah and Ruth learn that Ezekiel "will be the father of many, many children," though not "the offspring of the flesh."[19] Ruth further explains:

> There is more, Yezekiel. He showed me that out of grief will come vision, out of poverty will come richness. This wealth will be given from above, but it will not be for you. It will be given *through* you for others.[20]

The themes here are familiar to readers of O'Brien, as will be the novel's critique of "modernists" already among the captive Israelites, urging them to heresy and apostasy. Most extraordinary, though, is O'Brien's approach to the famous vision of Ezek 37, in the valley of dry bones. Rather than portraying this famous scene directly, O'Brien has the novel's prophet first experience the harsh reality of death and Babylonian "burial" suffered by a friend of the novel's prophet, who "lies in a heap of carnal refuse, corpses half stripped of their flesh by carrion bodies strewn all about."[21] Then O'Brien's prophet is anointed as priest, according to the precise commands given by Moses in the desert. Thus "Israel in captivity"

---

18. O'Brien, *By the Rivers of Babylon*, 263.
19. O'Brien, *By the Rivers of Babylon*, 365.
20. O'Brien, *By the Rivers of Babylon*, 365.
21. O'Brien, *By the Rivers of Babylon*, 373.

no longer "suffers from one less priest," and the ancient Israelites learn (as modern Catholics might) "acceptance of our chastisement."[22]

Yet O'Brien's understanding of this acceptance is not passive, for a priest can "offer [his] very self as a living sacrifice,"[23] and it is the awesome revelation of divine glory from the "Lord of Life" that finally brings consolation in the novel's valley of dry bones. As O'Brien's Ezekiel enters this famous valley, he asks the fundamental question of any prophet:

> What service can I offer you, O Lord Most High, I who am so poor in holiness, who can offer no sacrifice, who have no little learning, who am a ragged remnant of your Temple in this desolation.[24]

Ezekiel then makes the pledge to God required of any prophet: "Do unto me according to your holy will!" His fearlessness in the desert is then shown, as a "black snake" slithers away and a scorpion halts as Ezekiel whispers the name of the Lord.

Then follow two of O'Brien's most poetic paragraphs which, especially in the context of his broader artistic vision, could be read both as an inspired account of prophecy and of artistic creativity infused by divine life. For "into the empty reservoir" of O'Brien's Ezekiel comes the water of life, "rising within" until it becomes "a river . . . uniting with other rivers that become one river coursing towards the sea." As with the "great sea" that the nun Piccarda makes a metaphor for God's will in the *Paradiso* of Dante,[25] here "all these waters turn and flow upward to heaven, until Ezekiel sings the "great song" that he "was created for":

> "O You whom I cannot see, cannot hear," I sing as the river flows within me. "O You whom I love, O you who have poured out upon me in my desolation the love of she who is the delight of my heart, and he who sacrificed himself for me, and the messengers whom you sent to anoint me as your servant, I praise you. Thus shall I forever lift up my poor hands to you, and my blind eyes to you, and my deaf ears to you, and from out of the depths I will cry unto you, and praise your glory!"[26]

---

22. O'Brien, *By the Rivers of Babylon*, 383.
23. O'Brien, *By the Rivers of Babylon*, 385.
24. O'Brien, *By the Rivers of Babylon*, 390.
25. Dante, *Divine Comedy*, 3:84–87.
26. O'Brien, *By the Rivers of Babylon*, 391.

In response, the Lord of Life gives the miracle that makes Ezek 37 such a famous Scripture. The "dry bones live," and spiritually awake readers might also, as "behold, a great storm wind comes," and within "a mighty cloud" is "fire." O'Brien's final word in the novel makes clear that the Most High's holy presence is here manifest, with the help of the famous Hebrew letters for YHWH, the great "I am" revealed in both the Old and the New Testaments.

There is Fire.

יהוה

It is too early to say where *By the Rivers of Babylon* and *Letter to the Future* rank in O'Brien's oeuvre. However, both clearly continue the quality and relevance of his Catholic theological aesthetic. O'Brien's two most recent novels confirm what longtime readers have come to expect from his work: a challenging, often discomfiting experience of the sacred, in which Christ both comforts and chides not only our hearts and minds as twenty-first-century Catholics, but more importantly speaks to our eternal souls. Are we really ready to live in the holy presence of God? The capacity of O'Brien's novels to help us take this question seriously makes his art extraordinary, and well worth the time needed to read his work carefully. To be introduced to the novels of Michael D. O'Brien is not only to become aware of another talented novelist, it is to enter the presence of the One whose grace speaks to all of us, even in the darkest of human hours. O'Brien's words have most been attacked through the most effective means of the modern desert that is often the academic world—by being ignored—yet the truth and beauty which these words achieve remain because they point us to the eternal *Logos* who is always alive.

"David Schäfer's Vision" from *Father Elijah*

"The Victory of Christ": *Father Elijah*

> It is a dark century... to look into this darkness and see there the victory of Christ is the essence of hope.
> —Dottrina, in O'Brien, *Father Elijah*, 61

NO NOVEL FROM O'BRIEN offers a more striking icon than the cover of *Father Elijah*. A man clad in the simple garments of a Middle Eastern peasant tilts his head towards a small cup, the color of its liquid apparently red but obscured by the utter blackness surrounding it. Above the man are many symbols of the ideologies that have clashed throughout the twentieth-century; to the left is the Star of David of Judaism, the crescent moon of Islam, the cross of Christianity; to the right is the swastika of Nazism and the sickle and hammer of Communism. Above all these, and apparently on collision course, is the dove that since Christ's baptism has been a common symbol of the Holy Spirit; against it on the right is a far less common symbol, a black panther apparently ready to pounce upon and try to devour the divine bird.

There is much about the novel not answered by its iconic painting, but readers can be sure they are entering a novel of the twentieth century, as befits a novel published in 1996, and that the novel will test, on some level, the spiritual choices of readers themselves. This present-tense element of the cover is important, because of the ancient terms that O'Brien puts in the subtitle: apocalypse is a word, derived from Greek, that means "revealing" or "unfolding," and is most well known as the Greek title of what becomes in English the book of Revelation, the final vision of St. John the Divine at the close of the Bible. O'Brien's preface to the novel, though, opens with a broader definition that could be applied to *Father Elijah*: "An apocalypse is a work of literature dealing with the end of history." As this novel unfolds, we learn to see that literature can be both fictional and historical.

Father Elijah begins in the monastery of Mt. Carmel, one of Catholicism's holy places, site of the prophet Elijah's famous retreat, and well known to Catholic readers through the poetry of St. John of the Cross. This novel thus begins with monks who understand that their "vocation is a call to listening," "to adoration of the One who dwells among us."[1] Elijah is such a monk, committed to silence, to listening for the voice of God, but the novel opens with dialogues between his two closest companions at the monastery, Brother Ass and Father Prior. Both of these seemingly "minor" characters are crucial in the novel.

After its initial, ancient setting, the opening scenes of the novel also present more contemporary spiritual conflicts. As Elijah boards a plane for Rome, having been summoned there, elements of anti-Catholicism become clear. Some minor examples are first presented, but a conflict far more serious is introduced when Elijah begins to read magazines extolling the rise of a highly popular European President whose policies sound humane, even spiritual. The President has told the International Court of Human Rights: "Mankind must turn toward the future and accept a view of our destiny that embraces everything human, in its totality, including the concept of man as spiritual being."[2] Casual readers might imagine a Catholic cleric to be supportive of this sentiment, but the President's role as antichrist in the novel's enactment of themes from the book of Revelation is at the heart of this novel. By initially stressing the popularity of this President, O'Brien lays the foundation for the President's credibility, or how this antichrist will deceive the world.

Once Elijah arrives in Rome, he is welcomed by Monsignor Billy Stangsby, a convert from Anglicanism who brings a Chestertonian flair and humor to the novel. A more important meeting, though, occurs as Elijah is taken to meet the Pope. Right from the first description, it is very clear that this Pope is "modeled after" John Paul II; not in the usual manner of historical fiction, but described at a level of detail so there can be no doubt that this novel's Pope *is* John Paul II. "Dottrina" is also very specifically Cardinal Josef Ratzinger, later to be Pope Benedict XVI. No other characters in the novel, however, represent specific historical persons. Why is it important for John Paul and Benedict to personally

---

1. O'Brien, *Father Elijah*, 17.
2. O'Brien, *Father Elijah*, 25.

appear in the novel? There was an obvious risk in bringing so specific a historical reference into the novel. As the 90s end, and the papacy of John Paul II soon thereafter, does the apocalyptic vision of *Father Elijah* become irrelevant? Is the novel, in an important sense, a failed prophecy?

It is not in response to this question, but certainly relevant to it, that O'Brien revised stylistic elements of *Father Elijah* in the late 90s, and altered the description of the novel's Pope to make the details of the character less specific. This revised version was published by Ignatius Press in 2018. Universal rather than topical reference is a common choice for many artists, so O'Brien can't be faulted, but the original description does fit with the "mid-90s" setting of the novel as first published. My own preference is for the original version, for two reasons. First is the exceptional influence of John Paul II on all of O'Brien's fiction; it seems entirely fitting, in my opinion, that this Holy Father appears directly in *Father Elijah*. Second, the historically specific details, paradoxically, can cause us to rethink the meaning of apocalyptic prophecy. The meaning of *Father Elijah* is relevant not only to specific calendar dates, but moreover to the spiritual lives of readers in any age.

The novel then shifts scene from Rome to Assisi, where the influence of great saints like St. Francis or St. Clare still evidences the church's divine strength, despite the contemporary influence of men of power, such as the President, who do not recognize it. Though O'Brien's narrator laments that the peace of Assisi "could not be described without resort to crudely rendered metaphors," perhaps he comes close by describing how his time there brings Elijah "a joy unlike any other joy he had ever experienced. Unexpected joy in a dark time."[3] God's work through St. Francis is perhaps most famously remembered through stigmata, bleeding of the hands like the wounds of Christ. Many dismiss such miracle as myth, but in twentieth-century Italy another famous cleric, Padre Pio, also had stigmata. In the tradition of such figures is the monk Don Matteo, who in O'Brien's novel welcomes Elijah to Assisi and instructs him spiritually while he is there. Holy men such as Saint Francis, Padre Pio, and Don Matteo are all essential actors in the drama that is *Father Elijah*, for they act as guides and models to Elijah himself.

Don Matteo directs Elijah to view some Renaissance-era paintings, from 1500, by Luca Signorelli. Though relatively obscure, these frescoes do still exist, and remain vivid portraits of the last judgment. Elijah and

---

3. O'Brien, *Father Elijah*, 80.

Billy especially notice a mural called *The Damned Cast into Hell*, which both repulses and scares Billy because of its drunkards. Elijah, though, notices the stranger feature of the painting: "the Lord with the figure of Satan whispering in his ear."[4] Gradually, Elijah realizes the truth: "The figure held in the devil's embrace was not Christ but Antichrist."[5] The point here does not relate to Signorelli's own beliefs—great art must be allowed multiple purposes—but rather to how easily a casual observer might confuse illusion and reality. As Elijah himself wonders, "Couldn't a flesh-and-blood Antichrist far more effectively create the *appearance* of goodness, while hiding his attachment to evil?"[6] Or, to put it as the book of Revelation makes us ponder, why will so many mistake the reign of antichrist for the return of Christ?

Another element of the biblical apocalypse is then presented when Billy tells the story of a most unusual encounter that occurred as he drove the highways of Britain. Not usually given to mysticism, even Billy had to obey after repeatedly hearing a voice say that he should stop and pick up the next hitchhiker he sees on the road. There seems nothing unusual about the man picked up, until he says, "The first trumpet has sounded"; when Billy asks his name, the reply comes, "My name is Gabriel." The real wonder, though, comes next; for then, as Billy puts it, "I looked over to the passenger side and he wasn't there."[7] Either Elijah or the novel's readers might question Billy's sanity, but then he also reports a conversation with a policeman on the highway, who tells him, "You're the fourth person to tell me that very story this morning."[8] Is Billy's story simply a fantastic element of O'Brien's fiction, or does it remind us of the miraculous events that must occur if the book of Revelation were to become historical?

In the next chapter of the novel, we see the first stage of the mission that the Pope has given Elijah: to convert the antichrist, the President. This mission, however improbable, reminds us that the biblical antichrist is a human being, though ruled by Satan, and retains some free choice through the divine image given to all people as part of their human nature. O'Brien's antichrist remains, in many ways, as Elijah later tells Billy,

---

4. O'Brien, *Father Elijah*, 115.
5. O'Brien, *Father Elijah*, 116.
6. O'Brien, *Father Elijah*, 117.
7. O'Brien, *Father Elijah*, 134.
8. O'Brien, *Father Elijah*, 135.

"a normal human being."[9] To this normalcy, though, has been added tremendous wealth and power, so that Elijah's first meeting with him occurs at the President's palace in Capri, on grounds built over the ruins of the residence of the corrupt Roman Emperor Tiberius. The comparison is obvious, though the President himself, a history and archaeology buff, tries to qualify it by claiming that modern historians have shown Tiberius's evil to be exaggerated. He also makes the obviously utopian, probably dystopian, claim that "all people should be able to live like this."[10] Both normal humanity and extraordinary wealth are part of the appeal of this antichrist.

However dubious the President's claims, more substantial, within the novel, is his discovery of medieval translations of Aristotle deriving directly from the Arab Averroes. Whereas most Aristotelian texts in the West, so important to Catholic theologians such as St. Thomas Aquinas, derive from Latin translations, the new texts, says the President, "breathe with the very soul of the mystical East, but they breathe through a mind that transcends both West and East."[11] Such texts are thus important to the New Age spirituality that this antichrist will advocate to replace Catholicism. Somewhat surprisingly, the President has long followed the political career of David Schäfer, and tells Elijah: "Had you chosen a different path for your life, you might be standing where I am now standing, in the position of maximum influence." Father Elijah replies, "I have found something much greater. The greatest thing in the world...."[12] But at this crucial moment the President is distracted.

Along with his great wealth and extraordinary archaeological discoveries, Elijah finds the President "noble, even spiritual," evincing a sincere humility. Billy points out that virtues such as humility can be feigned, citing the example of Dickens's Uriah Heep, but O'Brien's point again concerns why so many will not, according to the Bible, recognize the apocalypse. As Elijah reminds us:

> The apocalypse is not melodrama. If it were, most people would wake up and see the danger they are in. That is our real peril. Our own times, no matter how troubled they may be, are our

---

9. O'Brien, *Father Elijah*, 155.
10. O'Brien, *Father Elijah*, 147.
11. O'Brien, *Father Elijah*, 150.
12. O'Brien, *Father Elijah*, 153.

> idea of what is real. It is almost impossible to step outside of it in order to see it for what it is.[13]

This "impossible" task is a central aim of O'Brien's *Father Elijah*, which aims not only to help us recognize a real antichrist, but also our role in opposing this antichrist in order to remain faithful to the risen Christ. In this fundamental sense, then, the novel seeks to alter our conception "of what is real."

The exciting but tense meeting between Elijah and the President is followed by a meeting of Elijah and the Pope. One of the most spiritually important chapters in the novel, O'Brien slows the suspenseful pace in order to allow Elijah, and the reader, to sit down and be spiritually fed by a father who loves him rather than by a politician seeking to manipulate. The Pope is able to do this because he sees, first, that Elijah, like most modern men, suffers from "that great wound . . . The temptation to absolute despair." One might not guess this weakness upon a casual glance at Elijah's clerical robes or monastic obedience, but the Pope cautions: "I must warn you, as I warn myself daily and have repeatedly warned our shepherds: no man knows his own soul so well that he is invincible to the tactics of the enemy. No man."[14]

The issue of spiritual readiness and vigilance is then raised by the Pope by contrasting modern men with child martyrs of the early Christian centuries; such souls, he teaches Elijah, were

> so young, but they had learned the only thing they must know. They knew something that we, who wrestle endlessly with our prodigious intellects and our complicated emotions, can rarely know. You ask me if they chose? I believe they did. They had clarity. They had the eye of childhood.[15]

Restoring this clarity of vision is a primary purpose of O'Brien's art, and the meeting between Elijah and the Pope exemplifies the capacity of this novel to at once be didactic, a novel of ideas, and yet to retain the concrete mystery typical of great narrative art.

Elijah perhaps speaks for O'Brien the artist when he affirms the contrast between modern men and Christian souls of the past: "I have often sensed, Holy Father, that the people of our generation move as if in

---

13. O'Brien, *Father Elijah*, 157.
14. O'Brien, *Father Elijah*, 161.
15. O'Brien, *Father Elijah*, 162.

a thick, but invisible, cloud. Every faculty of perception is clogged."[16] This clogging leaves us vulnerable to the deceptions of people like the President, themselves manipulated by demonic forces, and unable to face the true challenges of the apocalypse. The Pope asks Elijah, and all readers:

> Do you understand that in those days every human being will be put to the test. Each will be asked to render an account of himself? Do you realize how universal this trial will be? How dreadful will be the cost of faithfulness?[17]

Do we? Soon after his meeting with the Pope, Elijah has spiritual, supernatural conversations with some modern people who certainly do: African nuns witness to the horror of genocide, but also to the power of Christ over death.

The spiritual challenge of the novel thus clarified, O'Brien can return to suspenseful story. Billy somehow gains information about the President's political program and, just as suddenly and mysteriously, he is poisoned and lands in hospital. Elijah investigates, trying to wade through the Vatican bureaucracy to gain answers, but the chapter ends with him in prayer, with Christ. Elijah cries out: "My God . . . my God. Where are you?"[18] O'Brien puts Christ's response in italics, a simple aesthetic technique also well used by George Herbert, a seventeenth-century Anglican poet who similarly allowed Christian faith to create great art. After scenes where Elijah walks through the harsh streets of Rome, seeing both satanic activity and humanity in its most degraded forms, O'Brien's Christ calms Elijah's fears but also challenges him to act faithfully:

> *My son, I ask you to go down into the lost places. Go without fear. . . . No man can save another. Only I can save. Yet My strength is within you. My strength works most effectively in your weakness. When will you trust me? . . . Have no fear. Walk into the darkness and bring back souls from it. I am with you always. . . . You are to do only this: you are to look neither to your left nor to your right. You are to go neither ahead of Me nor behind Me. Wait for Me and I will act.*[19]

Elijah, after struggling with fearful questions, finally has no verbal response. Rather, O'Brien portrays Elijah's interior life at this crucial

---

16. O'Brien, *Father Elijah*, 163.
17. O'Brien, *Father Elijah*, 163.
18. O'Brien, *Father Elijah*, 192.
19. O'Brien, *Father Elijah*, 192.

moment of the novel as an experience of the Holy Spirit: "The fire of Presence on this altar was the embrace of total love; it burned but did not consume."[20]

The following chapter resumes Elijah's mission to speak truth in love to the President. Even the sad death of Billy, under suspicious but not clearly criminal circumstances at the hospital, gives only a minute's interruption to the business of elite European social life, from evening galas to academic conferences. Elijah finds some spiritual refuge in the Roman catacombs, at the tomb of a young Roman martyr named Severa. There Elijah meets secretly with the Vatican secretary of state to discuss the President's plot against the church, and there he draws spiritual strength from the early martyrs of the church. Inspired by these meetings, the chapter closes with an extraordinary letter from Elijah to Don Matteo in which O'Brien offers some of his most inspired reflection on the book of Revelation.

Elijah sees a "sphere" on the wall beside his bed, and somehow knows that it represents the "multidimensional" form of the book of Revelation, which is not to be read in a linear, chronological manner, even though John was forced to use the two-dimensional form of letters on a page to write it down. Rather, in this divine vision,

> The Holy Spirit employs powerful symbols to help the reader suspend his normal ways of perceiving and draw him into a much larger awareness of the vast, multifaceted conflict between good and evil that will occur as the culmination of history. He is interested not so much in imparting information as implanting in us the tools of awareness.[21]

Is it too much to claim the same of *Father Elijah*? To do so is not to pretend that this work of literature is Scripture, or that O'Brien is a biblical prophet following Daniel or John, but rather that this novel intends not the "inside information" of historical prophecy, but rather an awareness of the spiritual struggle that both history and Scripture often describe.

Another way to say this is that the President does not represent any one single political figure, but rather is a type of antichrist who might arise in our postmodern age. Another key paragraph in Elijah's letter to Don Matteo makes this vital point clear:

---

20. O'Brien, *Father Elijah*, 193.
21. O'Brien, *Father Elijah*, 234.

> We often forget that in every age the spirit of Antichrist has been active, capable of deluding souls and dragging to perdition entire nations and peoples, without resorting to the high drama of an Apocalypse. There have been many apocalypses since the time of Christ—the reigns of Nero, Hitler, and Stalin, for example. They are prefigurements of the reign of the Man of Sin. They are also warnings. Reminders that we must not perceive the struggle against Antichrist as simply a magnificent mega-drama reserved for a distant future. The actual battle against that spirit is waged from the very beginning of human history and continues uninterrupted to this day.[22]

Again, we must ask, how do these ideas apply to *Father Elijah*? Perhaps a clear answer comes later in this same letter: "With prayerful reading, the book assists in the conversion of attention into holy vigilance, the spirit of the watchman."[23] The chapter with Elijah's long letter concludes with a reassuring response from Don Matteo: "Your vision is from the Lord. Trust in Him and He will act."[24]

The spiritual purposes of this novel are developed through three long chapters in the middle of the book, each focused on Elijah's relationship with Count Smokrev, an elderly man whom he meets in Warsaw just prior to attending one of the President's conferences. Although not uncommon in other literary novels—think of the Tom Bombadil chapters in Tolkien's *The Fellowship of the Ring*—these chapters are not essential to *Father Elijah*'s broader plot, and an "efficient" editor might have demanded their deletion from an already long novel; we must thus ask why O'Brien thought it essential to include these chapters. Regardless of our answer, these chapters certainly include some of the finest writing in all of O'Brien's novels, and within them are ideas essential to the theological aesthetic of *Father Elijah*.

"Warsaw" is the first of these chapters and the scene of the conference. It allows Elijah to returns to his Polish youth as David Schäfer, and to reflect on his religious identity. He states this clearly but yet confuses inquirers when he affirms that he is "a Catholic" and "a Jew."[25] How is it possible to be both? Must a Catholic also be a Jew, or is the point here solely Schäfer's personal background? Why is the relationship of Catholic

---

22. O'Brien, *Father Elijah*, 235.
23. O'Brien, *Father Elijah*, 236.
24. O'Brien, *Father Elijah*, 237.
25. O'Brien, *Father Elijah*, 242.

and Jew different from the religious syncretism and monism that, as we are soon to learn in the novel, is central to the President's own worldview? Such questions are certainly difficult, the kind that Dottrina, as Cardinal Ratzinger, will take up in a key encyclical written just after *Father Elijah*, *Dominus Iesus*. O'Brien also uses Elijah's past, however, to explore an even more controversial topic in contemporary Christianity: homosexuality.

The story is told more fully in *Sophia House*, but the outlines of this prequel are already clear in *Father Elijah*. As a young Jewish boy in the Warsaw ghetto of World War II, David Schäfer was hidden from the Nazis by Pawel Tarnowski, a bookseller who has made it his mission in life to "put good books into the hands of people, so that "perhaps good thoughts are born in the mind."[26] Sexual subtext certainly seems implied, though, when the older Elijah recalls how Pawel would not let the boy David share his bed, even on the coldest of nights. *Sophia House* makes clear that homosexual inclinations were a problem for Pawel, but rather than an "orientation" he chose, it was violently inflicted on him and he fought against it. This fact, clear in *Sophia House*, is also strongly implied by a remembered wartime conversation, recorded later in *Father Elijah*. Pawel told David of "a wound inflicted by the *sitra ahra*," which O'Brien's footnote translates as "the kingdom of darkness,"[27] but by resisting it Pawel became "a father of the soul" to David.

Pawel had allowed himself to be arrested by the Nazis while pushing young David out onto the roof of the bookshop, and it is years later, through apparently providential acts, that Elijah has confirmed what he has long suspected. A Polish woman tossed him a medallion that read: "Madrosc—Wisdom!" This seemingly insignificant object had significantly altered David's political trajectory, which the President recalls as potentially making him a very important person, for the medallion "had raised the fundamental doubt which set his life upon an entirely different court." What is this doubt? Rather than doubt, it was certainty of a different kind that David also found attached to the medallion, in a "few words on a scrap of yellow paper": "I give you my life. I carry your image within me like an icon. This is my joy. I go down at last to sleep, but my heart is awake. Pawel."[28]

Awakening to the reality of divine, eternal life is a central theme of *Father Elijah*, and making this awakening personal, in an individual soul,

26. O'Brien, *Father Elijah*, 255.
27. O'Brien, *Father Elijah*, 256.
28. O'Brien, *Father Elijah*, 251.

is an essential parallel to the political awareness required by the apocalypse. Count Smokrev is a special challenge to Elijah's spiritual life, for Smokrev is at the end of a life in which he has not only repeatedly chosen evil, but also come to view spiritual impulses of any kind as a grand illusion. In his first meeting with Father Elijah, Smokrev tells him:

> I know that there is no love in the world. We are all creatures of various kinds of desire. Even the idealist who talks of love, love, love all the day long will make a few sacrifices to convince himself of his fantasy. But I tell you, his fantasy is a *pleasure* to him; he *desires* it to be true, but he will abandon it at the very instant it becomes unmitigated suffering.[29]

Smokrev goes on to accuse Pawel of flagrant vice, but these claims are entirely false, indicative not of objective reality, but of Smokrev's own sin. Nihilistic cynicism of this kind, which is often termed "postmodern" today though Smokrev's view of love to my mind recalls Iago[30] can only be faced by great spiritual strength, especially since, though this revelation is delayed, Smokrev has very directly caused great suffering in Elijah's life. Seeking this strength, Elijah turns to its source in the chapel of a convent where he can enter the presence of the sanctified Eucharist, the Blessed Sacrament. Eventually Christ's voice speaks within him, "*I ask you to love My enemy in My name*," but Elijah replies,

> I am afraid, Lord, I am afraid. Soon I must face the lion. I fear him greatly. This corrupt one, I fear him also. He exhausts my every resource, and he has weakened me for the meeting with the lion.[31]

Elijah's honesty allows the Lord here to again state perhaps the most consistent and important theme of the novel: "*My strength is most effective in weakness.*"[32] Accepting the truth of the Lord's words here, however, is surely difficult; even Elijah, as the novel goes on, will lament many times the weakness of the church. The paradox here raises a very fundamental human question: In our constant quest to be strong, can we be weak enough to let the Lord work within us?

Such questions are never easy to answer, but O'Brien makes the issue even more complex in the second of the three Smokrev chapters, entitled

---

29. O'Brien, *Father Elijah*, 261.
30. Shakespeare, *Othello* 1.3, 826.
31. O'Brien, *Father Elijah*, 263.
32. O'Brien, *Father Elijah*, 264.

"The Confession." The chapter begins with a message from Smokrev that excites the cleric in Father Elijah: "I wish to confess. . . . Come quickly." Upon Elijah's arrival, though, Smokrev clarifies: "You misunderstand me. I wish to confess to you as one man to another. I didn't mean your sacrament."[33] Inadvertently, however, Smokrev's words raise another key theme of these chapters: What is the meaning of sacramental confession? For Catholic sacraments to be valid, normally free will or a rational mind is required (as, most obviously, in marriage). Yet often a sinner cannot understand the very nature and gravity of the sin being confessed; does Christ come for them, even in their sins?

The origins of Count Smokrev's lust, which is not merely sexual but also—as in the classical Augustinian conception of lust—reflective of a willfulness that desires power and control over all things, is fully manifest as Smokrev "confesses" his first friendship, with a peasant boy named Piotr. Raised as a Polish aristocrat, Smokrev himself had as a child been a devout believer, until his mother interrupted sacramental life in favor of "less traditionally religious" practices.[34]

In Piotr, though, the youthful Smokrev had found a true friend with whom to share games, fishing, and all the fun to be found in God's green countryside. The elderly Smokrev vividly recalls the day "when desire burst through the membrane that separates chaste love from lust."[35] Falling asleep beside each other after a hot day outside, Smokrev had awoken and attempted to touch Piotr's face; sensing sexual tension, Piotr had refused. When Smokrev claimed such touching as his right, because "You work for us. You belong to us," Piotr quickly left. He returned the next day, apparently ready to forget and forgive, bringing his pet rabbit, Ludmilla. The young Smokrev, though, thinks to himself, "Who is this peasant to play the prince!"[36] He then grabs the rabbit from Piotr and tosses it into the jaws of a savage dog, who tears the rabbit to pieces. Piotr's horror, Smokrev admits, "was a pleasure to me," and as an elderly man he recognizes this moment as "the first step in a long career" that "might give me the power to rule over everything."[37]

The story of Smokrev's relationship with Piotr did not end in this violent, painful way. Years later, a middle-aged Smokrev has come home,

---

33. O'Brien, *Father Elijah*, 266.
34. O'Brien, *Father Elijah*, 277.
35. O'Brien, *Father Elijah*, 277.
36. O'Brien, *Father Elijah*, 281.
37. O'Brien, *Father Elijah*, 282.

and found that Piotr, "the apollonian youth," had become a "large, jolly" baker. The soul behind the older Piotr's "still kind" eyes was slowly unveiled, as Smokrev recalls his former friend's reaction: "He smiled. I couldn't believe it. He smiled."[38] When Smokrev warily recalls Ludmilla after some friendly small talk, Piotr at first pretends not to remember, then affirms forgiveness and most tellingly uses the same term of affection from their long-past youths: "Nothing to forgive, *dziecko*. Nothing to forgive." Smokrev, by then jaded by years of willful self-interest, did not respond but instead "roared out of town and never returned."[39]

In the third and final chapter of this section, "Another Confession," the sacramental role of the priest becomes especially important. One does not expect this at the start of the chapter, for Smokrev speaks of his words thus far as "all theatrics, setting the stage," and Elijah himself rises to leave at one point, convinced that Smokrev is "playing games." The serious possibility, however, that Christ will come to Smokrev is suggested when Elijah reflects upon the meaning of the sacrament of reconciliation, popularly known as confession:

> A priest of Christ knows that he is a man like other men. He too could commit the sins told to him through that screen. He stands there as a sign of contradiction set down in creation. A sign of mercy and truth. The truth sets us free, and mercy heals us. He stands as a living presence of Christ before men, and in the place of men before Christ.[40]

Can Elijah be such a priest for Smokrev? It is Smokrev himself for whom homosexuality has been a symptomatic expression of a lust for power and self-preservation that has influenced his behavior all his life. On his choices during the Holocaust he is particularly repulsive:

> Hundreds of thousands of people destined for burning. Trash. Human waste, already erased by the state. No future, no hope. No rescue. No savior. No God. No nothing. They were already dead, even though they continued to walk around for a few miserable weeks or months or years. There were so many, many beautiful young people. I kept a stable-full.[41]

---

38. O'Brien, *Father Elijah*, 286.
39. O'Brien, *Father Elijah*, 287.
40. O'Brien, *Father Elijah*, 292.
41. O'Brien, *Father Elijah*, 293.

Even Elijah is momentarily dismayed, "looking down at his hands," but the wounds Smokrev can inflict will yet become more personal. Can God himself forgive such a man? Ironically, this question never occurs to Smokrev himself, who is convinced by his own experience that God either does not exist or certainly is not worth worshipping. Smokrev reminds Elijah that "millions of victims" during the Holocaust "were pleading with Heaven as they fell into the flames," asking, "Where are you, Saviour of the World?"[42] Can there be a persuasive response to the problem of evil posed by the Holocaust, just one of the many dark moments of the dark twentieth century?

The problem of evil is of course a very ancient theological question, and Elijah begins his response with the traditional Christian answer: free will. Human free will "is part of "the fundamental structure of the universe."[43] Rhetorically, but logically, Elijah asks, "Should a soul who has chosen to reject the light be permitted to annihilate the laws sustaining those who have chosen to follow the light?"[44] Could God "have prevented the possibility of evil without turning every living thing into a puppet, a mere part in a clockwork?" Rather, God creates "a universe in which there is freedom," where "beauty was made to increase and multiple unceasingly, where unique beings love one another and create ever more life."[45]

Of course, there are counterarguments to this view, but intellectual debate is not what is most relevant here, now, for Smokrev's soul. So Elijah turns to a different tradition in theodicy, one which focuses on Christ's ministry in the world as God's primary response to human suffering and evil. Christ himself speaks through Elijah to tell Smokrev:

> *I will go down into my own creation as once I did so long ago, when I walked with Adam and Eve in the garden. As I did when I came to Jerusalem as a man. I will go down into my creation and I will suffer in it. I will suffer with it. And this shall be my Word, as once it was my Word on Calvary.*[46]

As already noted, it is crucial to O'Brien's Catholicism, and theological aesthetics, that the "Word" of love given by God on the cross

---

42. O'Brien, *Father Elijah*, 294.
43. O'Brien, *Father Elijah*, 293.
44. O'Brien, *Father Elijah*, 296.
45. O'Brien, *Father Elijah*, 295.
46. O'Brien, *Father Elijah*, 297.

continues speaking in history, even to evil individuals. Even, we should say, to ourselves, for sin and evil afflicts all of us; yet sin cannot, Elijah insists, alter the divine image within us:

> In every person's soul there is an icon of what he is meant to be. An image of Love is hidden there. Each soul is loved beyond imagining. Each soul is beautiful in the eyes of God. Our sins and faults, and those committed against us, bury this original image. We can no longer see ourselves as we really are.[47]

Even Smokrev's soul begins to be moved by this theodicy, until finally evil moves with him to utter lies that he hopes will shake Elijah's faith in divine love: Pawel, Smokrev claims, took the young David Schäfer "into his bed," so Smokrev "gave" Pawel "what he deserved, a meeting with the SS."[48] Elijah knows the first claim to be a lie, but the second one is partially true. Seeing his own betrayer in front of him, the man directly responsible for the death of the man who saved his life, probably prompts feelings of revenge even in Elijah.

This is exactly what Smokrev is hoping, for he calls Elijah to stand up, choke him, and thus prove that any claim that the priest of his Christ loves this unrepentant sinner is simply illusory rhetoric. Elijah does stand, but instead "he took Smokrev's face in his hands, and he kissed him on one cheek, then the other."[49] Smokrev is shocked and horrified, but when Elijah also calls him "dziecko" and says, "I love you," there is an apparent exorcism:

> The darkness fled outward to the farthest corners of the room. Elijah closed his eyes, and he saw an interior image of a small boy in a golden crib. The child was crying in the night. He screamed but no one came.[50]

Smokrev soon dies of the lung cancer that had been afflicting him, but not before admitting his lies about Pawel and giving Elijah two crucial gifts: an icon of St. Michael fighting Satan in the apocalypse, and a small tin containing scraps of Pawel's writing. Physically, Smokrev then dies, but spiritually Elijah seems to have saved his soul and prepared him to meet the eternally alive Lord of the universe. Can we believe in the

---

47. O'Brien, *Father Elijah*, 305.
48. O'Brien, *Father Elijah*, 310.
49. O'Brien, *Father Elijah*, 311.
50. O'Brien, *Father Elijah*, 312.

possibility of this conversion? That is not at all an "academic" or "speculative" question for O'Brien. Rather, upon it hinges the question of whether Elijah's mission to convert the President is futile, and whether our own hearts are as awake as Pawel's, on the train to Auschwitz, trusting even in the midst of extreme evil and suffering that God's mercy and love is ultimate reality.

Following Count Smokrev's death, O'Brien develops two plot lines that similarly prepare Father Elijah for his ultimate mission to the President, yet differ from each other in that each expands upon different themes of the novel. Anna Benedetti is an Italian lawyer whom Elijah meets at the President's social gatherings. She has become a World Court judge through the President's influence, but from the start her friendship with Elijah suggests that she retains an independent ideological outlook. With Anna widowed, the potential for a romantic relationship between Anna and Elijah tests his priesthood, but finally Elijah helps Anna, an agnostic but deeply humane person, to know the reality of eternal, divine love. Father Elijah also offers this, in a far different way, to Father Smith, an American cleric and editor whose world has been turned upside down by corruption in the post–Vatican II Catholic Church. Drawing on narratives familiar to anyone who has followed the liberal vs. conservative skirmishes commonplace in post–Vatican II Catholicism, O'Brien depicts how Elijah both comforts Smith and tries to remind him of the eternal center of justice and love that is the living Lord.

In a summary of the novel, the relationship between Anna and Elijah can sound like the kind of romance seemingly required by a major motion picture. The novel never includes any physical intimacy between the two, and no honest declarations of their romantic love for each other. Rather, the relationship explores the issue of how a faithful priest might feel human attraction towards someone, but yet choose instead to point that person towards God. Anna feels a similar attraction to Elijah, but desires above all justice, to find those responsible for what she has come to believe was the murder of her husband, Stefano. By creating the possibility of a stereotypical romantic relationship but then turning it towards eternal concerns, O'Brien subverts the expectations not only of Hollywood thrillers but also anti-Catholic, anticlerical stereotypes.

The Anna-Elijah relationship also brings a lot of suspense to the novel, as the search for Stefano's killers unfolds, and this is important for readers who may not grasp the issues raised by the case of Father Smith. Initially a successful editor of an American Catholic journal, the

Catholic New Times, Father Smith considers himself "neither liberal nor conservative, despising those political terms."[51] However, he is caught in the vortex of post–Vatican II Catholic politics, when "the truly moderate" became "considered ultraconservative" and the "conservatives to be sociopaths."[52] How were such shifts possible? Spurred by reforms and the "aggiornamento" of Vatican II, many made the mistake of thinking the church reformable through human means.

Catholicism has always viewed the church as created by God—Eternal Father, Risen Lord, Comforting Spirit—at the human hour recorded in Acts 2, but certain, due to divine holiness, to survive into eternity. Human sinfulness remains, but cannot detract from the eternal essence of what God created in the church. This transcendent ecclesiology was often ignored, in the post–Vatican II era, by those focusing solely on the human reforms rather than the traditional doctrine often reaffirmed by the council's documents. Such error forgets, as Elijah tells Smith, that "the true centre" of the church is Jesus Christ, who remains "the same yesterday, today, and forever." Such is eternal reality, but in this world, Elijah also reminds Father Smith, the priest's vocation is to "spread the Gospel, teach, feed, protect—and conform ourselves to the image of the One who carried a Cross and died on it."[53]

The ominous but often forgotten implications of this vocation become clear, and the novel's ecclesiastical ideas become tragically concrete, when Smith is framed for embezzlement and an alleged sexual affair. Such melodrama might seem extraneous to O'Brien's novel, and we must ask whether the Smith plot is necessary. However, it does parallel the Anna Benedetti plot, and directly connects to it, when the story of Anna itself turns sinister. The dark side of the President, normally hidden by his public image, is finally revealed. As Anna has long suspected, the President was responsible for the murder of her husband, a devout Catholic lawyer and politician named Stefano Benedetti. Anna has remained in the President's circle primarily in the hopes of learning how her husband was killed, and thus to bring the killers to justice.

As many legal cases remind us, however, if ultimate human justice is to be found, then divine, eternal justice must also exist. Anna is not herself a believer, but Elijah brings her to Don Matteo, and the old monk tells her: "The Lord asks me to tell you that your martyr is with him .

---

51. O'Brien, *Father Elijah*, 370.
52. O'Brien, *Father Elijah*, 370.
53. O'Brien, *Father Elijah*, 384.

... He who shares the name of the first martyr."[54] How can Don Matteo know Stephano's name, never having had any opportunity to learn this information? This clearly supernatural moment, possible solely because Matteo communes with the divine world where Stefano now lives, should convince the rational Anna, but it does not; why not? On an existential human level, the consolations of eternity are not enough to salve the bitterness in Anna's soul. Later in the novel, Elijah tells her: "Some day you will rejoin Stefano," but Anna replies, "That's too theological. I can't think along those lines. I want Stefano's killer."[55]

Anna's desire—aided by the disguised romance with Elijah that the two of them dissemble through correspondence they know will be intercepted—becomes fulfilled at one of the President's gatherings. Through the subtle awareness of facial response and telling statements that Anna has gained through courtroom experience, she recognizes the killers. They are at once "utterly sane and utterly psychopathic," traits Elijah remembers seeing in Adolph Eichmann.[56] In the most revealing moment, when the killers have been lulled into complacency by Anna, one of the President's men says to the primary killer, Chirurgo or Surgeon: "Tell us, doctor, what is it like to take apart a living human being? Chirurgo didn't blink an eye. He tilted his head a little and said, 'It's a science.'"[57]

The entire scene recalls Anna's first awareness of the President's hatred of Stefano, when a shadow had passed across the President's face, very briefly, unmistakably revealing his malicious inner spirit. Such revelations, given the deceptive nature of human sin and crime, are often our only means of recognizing evil. By giving Anna not only the stereotypical "female intuition" to recognize such revelations, but also the legal mind to understand their necessity in solving crimes, O'Brien depicts the battle against evil in human terms that complement the spiritual warfare also occurring within the novel.

The brutal nature of the President's circle is fully made clear, though, after a period in which the correspondence of Anna and Elijah has suddenly become cut off. Elijah receives an envelope containing a brass reliquary that he had given Anna as a parting gift, one that contained both the rosary beads of African martyrs and a priceless piece of Christ's cross (given to Elijah by Don Matteo). In the reliquary now "was a mass of

---

54. O'Brien, *Father Elijah*, 418.
55. O'Brien, *Father Elijah*, 454.
56. O'Brien, *Father Elijah*, 455.
57. O'Brien, *Father Elijah*, 459.

material that appeared to be semi-liquid. It was dark purple, almost black, and bits of solid matter were embedded in it. It smelled of putrefaction."[58] Whose blood is this—Anna's, the African martyrs, or is all congealed on the sliver of wood, Christ's cross? Scooping the "sliver of wood" and other materials "back into the reliquary," Elijah turned to the cross by her bed and cried out, "Save her!"[59]

The novel's most suspenseful moments follow, though we can guess from the outset that eternal rather than temporal salvation is now Christ's will for Anna. Elijah has one final moment of emotional intimacy with Anna through a letter that he finds in the Foligno estate where he had earlier visited her. Much of Anna's final letter is hopeful and uplifting, as she reports compiling damning documents proving the President's guilt, feeling that her children have a bright spiritual future, and even going to hear Mass for the first time in twenty years. She cautions that this is not yet the faith Elijah hopes for but, prophetically and ominously, she also says, "I feel Stefano very close."[60] Perhaps most importantly, after acknowledging that there were moments when their charade of notes gave her romantic pleasure, she understands and values the real spiritual relationship between her and Elijah:

> You are a father without a child. I am a child without a father. Let us be this kind of love for each other. It is no less a love than what has come to Gianna and Marco. The form of it changes, and the season, and the harvest. But it is love.[61]

Most tragically, however, the printed letter also contains a "hurried scrawl": "O God. They are here."[62]

There then follows another suspenseful chase in which Elijah first finds then tries to preserve the evidence that Anna has compiled against the President. All seems secure when Elijah finally delivers it to the Pope, but then follows a scene in which, after sending Elijah from the room and ordering him "not to intervene for any reason," the Pope is first intellectually and then physically attacked by a dissident cleric. Cardinal Vettore represents everything sought by the liberal church that has demonized Father Smith, but Vettore himself has been converted to the

---

58. O'Brien, *Father Elijah*, 473.
59. O'Brien, *Father Elijah*, 474.
60. O'Brien, *Father Elijah*, 478.
61. O'Brien, *Father Elijah*, 479.
62. O'Brien, *Father Elijah*, 479.

President's purposes. In the course of his interview with the Pope, the friendly, somewhat rational face of this movement gives way to physical violence as Vettore strikes the Pope before running out. Only later, long after Vettore has escaped, do the Pope and Elijah realize that he has stolen the evidence that Anna compiled. The Pope has already stated clearly, however, why this point is now moot: "Even if the President is brought down, the enemy will raise another like him."[63]

More suspense follows as the Pope prepares an escape route for Elijah (who has already been convicted of Anna's murder in the popular media), but within this tension intersect several moments in which O'Brien's transcendent, supernatural concerns remind readers that this is not another crime thriller. For example, on the escape route that the Pope has prepared for him, for some inexplicable reason Elijah turns north towards Capri, towards the President's palace. Is the Holy Spirit guiding him, or his own will? Readers can't be sure, but on Capri, he meets "Raphael," who appears to Elijah as an eight-year-old boy but does things—like the hitchhiker named Gabriel picked up earlier in the novel by Billy—which could be possible only for an angelic being.

On Capri, Elijah certainly could not have found the President, as he eventually does, without Raphael's aid. As in so many critical moments in the Bible, angelic aid here is an important element of divine providence. Rebel angels clearly guard the President, and their voices assault Elijah to convince him to turn back; most ominously they chant, in his mind, "What happened to her will happen to you."[64] It is a very civilized President whom Elijah finally encounters, however, a man only mildly disturbed by the entrance of spiritual forces that could turn his world upside down. The President feels "only a hint of disturbance from the guardian spirits," perhaps because he is completely captive to the demonic side of the war that began in heaven with Satan's rebellion. There is a numbing power to the President's sanity, though, and as he argues with Elijah for his New Age/ancient demonic religion and denies any involvement in Anna's murder, there is "the cessation of the [demonic] voices," for they are seemingly satisfied by the President's "stroke of genius" and await only "the storm of applause" that normally follows his rhetorical performances.[65]

---

63. O'Brien, *Father Elijah*, 518.
64. O'Brien, *Father Elijah*, 525.
65. O'Brien, *Father Elijah*, 535.

Father Elijah's mind is numb, but he reaches into his pocket and touches the brass reliquary, and into his soul flood many spiritual symbols that remind him of divine reality; he sees, among many other images from his past, "a chalice raised on a million altars."[66] Elijah is inspired to ask about Stefano Benedetti; when the President lies, "a shadow passed across and behind his eyes."[67] When Elijah brings out the reliquary, the President's self-assurance seems gone, saying, "Put that away," while also claiming not to know what it is; Elijah reminds him:

> You know very well that it contains a splinter of wood soaked in Christ's Blood. Here also are beads from Africa, where holy blood was spilled. And here too is Anna's blood.[68]

In what might be *Father Elijah*'s most important demonstration of the meaning of priesthood, Elijah confronts evil not just with ideas or symbols, but rather with the historical and spiritual reality of the cross itself. The point here is not only the relevance of historical relics or even martyr's lives, but rather to show how all suffering and evil is overcome by the blood Christ sheds for us. The President throws this holy relic into the fire, attempting to destroy it.

Undaunted, Father Elijah fearlessly grabs the reliquary from the fire, burning into his hand, as he tells the President, "The sign that has defeated you and will continue to defeat you until the end of time."[69] Though the demonic spirits in the President fight back, finally "the scorched flesh in the shape of the cross was lifted high over the most powerful man in the world," and Elijah can offer, as he did with Smokrev, both a direct call from the Lord himself and "a moment of choice" to decide finally whether or not to accept God's mercy. As with Smokrev, there is clearly an exorcism involved here, for at one point "the personality that looked out through [his] eyes was not the President's."[70] Raphael then appears to lead Elijah to safety; as Elijah leaves Capri, he hears the alarm bells and sirens which make clear the President has awoken and, unlike Smokrev, has chosen this world rather than God.

Elijah then flees, back along the escape route planned by the Pope, arriving in modern-day Turkey near the ruins of the ancient city of

---

66. O'Brien, *Father Elijah*, 536.
67. O'Brien, *Father Elijah*, 537.
68. O'Brien, *Father Elijah*, 537.
69. O'Brien, *Father Elijah*, 537.
70. O'Brien, *Father Elijah*, 542.

Ephesus. O'Brien's narrator first recalls the extraordinary evangelization of the area by St. Paul many centuries ago, but it is another historical place that is the raison d'être of Elijah's journey here and, like the other place names used throughout the novel to entitle chapters, is the title here. "Panaya Kapulu" is the Turkish name for House of the Holy Virgin, for this is the place, according to many Catholic historians, that the apostle John brought Mary the mother of Christ after Jesus' command from the cross that John take Mary as his mother and Mary take John as her son (John 19). Archaeological ruins testify to this place's historicity, but it is to a related place, one unknown to history, but according to Catholic doctrine certain to exist, that Elijah next takes Father Prior and Brother Ass, whom the tumults of the world have reunited with Elijah in the desert.

Taking his friends on a long, mysterious hike, Elijah finally brings them to a cave and tells them simply to "rest here, and then after we have prayed, I will ask you what has been revealed to you."[71] Father Prior remains highly intellectual, asking about the archaeological ruins found by Elijah in the place, which date the cave in the Roman era, first century AD. Brother Ass, by contrast, sleeps quickly and is given a long vision in which he seems to be speaking the words of Christ's apostles after first learning that Mary has died. Then, as according to the Roman Catholic dogma of the assumption of Mary, Brother Ass's vision recounts how Mary after death was brought "body and soul" directly into heaven. Father Prior recognizes then where Elijah has brought them: "We are in the tomb of the Virgin."[72] Brother Ass is given the more important, present-tense insight, a "smile of surpassing sweetness" crossing his face: "She is very beautiful ... beautiful ... She is so good."[73] After the President's moment of choice, and in Elijah's desperate hour, why now are the Marian doctrines of Catholicism particularly relevant within the novel?

The theological challenge posed by this question is minor, however, compared to the conundrum to which Elijah again turns: the problem of evil, or of why a good God allows the innocent to suffer for so long. Has not this already been covered in the novel? The President has made the opposite choice to Smokrev's, but is not the problem of evil the same? Here, O'Brien acknowledges that the depths of this problem go beyond

---

71. O'Brien, *Father Elijah*, 555.
72. O'Brien, *Father Elijah*, 559.
73. O'Brien, *Father Elijah*, 559–60.

intellectual argument. "Oh, yes," Elijah "knew all the replies, back and forth, up and down, inside out":

> Freedom. Human will. Man could not love if he were unable to choose love, and with this choice came the ability to choose love's opposite. Elijah could argue an atheist into silence, if one would listen, and he could go farther to implant the questions that lead a soul in darkness to fairest hope. But beyond that there would loom the wider and more perilous questions still. His convert would have to face it eventually, for he, Elijah, was still facing it after all these years.[74]

He still faced, in other words, the Holocaust, Pawel and the rest of his family, his wife Ruth and their unborn child murdered later in Israel, now Anna also cruelly murdered. How can a good God with power to intervene allow this to happen?

Against such despair, the hope and promise of God's redemption of the human race begun in Mary, which Catholicism understands through the doctrine of the immaculate conception, is especially important. Elijah now understands:

> Did not Mary's womb contain the impossible, the unthinkable? In that sacred little room of hers was nurtured the seed that would save the world from darkness. Encoded there, as if on a double helix, were the martyrs and mystics, the cathedrals and the statues, the Christian East and the West, the songs of the monks, the encyclicals, the poems, the millions of children who might not otherwise have been.[75]

Mary is the supreme example of the Pauline paradox so important to O'Brien: "Your strength is to be found in weakness."[76] In spite of the grace embodied in her, Mary never exalts herself, but because of her great humility, she points always to the only ultimate answer to the problem of evil, the living theodicy who is Christ himself:

> Our faith can never be a system of religious thought, a set of ethics, or a beautiful culture. That is why miracles and visions can never be enough. When everything is stripped down to its essential form, our faith is a belief in One who loves us; in Jesus, true God and true Man, the only Christ, dwelling in the heart

---

74. O'Brien, *Father Elijah*, 562.
75. O'Brien, *Father Elijah*, 566.
76. O'Brien, *Father Elijah*, 567.

of His Church, He who was, who is, and who is to come. That is why our home is the Universal Church, the throne on which You reign, a Church that is within time and yet outside of time. That is why her doors stand ever open to Anna and Severa and Smokrev and Billy and me and even to this possessed man who desires to rule the world.[77]

This insight is arguably the theological high point of the novel, but in its final chapter, "Apokalypsis" (the ancient Greek word for the book of Revelation), Elijah is led to an even higher viewpoint, at least physically, to view the end of the world. Again, angelic aid leads him, as the same child who brought Elijah to the cave of Mary's assumption reappears to lead him high up a mountain, then into a desert for forty days of fasting.

More dark nights of theodicy await, but eventually the biblical pattern recurs; as for his ancient namesake, in "a breeze" the Lord speaks, "Look up." In the sky, Elijah sees Christ on the cross, "with light streaming from the holes of the wounds," and hears:

> *This is a vision of what is not yet, but is soon to be. On that day, every human creature will see his soul stripped bare before his eyes. Then he must choose. You are to give witness for Me against the Man of Sin who seeks to set himself in My house, to usurp the throne of God.*[78]

O'Brien closes the novel by linking Father Elijah and Brother Ass to the return of Elijah and Enoch, prophetic witnesses whom Catholic tradition often argues will confront the antichrist in the final days. The final page of the novel is actually Scripture, Rev 10:10—11:13, which describes this confrontation and includes these wonderfully consoling words about God's witnesses:

> After three and a half days a breath of life from God entered them and they stood up on their feet, and great fear fell on those who saw them. Then they heard a loud voice from heaven saying to them, "Come up hither!" And in the sight of their foes they went up to heaven in a cloud. [Rev 11:11–12][79]

So, far from conclusively answering our questions, the passage from Scripture raises many more: Are Father Elijah and Brother Ass the witnesses prophesied in Revelation? Why would O'Brien not show their

---

77. O'Brien, *Father Elijah*, 567.
78. O'Brien, *Father Elijah*, 583.
79. O'Brien, *Father Elijah*, 597.

descent into the city to confront the President? Why might O'Brien's apocalypse close in mystery, pointing us back to Scripture, rather than following Elijah to his earthly end? Despite these uncertain questions, how does *Father Elijah* yet clearly affirm the ultimate victory of Christ?

"The Sojourners" from *Strangers and Sojourners*

"Places of True Home":
Strangers and Sojourners

> Perhaps there are places within us, places of true home, that do not yet exist and are carved from the stone of our hearts only by suffering. Perhaps. Who will tell me if this is true?
> —Anne Delaney, in O'Brien, *Strangers and Sojourners*, 193

THE THEOLOGICAL SUBLIMITY OF *Father Elijah*, essential to its subject, is a hard act to follow. That it was also O'Brien's first published novel, and sold well, made the task all the more difficult. Yet, as already noted in my preface, this was certainly not O'Brien's first novel. For many years he had been working on a series, alluded to by the references to *Sophia House* in *Father Elijah*, and so it was a natural decision to next publish the series' first title, chronologically, *Strangers and Sojourners*. The back cover of the novel, when first published, called it the first part of a trilogy—the novel's main family continues through *Plague Journal* and *Eclipse of the Sun*—but eventually O'Brien would place this trilogy within a series of seven books, including *Father Elijah*, that became known as *Children of the Last Days*. Printings of *Strangers and Sojourners* published after 2013, in fact, include an afterward that lists all seven novels in the *Children of the Last Days* series, giving a synopsis that connects each novel.

It is *Strangers and Sojourners* that first gives the series' title. An older brother of Pawel Tarnowski, Jan, has emigrated to British Columbia, on the West Coast of Canada. Somewhat unhinged, understandably, by the horrors of the Holocaust, Jan appreciates the tolerance and gentility of his new neighbors, but is also disturbed by their naïve view of world affairs. To awaken them each day at three o'clock, with a daily reminder of both the reality of evil and Christ's crucifixion, Jan builds an "endofdevorldkluk" (an "end of the world clock") and when introducing it tells his listeners, "You don't know it, but you are the Children of the Last Days."[1] Jan combines social eccentricity and mad prophecy in a manner that is at once comical and serious. Many other aspects of the novel, and of subsequent novels in the series, allow O'Brien to successfully transfer many of the apocalyptic and theological concerns natural to the Europe of *Father Elijah* to a much earlier twentieth-century setting in Canada.

Though often concerned with local issues, the Canadian characters of this series must face the same serious questions as any citizen of the "progressive" twentieth century, which included both rapid technological progress and the sad reality that more people died in its wars than in all previous centuries of human history combined. Why? Perhaps the Holocaust itself best sums up the paradox: how could any human beings, let alone a nation as culturally developed and well educated as modern Germany, allow such atrocities to happen? Perhaps most troubling of all, where was God when such horrors occurred? Can one have any faith in either God or humanity, after the Holocaust?

These troubling questions, elements of the vexed issue that theologians call "the problem of evil," are a recurring concern of the *Children of the Last Days* series. One of O'Brien's responses to these questions is given through a character always in the background in *Strangers and Sojourners*, one who also reappears in most of the other *Children of the Last Days* series, unifying them as much through the constancy of his stance as the appearance of his person. Father Andrei is a priest who works the trapper line of interior BC, but his "occupation" and "territory" barely begin to suggest his spiritual significance. O'Brien does not introduce him until halfway through *Strangers and Sojourners*, and even then naming him only as "the hermit," but his initial words in the novel are the same as those first spoken by John Paul II at the beginning of his pontificate: "Don't be afraid."[2]

Surely this is no coincidence. Consistently, Andrei's presence offers authentic spiritual comfort—the love of the living God—but he also challenges, through wisdom, in a way sure to make any North American feel a bit uncomfortable. Addressing not only the novel's main character, but also the general reading audience's need for the "dark way" or *via negativa* of John of the Cross, Andrei teaches:

---

1. O'Brien, *Strangers and Sojourners*, 414.
2. O'Brien, *Strangers and Sojourners*, 299.

> The world is full of hatred because it refuses to be poor. It wants to conquer fear with power. But you will conquer in another way, the unknown way. First, perhaps, you will forget. You will not see. You will not understand. Later you may see, and then you will know that the false self must die in order for the true self to be born.[3]

An obvious distinction between this novel and *Father Elijah* would seem to be the relative emphasis on the roles of clerical and lay members of the church. The role of the family, and of married life, is clearly vital in *Strangers and Sojourners*, but Father Andrei is present throughout the series, even when absent from particular scenes, and thus is a crucial reminder of the unity of the body of Christ.

Within its various twentieth-century settings, then, the *Children of the Last Days* series allows O'Brien to consider the most profound philosophical and theological themes. A short preface to the novel suggests such sources as "G. K. Chesterton, Christopher Dawson, Catherine Doherty, Dante, and a host of people whose greatness will never be known,"[4] but the title of the novel clearly alludes to a well-known scriptural concept. *Strangers and Sojourners* alludes to Heb 11:13, a passage quoted later in the novel itself. As well, one of the novel's epigraphs is 1 Pet 2:11: "Beloved, you are strangers and in exile." These Scriptures are the source of one of St. Augustine's most influential ideas; the great early church father reminded citizens of the city of man that their true and only final home must be in heaven, in the city of God. The novel's title thus poses the question implied by my epigraph above: Where is our true home? Is our true home only the eternal world, or do we begin to find it within ourselves in this life, perhaps through suffering, as suggested also in the epigraph? How can we know the answers to such questions?

The novel explores these profound questions through a wide variety of characters, many of whom are realistically depicted. In a short preface to the novel, O'Brien admits that some of the novel's characters "are composites of real people," but historicity does not make them less spiritual. Rather, the preface continues, "their nobility and their failings are drawn from the drama of personal histories—the holy and mysterious material we presume to call 'ordinary' lives."[5] As with all of O'Brien's fiction, the

---

3. O'Brien, *Strangers and Sojourners*, 300.
4. O'Brien, *Strangers and Sojourners*, 11.
5. O'Brien, *Strangers and Sojourners*, 11.

mysterious yet holy reality of the novel's subject matter is suggested by its cover icon, which depicts a family, child between mother and father.

The child has a book open, and in the loving gaze towards his mother is surely the commonplace longing any child has to learn from parents. This icon thus suggests the long tradition of Catholic painting in which Christ looks to Mary, while she begins the long human quest to understand the divine Word. What natural and supernatural learning is implied in *Strangers and Sojourners*? As in *Father Elijah*, there is a dove, symbol of the Holy Spirit, rising on the left side; on the right, however, is a white horse without a rider. Is the horse in opposition to the Holy Spirit, or in harmony with it? What do both symbols offer the icon's family? At the top of the painting, forming a horizontal horizon, seems to be the British Columbia sky, with evergreen trees thickly covering the land below. How will this horizon shape the family's future? How will the horizon of eternity shape their time?

The opening scenes of the novel, dated at precisely the start of the twentieth century, January 1, 1900, suggest some responses to these iconographic questions. Initially, the white horse is clearly associated with the occult practices, such as the attempt to communicate with dead spirits, that are familiar to any student of early twentieth-century British literature and have a much longer history, of course, such as Saul's necromancy with the witch in 1 Kings. O'Brien clearly depicts the demonic character of the occult, but in *Strangers and Sojourners* there is a more common human reality behind such practices; the mother of the family depicted, the Ashton family of England, has died. Heartbroken, the father has been drawn deeper and deeper into the occult, despite his own intellectual learning, in the hope of contacting his dead wife's spirit.

From this painful opening emerges the central character of the novel, the younger daughter of the family, Anne. From the start, she recoils from occult practices, but the inevitable question—what then should I believe?—haunts the rest of her life. Anne's courageous struggle to find faith, fueled by a very valiant spirit that enables many brave actions throughout her life, becomes the concrete means to explore the major philosophical and theological questions that the novel raises. As taught in the "personalism" espoused by John Paul II, it is the acting person who becomes a word of meaning through which the Word reveals meaning to the world.[6]

---

6. John Paul II, *Acting Person*.

In this revelation, Anne is never alone. Her life interacts with and is affected by numerous other characters—one hesitates to call them "minor"—who are also important individuals, and meaningful words, within the novel. The novel's second epigraph comes from *Paradiso*, when in heaven Dante has this famous moment of insight: "Within its depths I saw ingathered, bound by love in one volume, the scattered leaves of all the universe."[7] The novel takes place firmly on earth, yet Anne eventually also sees that the "universe is not flat. It is deep, multilayered, complex, always astonishing."[8] A highly relevant example of this, when she considers marriage, is the apparent reality of "a male and female principle in biology." Nature does seem divided, relatively equally, between male and female forms, and perhaps this is not simply a matter of physical survival. Perhaps, especially in the case of human life, "the unifying principle would seem to be love." But "what is love?"[9] Ann wonders, for the quest to know the reality of love can be said to define Anne's life, and O'Brien explores this sublime theme from many angles.

Most important, at least to Anne, is the man she meets and marries after she becomes a teacher in Swiftcreek, British Columbia. Stiofan O'Dulaine, an Irishman known in the new world as Stephen Delaney, does not at first seem a likely match for Anne. He lives alone in the bush, and she dubs him "the Centaur." Though there is some attraction on Anne's part to Stephen's animal form, they are not brought together in romantic scenes in which either makes the independent, willful, "free" decisions thought to be required for modern notions of romantic love. Rather, in a realistic scene of a frontier society with very limited medical resources, Anne first becomes intimate with Stephen not sexually, but in the far less attractive reality of his viral illness in an epidemic. All available doctors are needed to care for children and the elderly, so Anne stays in Stephen's rustic cabin to nurse him back to health.

This often thankless and even grotesque task, performed mainly while the man is unconscious and incontinent, itself seems fatal to any romantic future. Then, once he does regain health, the long-standing mistrust between the Irish and English seems to render any potential romance impossible. In Stephen's case, this wound has been made much more painful because British soldiers killed his father. In addition to his deep pain, Stephen has brought a devout, mystical Catholicism with him

---

7. Dante, *Divine Comedy*, 3:33.
8. O'Brien, *Strangers and Sojourners*, 99.
9. O'Brien, *Strangers and Sojourners*, 100.

to the New World, and it seems unlikely that this faith can coexist with the agnosticism that the occult experiences of her English family have bequeathed to Anne.

As O'Brien did to depict the interior prayer life of Father Elijah, in this novel the interior thoughts, often doubts, of the couple are also conveyed through italics. Considering marriage, Anne wonders, *"Am I mad, mad, mad to do this?"* Stephen thinks: *"Woman, you seem so calm. Are you not afraid of this thing that is happening to us? If you saw my past, would you still wish to marry me?"*[10] There is more to his past than is initially revealed; the early scenes of the novel depict his father being captured and killed by English soldiers, but only later do we learn that Stephen himself killed one of those English soldiers, in retaliation.

So the two seem an unlikely match from the start, and O'Brien makes very little attempt in the novel to make the marriage that nevertheless occurs seem romantic or providential. Rather, though the marriage includes the typical consolations of the flesh and the joys possible whenever parents are open to and gifted with children, in many ways this seems a marriage of convenience; or, if that is too harsh, then at best this marriage seems a means to avoid the loneliness and material discomfort of the frontier. While the New World surely opens new possibilities, it also brings material challenges while retaining many of the spiritual conflicts of the Old World.

On a more basic level, perhaps one should simply say that this is a human marriage, for if humans in general are unfit for this world, not really made for its nature, there are bound to be some conflicts involved in any two humans attempting to make a life with each other in this world. Perhaps Tolkien had it right when he said that each person in a marriage should view their spouse as a fellow survivor in a shipwreck.[11] At the wedding of Anne and Steve, the full passage from Hebrews is read which gives the novel its title:

> All of these died in faith before receiving any of the things that had been promised, but they saw them in the far distance and welcomed them, recognizing that they were strangers and sojourners upon the earth. (Heb 11:13)

Yet if Anne and Steven are united by their basic human condition, their worldviews are so fundamentally different that one often questions,

---

10. O'Brien, *Strangers and Sojourners*, 141.
11. Tolkien, *Letters*, 50, letter 43.

in the novel, whether these two can die together, "in faith." The most basic of these conflicts has little to do with history or geography; it is rather the spiritual conflict that exists when one person in a marriage believes and the other doesn't, or believes in very different sort of deity. Even on their wedding day, O'Brien suggests this is the case with Anne and Steven; through the Holy Spirit in one of its traditional symbols, as the wind, God speaks to Anne after the wedding, but she can't hear:

> *It is good that you have come empty before the Presence,*
>   *said the wind.*
> *But I do not believe in the Presence, she replied.*
> *Be still, be still.*
> *I will, I will.*
> *Are you listening, do you hear?*
> *I am listening, but I cannot hear. I cannot hear!*[12]

Why is a good person sometimes unable to hear the voice of God? The spiritual angst in Anne is painful, but real; the italics here express the real words in her interior life. Her great virtue, though, is that she does not accept simplistic answers to the great metaphysical questions, no matter how popular these might make her with the culture around her. On the question of "What is love?" for example, she refuses to fall into romantic clichés, and instead keeps searching for something deeper. Seeking the principle that holds our world together, she asks,

> *Is it no more than the sensation of pleasure as life is bestowed on life, no more than a reward mechanism that ensures the complexification and affirmation of existence? If it is only that, and if the whole thing is meaningless, I think it a colossal waste of effort.*[13]

The independence of mind implied here in Anne means that throughout this life, even in marriage, she is haunted by loneliness, of the kind that any theist must say is inevitable to the atheist or agnostic. She thinks to herself, "*I am happy . . . I am lonely too. I love and am well loved but remain incomplete.*"[14] Later, in a diary, she writes, "*I have been depressed a great deal this winter. Why does this emptiness persist within me when I am so abundantly blessed?*"[15] In the honesty and authenticity of Anne's questions, we see not only the angst of the human condition but

---

12. O'Brien, *Strangers and Sojourners*, 145.
13. O'Brien, *Strangers and Sojourners*, 100.
14. O'Brien, *Strangers and Sojourners*, 167.
15. O'Brien, *Strangers and Sojourners*, 224.

also an example of how to continue to seek truth throughout a human life.

The conflicts within the marriage of Anne and Steven seem unresolved until her dying days, but throughout her life she has a series of relationships with men—nonsexual in nature—that allow her, and the novel's readers, deeper insight into the nature of love. This begins even before she meets Stephen when, working as a nurse on the battlefields of WWI, she nurses a dying man named Peter who falls in love with her and requests, as a last wish, a kiss from her. She complies, and finds herself caught in a romantic cliché; she is attracted to Peter, attracted both by his bravery and stories of painting in the wilderness of his native Canada, even after his death. Is this love or delusion?

The emotion endures long enough to help inspire Anne's own immigration to Canada after the war. There she meets Stephen, and at first the far more likely candidate to fulfill the romantic desires of her heart seems Rev. Gunnalls, a young Protestant minister who, before her marriage, woos Anne with long walks and intellectual talk. The latter appeals to the young teacher sometimes shocked by the absence of frontier culture, but there is a vaguely occult, "New Age" theology lurking inside Rev. Gunnalls's mind, even at this early point in the twentieth century. "Good and evil," he claims, are "just the opposite sides of the same things," approvingly citing Nietzsche. Anne has heard this before, however, and replies, "That's exactly what Father says."[16] Despite the allure of another romantic cliché—young professionals, a teacher and minister meeting on the harsh frontier—before long Anne ends the courtship and soon marries Stephen.

Her marriage does not bring her to belief, but at least to an appreciation of some of the wisdom and beauty of Catholicism. O'Brien uses another conversation with Rev. Gunnalls to develop especially the twentieth-century, North American reality behind this theme. Anne tells Rev. Gunnalls, "This Church, this thing that neither you nor I believe in . . . Doesn't its only power lie in being a voice in the consciences of men?"[17] The young reverend, still apparently enamored of New Age religion, critiques Catholicism as "so primitive a religion . . . so pessimistic . . . so damn critical," but she stands her ground, arguing: "Maybe it's realistic. Perhaps there's something to criticize, something in the atmosphere that's

---

16. O'Brien, *Strangers and Sojourners*, 74.
17. O'Brien, *Strangers and Sojourners*, 210.

poisoning us all. Something that kills love."[18] He goes on to claim, like so many post-60s North Americans, that love does not need rules, but even a highly intellectual teacher knows enough about agriculture to disagree; Anne replies:

> Orchards need exquisite care, you know. Otherwise the fruit gets smaller and bland and the tree puts out a thousand new branches, then it dies prematurely. Only for a while do the beasts gorge on the fruit that lies rotting in the forest glades.[19]

At this moment Anne "glimpsed the difference between the minister and her husband." Stephen's "strength was the long, silent labor of the orchardist," whereas Rev. Gunnalls "was a flash of theoretical passion, ready for any heroic destruction." She finally wonders, "Which form of strength would be vindicated?"[20]

Even after her marriage, however, Anne remains a restless spirit, and at one point, midway through the novel, O'Brien suggests Anne's desires through a dream. Aboard a cruise ship, on the way to visit her childhood home in England, she has an emotionally intimate, though physically platonic, friendship with a painter also named Peter. Perhaps a projection of the WWI soldier, Peter has only become more attractive over the years, an artistic, cultural, romantic alternative to the base reality who is Stephen. Yet even in the midst of the dream, Anne recognizes the clichéd nature of this "romance," and rejects it as "so entirely predictable, a shipboard romance, a dime novel written badly, expressing pathetic sentiments. She would have none of it."[21]

After waking up in her home, beside her husband and children, Anne returns to the dream to tell Peter that "real love is a long apprenticeship," and after many years of giving love in marriage, "it's given back to you in a better form than you could have imagined."[22] Though this later Peter is entirely fictional, through imagining him Anne both learns truth and becomes able to articulate some of the wisdom gleaned from her marriage to Stephen.

What kind of truth should be learned from the imaginative world of art? This is a key question for O'Brien, given his vocation as painter and

18. O'Brien, *Strangers and Sojourners*, 210.
19. O'Brien, *Strangers and Sojourners*, 210.
20. O'Brien, *Strangers and Sojourners*, 210.
21. O'Brien, *Strangers and Sojourners*, 233.
22. O'Brien, *Strangers and Sojourners*, 252.

novelist, and *Strangers and Sojourners* explores it in a number of ways. The fictional painter Peter expresses some of O'Brien's key thoughts, such as when he tells Anne, "A painting is a word spoken into the void. It pushes back the darkness," qualifying this thought by adding, "Only to the degree that it's a true word."[23] Anne replies with Pilate's question, "What is truth?" causing Peter to allude to one of the most famous pronouncements on truth in modern aesthetics, Keats's "Ode on a Grecian Urn":

> I don't agree with Keats that truth is beauty and beauty is truth and that's all you need to know. We need to know a hell of a lot more than that. But I do know that truth doesn't do well without the help of beauty. It needs it so badly I think the world would collapse without it. Without it we couldn't grasp things intuitively, things we could never express by intelligence.[24]

There are moments when it seems, perhaps because of a lack of intellectual culture—of serious searching for philosophical beauty and aesthetic truth—that Anne's world with Stephen could collapse. Though her marriage is abundantly blessed, at her lowest points Anne cannot feel this. She looks at her children and thinks, "I will fail them, scar them, leave a legacy of insanity," and her spirit even cries out, "Kill me, God!"[25] At this time, Rev. Gunnalls has returned to live in Swiftcreek, and we fear the worst, but time proves to have changed them both. Gunnalls has already been through an adulterous relationship, admitting to Anne, without revealing the gory details, that he "destroyed a family." The sad experience seems to have changed his views on religion.

Previously he had thought, "All religions are the same, Anne, and each of them has its way of helping us adjust to an empty universe."[26] Now, though, Rev. Gunnalls respects orthodox Christianity. He tells Anne, "I found, you see, in a long crucible of pain, that all religions aren't the same."[27] Perhaps most crucially, he has learned the importance of forgiveness, even if this education has been ironically self-centered: "I began to find it more important to forgive my enemy on the day that I found

---

23. O'Brien, *Strangers and Sojourners*, 242.
24. O'Brien, *Strangers and Sojourners*, 252.
25. O'Brien, *Strangers and Sojourners*, 260.
26. O'Brien, *Strangers and Sojourners*, 75.
27. O'Brien, *Strangers and Sojourners*, 309.

out that I *am* my enemy."[28] Anne here finds this view strange, but there is a growing wisdom in Rev. Gunnalls that allows him to laugh at himself.

For her part, Anne's understanding of both art and life is deepened not only through her marriage, but also through friendship. Nigel Lord Rockingham is a displaced English aristocrat, extremely eccentric and easily alienated from the rest of the town, but he seems to find a soulmate, or at least a protector, in platonic friendship with Anne. O'Brien's narrator explains this relationship, and hints at the narcissistic young man's fatal flaws, by explaining that with Anne and Nigel, "Their love of books might have dragged them into an infidelity of the spiritual kind, but the poet was so engrossed with himself that this proved impossible."[29] After claiming to be a poet constantly at work on a long, great poem, Nigel is found dead, a suicide, with no writing actually done.

This harsh reality is painful for Anne, but through it she is learning something essential to O'Brien's worldview. Nigel is a familiar figure in O'Brien's fiction, the empty, directionless aesthete for art's sake, whose values as an artist are in many ways opposite to the devout, purposeful art that O'Brien himself creates. But perhaps the deeper point here is that art cannot be the primary foundation of human spiritual life; as Jacques Maritain put it, "It is a deadly error to suppose that art can provide the super-substantial nourishment of men."[30] Art, even great art, is an insufficient foundation for human spiritual life; art can point to God or be a "bridge to religious experience,"[31] but it cannot replace religious life itself.

Anne also learns this error through another young man in the novel, Maurice L'Oraison. As a young teacher, Anne recognizes the intelligence of the young Maurice, who responds eloquently to poetry, and it seems a good thing when Maurice goes away to become a lawyer. Yet he comes back representing a government that steals the land of the people of Swiftcreek, and he later becomes one of the major villains of the *Children of the Last Days* series. In *Strangers and Sojourners*, Anne asks, after Maurice's fall, "Is this the shape that poets take when the poetry has been destroyed?"[32]

Maurice's fall is especially painful for Anne because he is the stepson of Anne's most steadfast friend in Swiftcreek, a rustic, down-to-earth,

28. O'Brien, *Strangers and Sojourners*, 317.
29. O'Brien, *Strangers and Sojourners*, 272.
30. Maritain, *Art and Scholasticism*, 29.
31. John Paul II, "Letter to Artists," §10.
32. O'Brien, *Strangers and Sojourners*, 451.

and often caustic middle-aged woman named Turid. Completely lacking the cultured background that might seem suitable for friendship with Anne, Turid instead can offer Anne honesty and loyalty, virtues that are foundations of friendship beneath any other intellectual bonds. When Anne's purely platonic, spiritual meetings with the Rev. Gunnalls cause scandalous gossip among the town's "elite" ladies, Turid stands by Anne.

The Creator's mysterious ways also affect Anne and her family through their friendship with the Tobac family. The Tobacs are of the mixed French and native ethnicity one often finds in western Canada, most famously in the Métis. The father, Thaddeus, is a trapper and devout Catholic who works hard to feed his family both physically and spiritually; the mother, Wanda, is a native who was scarred by a childhood in the residential schools that wounded so many Canadian natives, such that as an adult she struggles with mental illness, drinking, and, in her lowest moments, violence. On one snowy evening, Thaddeus is led by an anxious intuition to return home, and in the middle of the night finds Wanda stalking her children with a knife. The children, Jack and Sarah, mainly appear in the novel as young adults and are accepting of their mother's mental illness. They also offer true friendship, the kind of authentic love that they have learned from their father, when the eldest son of Anne and Stephen, Ashley, has his own physical and mental tragedies to deal with.

Just after the scene where O'Brien depicts Jack's nightmare as an eight-year-old child, and Thaddeus's intuitive intervention, Ashley is shown having a nightmare in which he looks into water and sees his own face all cut up. The older Jack comforts him, but Ashley feels it "too real. Too real."[33] As in the famous scene in Milton's *Paradise Lost* when Adam dreams of Satan only to awake and find evil all too real (4.639–52), so here Ashley's dream is not mere anxiety, but, rather, spiritual intuition. His cuts occur in a scene that O'Brien depicts in entirely naturalistic terms, though the novel as a whole develops its spiritual meaning. Ashley forgets his gun before setting off on a hike through mountains, and is suddenly confronted by a violent grizzly bear. He climbs a tree, but thinking how he will send warning to his brother Bryan to avoid this path, Ashley falls and is horribly mauled by the bear. Though just a wild animal, the bear here acts in the violent, nihilistic way that the novel as a whole links to satanic violence.

---

33. O'Brien, *Strangers and Sojourners*, 295.

The ensuing pain for Ashley is both physical and spiritual. He must undergo months of operations and rehab even to live, and is left so scarred that he will not go out in public. Jack Tobac eventually comes to him, embracing his friend despite the deformity. Jack's sister, Sarah, renews the romantic friendship with Ashley that had begun before his accident. Though their courtship sometimes seems painful, with Ashley turning his face away from Sarah as they sit together, the couple eventually marry and have children. Jack and Sarah, more than any other members of the Swiftcreek community, are able to love Ashley and help him through his darkest hours.

As with Wanda, however, Ashley cannot heal entirely, especially inwardly. One of the saddest moments of the novel comes later when Ashley asks his father, Stephen, to promise not to share any of his religion with Ashley's eldest son, Nathaniel. Yet Ashley does experience more of the self-sacrificial love so highly valued by Catholicism when he enlists to serve in World War II. Perhaps spurred by a death wish, he ends up on a ship suddenly attacked by an enemy sub. A fellow crewman named Wheeler had invited Ashley on the ship's deck, and when the attack started had suddenly given his safe chair; soon after, in the water, Ashley swims by the dead crewman. Though grotesque and traumatic, often later filling him with "survivor's guilt" and nihilistic thoughts about the meaninglessness of human life, Ashley also comes to realize that Wheeler sacrificed his own life, the safety of his own seat on the deck, so that by chance or providence Ashley's own life was preserved. In this novel, Ashley never seems sure which answer he believes, though after returning home he does regain enough faith and confidence to marry and live a full life.

Wheeler, we recognize, has paid a high price for Ashley to live this life, as has Thaddeus Tobac in raising the daughter, Sarah, whom Ashley marries. O'Brien further stresses the high cost of truth when Anne spends most of her inheritance (after her father's death) to buy the local town paper, *The Echo*. Many critique Anne's decision as foolish and self-centered, but the person seemingly most directly impacted by it, her husband Stephen, simply accepts it and offers encouragement. Anne herself seems unsure of the value of words against lies, especially after her application to teach again is rejected due to gossip about her and Rev. Gunnalls, but she tells him:

> Perhaps I should say that I still believe in truth, though I can't claim to have it totally and perfectly. And even if I did, yes, even then I would be incomplete. But it's all I have to give. I have

learned some things. And so have you. Shouldn't we speak of these things when the world is awash in nonsense?[34]

Anne uses her new platform to become an advocate for the Swiftcreek people against a provincial government that wants to flood their farm land to create new forms of energy and industry. Anne's words also become perhaps the sole opposition to men like MacPhail, who run their businesses without regard for human life. But perhaps Anne's most important words are given to Nathaniel, as she becomes a teacher and mentor to him, allowing him to become the family leader of the Delaney's through the next two novels in O'Brien's trilogy. Is this relationship the one depicted in the novel's cover icon, in which a child reading an open book gazes lovingly towards his mother?

The closeness possible between grandparents and grandchildren, especially in the case of an alienated parent, is one of the many conventional images of human relationships that *Strangers and Sojourners* enacts. O'Brien's point is more than the probable notion that for something to become as familiar as a cliché, there must be some truth in it. Rather, as the preface has suggested, Anne's trials point to the holy and mysterious reality of her inner life; what outwardly might seem a cliché is an interior spiritual reality that is unique to the word that God, working together with the noble yet often wayward paths of Anne's human will, writes through her extraordinary, "normal" human life.

One of the best examples of O'Brien's treatment of cliché in the novel comes when "normal" life recreates the "fictional" cruise ship of her midlife crisis, when she had rejected the romantic love of Peter in favor of the real love of Stephen. As an older woman, she takes an actual cruise ship back to England, after the death of her older sister. On it she meets "Peter Athelstone" who has almost every clichéd attribute attractive to the elder woman: recently widowed, a retired professional yet still wealthy, kind, polite, and a good conversationalist who is clearly attracted to Anne physically but also truly interested in her mind and heart.

In the midst of this cliché, Anne's subconscious produces a dream that she awakes from feeling "indescribably peaceful."[35] In her dream, she is remembering occult ceremonies from her youth, in which a wicked old man with a dragon on his staff shouts and seems to threaten her. Then a white horse with a rider on it appears, and drives the dragon

---

34. O'Brien, *Strangers and Sojourners*, 345.
35. O'Brien, *Strangers and Sojourners*, 518.

away. For readers familiar with Revelation or *Father Elijah*, the identity of the rider would be clear. Anne, however, cannot yet recognize the rider, and on waking she wonders if the rider was Alfred the Great, the great Anglo-Saxon king of English history and myth. The possibility of Christ's personal interest in Anne's history is mysteriously though subconsciously suggested.

On the cruise, Anne also meets another apparent cliché: Fran, a wheelchair-bound writer who seems to have all the flaws of the ugly American artist who writes for commercial gain and fame. Fran and Anne have some unpleasant conversations that seem to come to nothing. Fran does not seem especially friendly, at one point telling Anne, "Watch for the *New Yorker* magazine in May or June. There'll be a savage depiction of you in there. Now get lost."[36] Given the length of this novel, one might wonder whether this apparently sad relationship would best have been edited out.

Yet after returning to Canada, Anne reads Fran's account of the cruise, and learns first that Fran had taken the cruise initially as an opportunity for suicide. But then Fran had encountered "the once pretty" face of Anne, and saw in her eyes a "sufferin'" like only "me an the cripples know."[37] Fran's suicide plan, writes O'Brien's narrator, met "something immovable" in Anne, and Fran's article concludes by suggesting something almost divine in what she has found at sea:

> I have been defeated, and in the defeat I have won myself. It is
> a pleasure to die at the hands of Life. On its terms. Not mine.
> We are not alone. The vast sea sends messengers to us if we wait.
> They speak, they speak, though we hardly ever hear.[38]

Anne's impact on others, as perhaps an unconscious messenger of the divine, can also be heard in a final letter from Rev. Gunnalls. His denomination has formally "retired" him from ministry, in no small part because of the orthodox Christian faith that he has gleaned primarily from the fidelity of Anne to Stephen. In his final letter to Anne he writes,

> You said the other day . . . that I had helped to save your life. I
> have never told you, but it was I who was saved. Saved by your

---

36. O'Brien, *Strangers and Sojourners*, 508.
37. O'Brien, *Strangers and Sojourners*, 523.
38. O'Brien, *Strangers and Sojourners*, 525.

obedience, your word, which you refused to break. And saved by your humility.[39]

At the end of her life, Anne's faithfulness creates one of the novel's most moving scenes. Any depiction of a "death-bed conversion" carries the obvious risk of cliché, but O'Brien avoids this first by having Anne honestly express the agnosticism that has been the spiritual reality of her life. She tells Stephen, knowing that she is dying, that she feels "empty, nothing" in her illness, yet also affirms that her very "lack of faith" is a gift. He cannot understand what she is saying, "'No, no, no . . .' he said, attempting to correct this sick child,"[40] but she is moving towards faith. Anne then gives one of O'Brien's foundational theodicies, seeing God as an artist working to repair the fallen masterpiece of his creation; in Anne's dying words to her husband:

> Suppose there is a great Love behind creation, but the original unity of this vast work of art has been damaged, and all of existence as we know it, is merely a brief moment during which the artist repairs his masterpiece. If he is that beautiful, it would be unspeakably shattering to have a glimpse of his face.[41]

This insight then leads Anne to the key argument of theological aesthetics: the beauty of the world suggests the reality of a great Artist at work, and the reality of this Love eventually leads to a true knowledge of the living God. As Anne puts it:

> There is beauty in the world. There is no reason for it to be here. If it's all biology, all eating and getting eaten and the strongest devouring the weakest, then it's madness. Nothing more than madness. It's dying and drowning, and all love is illusion. But there is love, you see. Poor, weak, and broken love—a sign of something from a distant land.[42]

Again, Stephen doesn't understand, replying, "I wish I could give you my belief, my certainty."[43] Yet when both subsequently say to each other, "I love you," it does not come across as cliché. Rather, it is the reality of real married love, faithful and true unto one's dying days.

39. O'Brien, *Strangers and Sojourners*, 535.
40. O'Brien, *Strangers and Sojourners*, 542.
41. O'Brien, *Strangers and Sojourners*, 542.
42. O'Brien, *Strangers and Sojourners*, 543.
43. O'Brien, *Strangers and Sojourners*, 543.

Soon after this moving scene, Father Andrei visits Anne; it is unclear if it is "baptism" or "last rites" that occurs, but she reports that Father Andrei listens for two hours, then speaks some words in Latin, and very tellingly Anne says, "It should have happened many, many years ago" and that it was "so beautiful."[44] Perhaps most importantly, Anne no longer feels afraid. After Anne's death, Stephen believes she is with God, for as much as any human can she has followed Christ by laying down her life for her friends. She has been a spiritual sojourner; the final human word on her life is given to Turid: "'Tis a wee visit that we make t'this world."[45] Yet, with Stephen, readers can retain hope that Anne has gone on to a permanent home in eternity with God.

Anne's death allows us to reflect further on one of the most significant themes of the novel: the value of suffering. It is easy for anyone removed from the reality of suffering to become like Job's "comforters," rationalizing the causes of suffering and commending it as a surefire method of self-improvement. Cold comfort for anyone facing real suffering, but also a certain recipe for our own despair; can anyone believe in a God capable of "teaching" only through the level of suffering faced by the human world? Yet while the problem of evil, of theodicy, is a central problem faced by O'Brien and most serious literary writers, *Strangers and Sojourners* does raise a more basic human question: Would humans truly long for eternity if we were completely comfortable in the natural world? Is not our restlessness in this world a sign that our true home must be with God? St. Augustine's famous words, among the most famous words in all of Christian culture, remind us that "the heart is restless until it rests in God."[46] Augustine gives this insight early in *Confessions*, the account of his own conversion; by the end of this novel, O'Brien has allowed us to understand, even if her husband Stephen cannot, that Anne's restlessness led her to God, and her eternal home. It is true, at least for Anne, that suffering carves in her heart a place of true home.

Why does *Strangers and Sojourners* not end with Anne's passing? This might seem an obvious conclusion, given that the majority of the novel is about her life. O'Brien's main interest, however, has been her spiritual rather than physical life, and just as Stephen can believe in her soul's supernatural survival, so her spirit continues to leave a legacy in her family, and land, long after her death. The short, final section of the novel

44. O'Brien, *Strangers and Sojourners*, 545.
45. O'Brien, *Strangers and Sojourners*, 546.
46. Augustine, *Confessions*, 1.

suggests this via paradoxical rather than literal means, most obviously because its primary event is a forest fire that destroys much of Swiftcreek. This final section includes some of the most suspenseful scenes of the novel, but the fire's real significance is spiritual rather than physical.

This is shown especially by this final section's key scene. To escape the fire, the grandson of Anne and Stephen, Nathaniel, takes refuge in a mountain cave, a cave that will be just as important to his future as the cave his grandfather Stiofan entered when pursuing British soldiers back in Ireland, or his father Ashton entered as a young man reflecting upon the meaning of life. A Platonic "allegory of the cave" seems too exalted a description for such moments in O'Brien's fiction, but there is no doubt, at least in this novel, that caves take on symbolic significance as places of philosophical quest, sites allowing spiritual wisdom. In Nathaniel's cave he meets what first seems to be a bear; as his eyes clear of smoke, he sees:

> a shape that melted and flowed, a hybrid abomination of leopard and wolf, a coiled serpent, a bear. Gradually his vision cleared. It was a bear. It was very old; its snout was scarred and its flank matted with dried blood. Its eyes were black lodestones rimmed with red. It sat back on its haunches and opened its mouth.[47]

By its scars and age one could imagine this to be the very bear so dangerous to Nathaniel's father, Ashley, on that terrible day when he fell from the tree. Here, however, O'Brien will make clear the supernatural, demonic foundations of natural evil and random, destructive violence.

Not that bears themselves are demonic, of course, no more than are snakes despite the common misreading of Genesis. Rather, a demonic spirit has clearly entered this cave's "bear," a spirit whose primary urge is the destruction of Nathan and his family. The cave thus allows the moment of spiritual realism denied by those unaware of demonic reality. Nathaniel himself "had never before encountered darkness as a presence," but this "presence" seems capable, like a human person, of social relationships. The "presence" desires, for example, that Nathaniel will accept a job offer he has recently gotten from Maurice L'Oraison. Understandably, Nathaniel asks, "How did you know that? What are you?"[48]

Having established that, in some way, the spirit in the cave is supernatural, the bear begins to speak in the italics that O'Brien normally uses to indicate spiritual voices; the bear asks Nathaniel:

---

47. O'Brien, *Strangers and Sojourners*, 563.
48. O'Brien, *Strangers and Sojourners*, 563.

> *What do you want?*
> "I want truth"
> *There is no truth. Only knowledge. Only power.*
> "That's a lie"
> *Is it? Tell me what your "truth" is built upon? Tell me what I cannot blow away?*[49]

Nathaniel opened his mouth to reply but realized that he did not actually have an answer. "What was his concept of truth built upon? Vague ideas of democracy and freedom? Belief in man?"[50]

Conversation continues until a key moment, when Nathaniel says something he might have learned from his grandfather, a crucial principle also foundational to the life of his grandmother Anne: "The Truth will make us free." Jesus' famous words from the Gospel of John (8:32) have an immediate effect on the demonic presence; its spiritual significance is first suggested strongly by O'Brien's narrator:

> There was silence for an eternal moment as Nathaniel waited. Then the entire chamber filled suddenly with a choking smell that made him retch. Horror swept over him, as if he were blown in a hurricane of malice, an unthinkable force that would tear the hair, the nails, the flesh from his body. It was power. It was fear.[51]

The demonic presence continues its spiritual assault until, much like in Father Elijah's final encounter with the President, "Nathaniel grabbed the stone cross" that has been passed down to him and "lifted it high." By the cross of Christ, the "phantom bear" is "sucked out of the cave."[52] After he recovers from the ordeal, Nathaniel is not sure who he has been speaking to, perhaps "the ghost of our family bear."[53] When he emerges from the cave and returns to the burned town, Nathaniel has a final meeting with Jan Tarnowski. Jan is understandably upset about the fire's destruction, but Nathaniel points to the future: "The fire is finished, Jan . . . Make beauty."[54]

---

49. O'Brien, *Strangers and Sojourners*, 565.
50. O'Brien, *Strangers and Sojourners*, 565.
51. O'Brien, *Strangers and Sojourners*, 566.
52. O'Brien, *Strangers and Sojourners*, 567.
53. O'Brien, *Strangers and Sojourners*, 568.
54. O'Brien, *Strangers and Sojourners*, 570.

Again, these words would be a suitable conclusion to the theological aesthetic that O'Brien has so vividly pursued throughout the novel. One final scene is given us, though, since the fire does not take the life of old Stephen Delaney. The final words of the novel artistically point towards the eternal life that he is waiting to share with Anne. Stephen remains an important presence for his grandchildren, still "eloquent with silences," but inside him remains the spiritual heritage to be heard in eternity; in the novel's final paragraph, Stephen

> sings a word or two in a language that has almost ceased to exist, words that endure beyond forgetting, his face raised into the sky, an old man in a burned field, waiting for light.[55]

Why does O'Brien conclude here? Perhaps because there is no final conclusion to human spiritual life united to God. The "strangers and sojourners" theme pursued throughout the novel here finds its happiest expression; rather than the restlessness for God that must lead to impatience and depression—wanting what we cannot have can leave one depressed—here Stephen experiences the happier alternative: waiting peacefully for the eternal light he knows is coming, remembering the words of people of the past knowing he is soon to be with them. This is the peace of Christ, the peace that the world cannot give; in its silence one hears the Word that spoke, and will in heaven speak again, the human songs that Stephen already sings.

The final section of *Strangers and Sojourners* does set up the remainder of O'Brien's initial "trilogy" of novels, and the entire *Children of the Last Days* series, but in itself this is an epic and extraordinary novel. It richly fulfills the promise of O'Brien's preface to the novel, which sought to fictionalize "the holy and mysterious material we presume to call 'ordinary life.'" By the novel's end, we can see also the fulfillment of a further aim of that preface, to use the narrative of human life as a step towards gaining wisdom:

> The telling of stories is the abiding act by which people of all times and places pass down to the coming generations their hard-won fragments of wisdom. One can call it culture, or one can call it fun, but it will always remain indispensable. Wisdom is often purchased at great price, and much of it fades into disremembering because of silence or modest restraint, or because of

---

55. O'Brien, *Strangers and Sojourners*, 571.

shame and grief. Yet without the telling, we would soon cease to understand who we are.[56]

The suffering of Anne and Stephen Delaney, and their brief sojourn on earth, helps us to understand who human beings are in the eyes of God: flawed, but beloved, and capable of cocreating lives of great beauty and eternal significance. The art of fiction, of stories well told by an inspired storyteller like O'Brien, reminds us that God's holy purposes often cannot be seen or felt in a moment, but are rather revealed slowly, over the course of an entire human life. The word of Anne and Stephen Delaney's love has eternal meaning, for the Word of Love speaks through them.

---

56. O'Brien, *Strangers and Sojourners*, 11.

"The Last Homely House" from *Plague Journal*

"Father at Night": *Plague Journal*

> Anger, I knew, has its roots in fear. A father at night may be afraid of any number of things: sickness, poverty, chaos, isolation, the collapse of the roof, the car breaking down again, his own mortality ... or, even more to the point, his powerlessness in the face of reality. He may discover a secret in the fearful dark: he may actually learn to the depths of his being that he is not God.
> —Nathaniel, in O'Brien, *Plague Journal*, 192

WHY IS THIS "SECRET" important? With the manifest problems in our world, is it not obvious that men are not divine? If man is not God, then what is he? *Plague Journal* continues to ask the fundamental questions raised by *Strangers and Sojourners* by continuing to tell the story of the Delaney family. O'Brien's focus turns to Nathaniel, grandson of Anne and Stephen, now a middle-aged man who has followed his grandmother as editor of the town newspaper, *The Echo*, and his grandfather with an allegiance to the Catholic faith. He can barely recall his encounter with the demonic bear in the cave, however, and his faith is rootless and in many ways wounded by elements of modern life, most especially the contemporary plague of divorce. Nathaniel's wife Maya left him eight years ago, taking their youngest child, Arrow, and leaving him to raise Tyler (also known as Bam) and Zöe (nicknamed Ziz). Life suddenly becomes much harder for Nathaniel, however, when an increasingly totalitarian government decides to aggressively begin eliminating journalistic opposition. Falsely accused of sexually molesting his own children, Nathaniel and his two elder children become fugitives on the run from government police.

This simple, melodramatic plot cannot give us the epic novel that is *Strangers and Sojourners*, and is roughly half the length (at 271 pages, O'Brien's shortest novel), but even this apparent weakness allows considerable strengths. Most notably, as the title suggests, this novel is cast in the form of a journal that Nathaniel keeps as his situation becomes increasingly precarious. A third-person narrator also presents some of the suspenseful scenes in which Nathaniel acts, but for the most part the plot is conveyed through this main character's inner life. Yet the novel is not only a record of his emotional response to crisis, it is also the record of his spiritual growth, the awareness that his own assumptions and worldview must change to understand the radically changed world in which he lives. At one point in the novel Nathaniel describes himself as "a bad Catholic because I've been neither hot nor cold in matters of faith . . . simply mediocre for too many years."[1] Not, perhaps, the world's definition of a "bad Catholic," but one that would resonate with John Paul II, who exhorted his flock: "Do not be satisfied with mediocrity!"[2]

Nathaniel has inherited the integrity and honesty of Anne, allowing him to be an effective but also annoying (especially for the government) editor of *The Echo*, but also some of her spiritual agnosticism and insecurity. Over the course of the novel, the pressure of crisis moves Nathaniel towards the clear beliefs of his grandfather; yet he also inherits some of Stephen's anger and irrationality, and so Nathaniel's movement towards spiritual maturity is a major theme of the novel. Many aspects of *Plague Journal* cause us to reflect again on *Strangers and Sojourners*, but none more important than that moment in the cave when the demonic bear had caused Nathaniel to question, "What was his concept of truth built upon? Vague ideas of democracy and freedom? Belief in man?"[3] In *Plague Journal*, the crisis forces Nathaniel towards the intense examination of conscience that tends to make human answers to these difficult questions authentic and, ultimately, theological. In the process, the novel becomes not only a key connector within the *Children of the Last Days* series, but also in itself one of the most accessible, and moving, statements of O'Brien's foundational beliefs.

The social and political world that causes Nathaniel's crisis, at least externally, is an extension of problems hinted at in *Strangers and Sojourners* and in full bloom later in the series. We learn later in *Plague Journal* that the federal government—never given a Canadian political name—is engaged in a program of *unitas*, the same pseudo-theology that globally will be led by the President of *Father Elijah*. Early in the novel the social goals of this program are familiar to late twentieth-century Canadians,

---

1. O'Brien, *Plague Journal*, 143.
2. John Paul II, *Abbà Pater*, track 2, 1:17.
3. O'Brien, *Strangers and Sojourners*, 565.

as government is insisting on sexual education classes, in public schools, that go far beyond simple information about reproduction and rather aim to spread ideological propaganda about sexual ethics. Nathaniel's initial objection is a very simple, traditional one, that such education had always been the domain of parents.

A phone call then comes from a character remembered in *Strangers and Sojourners*, now a successful lawyer and rising figure in the federal government. Maurice L'Oraison calls to warn Nathaniel to flee because the government is about to arrest him and his children, making them noncitizens. The call is prompted, he explains, because of lingering doubts raised by Anne. In *Strangers and Sojourners*, doubts about the "dialectic between social progress and individual freedom"[4] led to Anne and Maurice clashing, we recall, over the government flooding of land around Swiftcreek, which had revealed the government's preference for "programs" over people.

Questions raised by the philosophy of John Paul II's "personalism" are at the heart of the disagreement between Anne and Maurice, but much more obvious ethical questions are raised when Nathaniel is accused of sexually molesting his children. Warning also comes from the opposite end of the social spectrum. Bill is the school janitor, but one who reads Dante and Dostoevsky in his spare time, a man whom Nathaniel believes to be "the only really educated man in the town." Bill tells Nathaniel, "I won't never believe that you are guilty."[5] Bill is soon killed and Nathaniel accused of his murder, clear evidence of the hidden savagery of *unitas* that reminds us of the murder of Billy and the framing of Father Elijah for the killing of Anna Benedetti in the novel *Father Elijah*.

Though the political problems of the novel fuels its suspense, as in *Father Elijah*, and though Peter Kreeft could be right in also claiming that the novel's social critique is as important as that of *Brave New World*,[6] this critique never becomes the developed focus of the novel. We don't have, to extend the analogy to Huxley, a "Mustapha Mond" type of character who explains things from the social engineer's point of view. Maurice L'Oraison could be developed into this kind of character, but the full social dystopian vision of *unitas* does not come until the next novel in the *Children of the Last Days* series, *Eclipse of the Sun*. Rather, because

---

4. O'Brien, *Plague Journal*, 59.

5. O'Brien, *Plague Journal*, 62.

6. Peter Kreeft makes this claim in a comment on the back cover of O'Brien, *Plague Journal*.

most of this novel presents events through the eyes of Nathaniel, rather than political argument we have rather a very personal account of what it might mean to be a father in the midst of crisis, a father trapped in a living nightmare. Nathaniel is driven not so much by self-preservation, but by the desire to protect his children. In his struggle to be a father to them, Nathaniel also learns, and teaches us, through his journal, much of what O'Brien sees as the essence of becoming a true human being.

Paradoxically, part of "becoming human" in this novel means "becoming elvish," as that conception—so different from the flimsy, flighty beings of Renaissance England—appears in the work of J. R. R. Tolkien. The role of children's literature in parenting is an important theme in the novel, as Nathaniel strives to preserve the creative, imaginative spirit that God implants in the hearts of children. In the background to this is the Christian view that adults must become childlike to enter the kingdom of heaven, a view developed and stressed by the twentieth-century British Christian literary group known as the Inklings, especially leading members such as Tolkien and C. S. Lewis. Nathaniel's children enjoy Lewis's Narnia series, and the fairy tales of George MacDonald (a late nineteenth-century Scottish writer who was a major influence on the Inklings), but for them,

> Tolkien is the master. Grandpa read it to them one summer when she was six and her brother eight. Some of the theology and the Oxonian witticisms went right over their heads, but they got the thrill of the quest, and the terror of Orcs raiding in the hills of the peaceful Shire. Black Riders made the hair on the back of their necks tingle. There were heroes and traitors, a hidden king, wizards, martyrs, brave men and women, creatures of every sort. The final climax made them tearful. By the end they longed to know real elves, the beautiful, beautiful elves, half man, half angel.[7]

The capacity to appreciate beauty is the positive, easily argued side of the importance of traditional children's literature. Nathaniel also writes at length about how "traditional fairy stories" preserve a "landscape with dragons," which "of course" doesn't mean belief "in the literal presence of dragons"; rather, it's a way to "develop the 'natural imagination,'" which knows that dragons are "a metaphor of malice and deceit, of evil knowledge, and of power without conscience."[8] O'Brien himself

---

7. O'Brien, *Plague Journal*, 78.
8. O'Brien, *Plague Journal*, 84.

wrote nonfiction about this topic,[9] but in the novel Nathaniel's fatherly commitment to children's literature helps us to understand Bam and Ziz's courage during the upheaval that they have to endure. Their bravery has been fueled by the example of hobbits like Bilbo or Frodo Baggins, and they are wise enough to understand that the dragon pursuing them cannot be tamed or reasoned with.

O'Brien's interest in Tolkien and the main themes of *Plague Journal* come together in the novel's cover icon, a painting called *The Last Homely House*, which depicts the house where Nathaniel and his children eventually take refuge. The Thu family, not coincidentally "boat people," refugees from Vietnam, have converted an abandoned boat into a home. In *The Lord of the Rings*, the "last homely house" is Rivendell, home of the elf lord Elrond, a home where the hobbits stop to rest and recover during their journey to Mordor. In the cover icon of *Plague Journal*, the father, mother, and two younger children of the Thu family wave to Nathaniel and his children, along with Anthony, the eldest Thu child, as they set out across the snow. Rather than a realistic painting or one in the style of Eastern Orthodox sacred art, the painting seems more in the tradition of folk art, perhaps even the peasant art common in Asian countries such as China and Vietnam. The boat is colored, though, in the Western Christmas colors of green and red, and ornaments or lights hang from its sail. But the most clearly symbolic element of the painting is universal in the Catholic world: the boat's sail is in the form of a slender gold cross.

There are levels of paradox in this folk art cover icon, however, that make its "word" as profound as the sacred art on the cover of O'Brien's other novels. In *The Lord of the Rings*, the "last homely house" is a magical place of exquisite artistry, crafted by the elf lord Elrond to provide a safe, secure home for the elves to live amid the growing evil created by Sauron and the pride of men. Rivendell is the opposite of the modern term, "homely," which means plain, even ugly; if "homely," the meaning must be the traditional way to form an adjective, and so to denote the "home" created from the people within rather than the materials of a house. A house is not a home, as modern Western society so often shows, but Elrond's elvish art creates a stable home of spiritual rest and recreation for the hobbits. The Thu boat house does the same for Nathaniel and his children, despite being a structure that most Western people would be too proud to dwell within.

9. O'Brien, *Landscape with Dragons*.

Before the arrival of Nathaniel and his children at this "last homely house," the novel flashes back to conversations between Nathaniel and his father, Ashley. An important character in *Strangers and Sojourners*, we recall that the younger Ashley had been badly scarred both by a wild grizzly bear and the horrors of WWII, the pain of life leading him to a despair soothed only by marriage to Sarah Tobac, Nathaniel's mother. Ashley seems to have done fairly well in life, becoming a school principal, but in *Plague Journal* it is also clear that he has entirely lost his faith in God. In this novel's dialogues with Nathaniel, it becomes clear that this loss of faith has been filled with almost blind trust in the promises of progressive, liberal democracy. Nathaniel disputes this trust as firmly as Ashley had rejected his father Stephen's trust in the Catholic Church, father and son bickering over the Western political state even long before its ministry proves so dangerous not only to Nathaniel's journalistic career but even to the life of his family.

While editor of *The Echo*, Nathaniel had followed his grandmother Anne in writing editorials on global politics that upset some Swiftcreek citizens; one, in particular, had warned that Canadian secular culture was becoming alarmingly close to the naïve liberalism within which arose fascist Germany. Though the comparison might seem alarmist, Nathaniel saw in both societies "a camouflaged despair" that makes citizens

> willing to elevate clearly evil personalities into positions of absolute power as long as the new rulers promise a secular redemption. If God is in fact dead, then it is permissible and even logical to do so. If there is no absolute good or evil, then why should we not employ evil men and evil means to bring about a perceived good—meaning, of course, any social good of which the collective mind is convinced. A reading of the culture of prewar Germany offers astounding evidence of just how swiftly and extensively the collective mind is convinced.[10]

Nathaniel also attempts to convince Ashley of this potential parallel—so hard for the proud citizen of Western democracy to accept—by also citing another text prophetic of Western dystopian totalitarianism: Aldous Huxley's *Brave New World*. Huxley's 1932 classic "predicted a society in which literature, religion, and the family would be neutered and all conflicts eliminated by genetic engineering." Over thirty years later, in *Brave New World Revisited*, Huxley "had come to believe that the

---

10. O'Brien, *Plague Journal*, 129.

totalitarianism of the immediate future would be less visibly violent than that of the Hitlers and the Stalins, but it would create a society that was 'painlessly regimented by a corps of highly trained social engineers.'"[11] Though this kind of totalitarianism in Canada is just beginning to show its malevolent face in the inexact future of *Plague Journal*, its full implications become clear in the next novel in O'Brien's series, *Eclipse of the Sun*.

Ashley and Nathaniel, despite being father and son, cannot agree on a political analysis of their own nation. Paradoxically, Nathaniel's views can be much more seriously entertained by a family foreign to Western democracy. The Thu family has survived the horrors of Communist totalitarianism, emerging not only with their faith in God, but even as living examples of why faith in humanity might still be possible. As "boat people," the Thu family has already survived demonic evil, finding in the safety of a loving home the spiritual sight needed to wisely support Nathaniel. The eldest Thu child, Anthony, will give the novel's clearest example of friendship, but his sacrifice will be possible only because he has learned how to truly be human from his earthly father, Matthew. In a moving scene after the Delaneys first arrive at the boat house, Matthew and Natano (as the Vietnamese accent terms Nathaniel) sit outside sharing some "home brew." When the language barrier causes Matthew to say, "You kill Bill," Nathaniel is momentarily dismayed until, his face shining by starlight, Matthew clarifies, "I believe you, Natano! I know you! I know you!" Matthew himself was once a state fugitive, on the run from evil men: "One time, before we leave Vietnam, I am like you. I run. I hide. I in big trouble. If they catch me, I dead."[12] Nathaniel begs to hear the full story, but before it's even finished, Nathaniel eloquently sums up the significance of the moment for the entire *Children of the Last Days* series:

> This Lilliputian tells a strange tale on the deck of a ridiculous ark, beached on the edge of a frozen lake in a cold northern land, on the far, far edges of a cruel century. Just before the end of an age, I have found a true man.[13]

What is a true man? As the hobbits find the essence of spiritual goodness in Elrond, so Nathaniel finds a concrete example of the answer to this complex, theoretical question in Matthew. Again, one naturally relates this moment of the novel to the papacy of John Paul II. As already

---

11. O'Brien, *Plague Journal*, 131.
12. O'Brien, *Plague Journal*, 148.
13. O'Brien, *Plague Journal*, 148.

noted, the first words of this papacy were "Be not afraid," which John Paul II quickly followed with his first encyclical, *Redemptor Hominis*, a reflection on how the incarnation of Christ redeems human nature. Whereas that text requires considerable theological sophistication to grasp its central points, *Plague Journal* gives us, in Matthew, an icon of humanity fully redeemed. As sacred art leads to the revelation of divine identity, and Tolkien's Elrond allows us to glimpse the artistic beauty passing from the world as the "age of the elves" ends, the Thu "homely house" helps Nathaniel and the novel's readers see what humanity should be despite the rise of the totalitarian state based upon *unitas*.

The Communism fled by the Thu family might seem the polar opposite of the "New Age" monism fundamental to *unitas*. However, in O'Brien's novels, characters with lived experience of Communism often give crucial spiritual insights to Western Catholics. Partly this is because such characters have suffered for their faith, often coming face to face with open, public ideology that explicitly and aggressively attempts to eradicate theism from a culture. In sharp contrast to Western Catholics grumbling about getting up on Sunday morning and going to Mass, the Thu family has learned to highly value the freedom of prayer. The contrast between this new generation of Delaneys and the Thu family is vividly depicted when the former first enters the boat house; Nathaniel tells us:

> Then we're commanded to kneel around the kitchen table—all of us. The family immediately obeys as if this is perfectly normal. It's quite a culture shock for us to be on our knees in a crowd of Oriental Christians. Tyler and Zöe look at me, I nod, and we obey. We do pray at home—usually at Christmas and Easter and funerals, but nothing like this, for we're lazy sprawlers, late Western Catholics. Now, to our surprise, we are immersed in stillness.[14]

This, as Robert Cardinal Sarah has written about so beautifully recently, is the power of silence.[15] In the quiet of the heart, the soul can hear God and become awake. Ironically, Christians living under Communism seem more likely than Western Christians to be awake, and ready to answer a fundamental question: Are you willing to die for your faith?

Also important, on a philosophical but also very practical level, is the metaphysical similarity between Communist scientific materialism

---

14. O'Brien, *Plague Journal*, 142.
15. Sarah, *Power of Silence*.

and Western consumerism. Famously pointed out by Solzhenitsyn in his 1978 address at Harvard,[16] and also a frequent theme of John Paul II (who himself lived in Communist Poland), the point here is not simply the problem of basing belief on empirical experiment; it is, more fully, the "practical atheism" that comes from believing that only the material is real, rendering the spiritual an unknowable realm of superstition that can be manipulated by the powerful. Matthew Thu feels "anger at both North American materialism and Marxist materialism" because, as Nathaniel now clearly sees, "he's one of the few people who knows that in essence they're the same thing."[17] This is a key link between the novels of the *Children of the Last Days* series, because the apparently unconnected *unitas* of the President in *Father Elijah* and the occult practices of the Ashton family in *Strangers and Sojourners* are each in their own way examples of the contradiction in terms which evolves from philosophical confusion: the "spiritual" materialist.[18]

The objective reality of evil, known to Nathaniel from the cave, but almost forgotten, is taught again to him through the life story of Matthew. Living in Communist Vietnam, Matthew's family and Catholic Church become used to enduring persecution. Nothing can prepare them, though, for the day when gun-toting young men enter the church after a morning service. Matthew escapes only after Father Tran, his boyhood friend, lays down his own life so that Matthew can climb out the back window. He lives for a few months as a fugitive, then returns home one night after learning about the privateers being paid to bring refugees over the sea away from Vietnam. The Thu family boards such a ship, but suffers further misfortune when the boat's engine stops working. They then become highly vulnerable to the pirates who terrorized the Vietnamese "boat people," and after a time the boat also runs out of drinking water. The Thu family begins regular recitation of the rosary, however, and reach first Indonesia and later California without ever seeing a single pirate.

---

16. Solzhenitsyn, "World Split Apart."
17. O'Brien, *Plague Journal*, 149.
18. Lewis, *Abolition of Man*, 689–730.

This "happy" ending is somewhat muted by the combination of racism and spiritual apathy that the Thu family discovers in North America, but their past has prepared them to show real Catholic love to the Delaney fugitives. Perhaps most importantly, at least within the novel, Matthew's example of fatherly love for his family inspires Nathaniel's determination and resolve to protect his own children and causes Nathaniel to remember the true nature of his vocation to fatherhood. Nathaniel's first-person narration also flashes back, in some of the novel's finest writing, to when his children were young, and he was first learning the true meaning of fatherhood.

Nothing Nathaniel has experienced thus far in his life could come close to the horrors known by Matthew, but O'Brien begins this key section of the novel by reminding us of what committed fathers everywhere similarly experience: "Every father knows that there are seasons in the life of a family when troubles seem to mount up and spirits burn low."[19] Nathaniel has not faced homicidal soldiers, but the massive amount of snow and shoveling familiar to Canadians did give him a growth on his spine, and surgery was delayed; then the family car was totaled by a reckless driver, and the toilet backed up after Tyler tried to put his toy truck down it to "make Daddy laugh."[20] On top of this, and perhaps most painfully, Nathaniel's marriage to his wife Maya was not going well. Unexceptional, perhaps, but still hard to deal with; "suffering finds us all sooner or later," O'Brien's narrator comments, "and when raising a family, you are especially exposed to the dangers of human existence."[21]

Yet Nathaniel's narrative here never becomes self-pitying, never ever implies that having children or a family is not well worth the struggle involved. There is a much more important lesson to learn, and, later in time, he is seeing that "children teach you most of the real lessons."[22] It was in the midst of this time of suffering that the then one-and-a-half-year-old Zöe taught him "the thing" he "most needed to learn."[23] The lesson had to do not only with suffering, but moreover with his own fear of or attitude to suffering. For all fathers everywhere know something of the desperate desire to protect one's family against suffering beyond human

---

19. O'Brien, *Plague Journal*, 187.
20. O'Brien, *Plague Journal*, 188.
21. O'Brien, *Plague Journal*, 189.
22. O'Brien, *Plague Journal*, 149.
23. O'Brien, *Plague Journal*, 187.

control, but Nathaniel recalls, during one late night with Zöe when, at some unconscious level, he knew that

> the cost of a happy family is the death of selfishness. The father must die if he is to give life to his spouse and children ... a father can provide a mountain of material goods for his family and defend it against all kinds of inconveniences, thinking he can rest easy, having done his part, and still have missed the essential point: he is called to be an image of truth and love.[24]

By "image" here O'Brien does not mean the word as it often appears in atheistic aesthetics, and still less a means to advertise glamorous figures in popular Western culture, but something much closer to what sacred religious artists, including O'Brien himself, typically mean by "icon." An icon is a concrete means by which humans see the otherwise abstract qualities of God. Fatherhood is among the most important "natural" means of this, but O'Brien's work is one of the concrete means for understanding what Catholic theologians and philosophers often claim: there is nothing that is not supernatural, in that God's intention and even presence is throughout his "natural" creation.

Nathaniel becomes this kind of "icon" of the fatherhood of God not by being a "super dad" who perfectly protects his children and supplies all of their material needs, or even a "super" teacher of religious wisdom. As for many men, life's circumstances make this impossible, but it is the reality of hardship which teaches him the really crucial lesson. In his hardship, Nathaniel gains "a heart that is willing to look at its poverty," and no longer believes that "we're in charge."[25] As a "father at night," Nathaniel learns that "he is not God," and here O'Brien allows us to understand the importance of this apparently obvious insight. For when, in a practical, concrete sense, we accept the weakness and poverty of the human condition, we become ready to trust in the God who is a loving Father beyond what we could ask for or imagine.

How did Bam and Zöe teach Nathaniel this crucial lesson? Partly it's the lesson human fathers often learn at the birth of a child—here is a miracle far beyond human capacity to construct, and therefore must come from some other source. The joy of birth is easily forgotten, though, in the many trials of raising infants, trials faced by both mothers and fathers. In the flashback scene, Nathaniel recalls that these trials were

---

24. O'Brien, *Plague Journal*, 190.
25. O'Brien, *Plague Journal*, 190.

not "meaningful" in any romantic or sentimental way, for often he felt "no gush of affection for this poor, squalling creature whom I had helped to make."[26] In the midst of another midnight attempt to console the inconsolable, Nathaniel remembered and began to sing some lines from "Whitman's old hymn to humanity," "Out of the Cradle Endlessly Rocking," which concludes with this verse:

> That strong and delicious word which, creeping to my feet,
> (Or, like some old crone rocking the cradle, swathed in sweet
>   garments, bending aside,)
> The sea whispered me.[27]

The words did not have the magical effect of calming Zöe. But from a perhaps unlikely poetic source, Nathaniel hears the notion that human beings are not struggling with meaningless suffering, but are rather words spoken with meaning and significance. Readers of O'Brien's fiction are by now aware of how this conception of "word" becomes so important to his sacred art, but in this novel the words of the music, combined with "rocking and stroking" the infant Zöe, give Nathaniel a true vision of the meaning of the word "fatherhood":

> I heard again the music I hadn't suspected was there: the song of poverty, a child breathing easily at last, the cry of a night bird, the poetry of wind, and the whispering of snow. And in the depths of night a train's horn echoing across the wall of darkness. It seemed to me a reflection of the final trumpet, of a great and awesome beginning lying somewhat distant. Then the life of my wife and children came before me with greater clarity than I had ever known. I had seen no star. I had heard no angels. Yet within my own arms lay a child as pure as an angel, and something more than an angel, for she was a living icon, "a strong and delicious word" never before seen, never to be repeated.[28]

O'Brien concludes this scene—perhaps the fullest, finest statement of his theological aesthetic—with a much simpler insight from the exhausted Nathaniel as he returns to bed: "Then, from the material of my little sufferings, I wove a word of thanks."[29] A simple, but highly significant moment in Nathaniel's spiritual life: he thanks God for the life he

---

26. O'Brien, *Plague Journal*, 194.
27. Whitman, "Out of the Cradle," 253.
28. O'Brien, *Plague Journal*, 196.
29. O'Brien, *Plague Journal*, 197.

has been given. The Father of Love has provided him what he needs to be a true father.

Plague Journal follows this sublime vision of fatherhood with what some might take to be a tragedy that shatters the vision's foundations, but which might instead be its paradoxical confirmation. Nathaniel is unable to continue evading the "hell-cops," or helicopters that chase him and his children. In surely the novel's greatest tragedy, the eldest son of Matthew, Anthony, who has selflessly chosen to become a fugitive with the Delaneys, is seriously wounded. Nathaniel himself is overwhelmed by these events, again made so desperate that he hears not the music of fatherhood, but rather the nihilism of his culture. Flannery O'Connor famously wrote of how "nihilism" has become "the gas you breathe,"[30] and here O'Brien gives a musical example of this reality; earlier in the novel we remember how Nathaniel hears a country music singer crooning, "nothing matters nohow";[31] as he tries to bring Anthony to safety, he will hear "classical guitar music in the background."[32] Anthony does matter, though, and O'Brien helps the reader hear his "word" through two very different reactions to the tragedy: the mysterious yet familiar presence of Father Andrei and a man whom Nathaniel thinks he knows much better and sometimes regards as his friend, Dr. Wooley.

As he so often does in the *Children of the Last Days* series, Father Andrei appears out of nowhere, standing by the highway to lead Nathaniel and his wounded children to the shack of his maternal grandfather, Thaddeus, whose small trapper's cabin is perhaps insignificant enough to evade government detection. Father Andrei might be critiqued as a classical deus ex machina, but this is the Catholic priestly variant of that theme; not appearing to make certain a happy ending, but simply becoming physically present in order to bring compassion to suffering. Every true priest is *in persona Christi*, as *Father Elijah* so vividly demonstrates, and Father Andrei reminds us that this means the priest must first be physically present, available, for those to whom he ministers. As he explains to Nathaniel, Father Andrei's interest in the Delaney family extends far back, to his friendship with Anne and Stephen, but his current ministry, in "retirement," is "here and everywhere."

---

30. O'Connor, "Letter to A.," 97.
31. O'Brien, *Plague Journal*, 61.
32. O'Brien, *Plague Journal*, 262.

If physical presence and comfort are essential to Father Andrei's ministry, however, there is no question that its purpose is primarily spiritual. He particularly ministers to Nathaniel's torn spirit, at war with the spirits of his age and now with the material reality of a New Totalitarianism. The soldiers of *unitas* have wounded the eldest son of his one true friend, Matthew, the "true man" who had survived the horrors of Communist materialism only to have to face a New Age "spiritual" nihilism employing all the weapons of Western power to publicly appear good while privately committing the most heinous crimes. A recipe for despair, no doubt, but Father Andrei ministers to Nathaniel's spirit through an ancient scriptural story, that of Joseph and his brothers. Father Andrei retells the story with detail and clarity, but there is a greater "point" to this narrative. Father Andrei wants Nathaniel to see, against all justice or reason, that even after the evil they have done, Joseph forgives his brothers, and only this forgiveness heals Joseph's own soul sufficiently to allow the peaceful reunion with the brothers' father that later occurs. Without saying so, Father Andrei has given Nathaniel the Catholic typological reading of Joseph's story, seeing it as prefiguring the forgiveness of enemies that Christ will give on the cross, making possible the return of the entire human family to the peace of their Father in heaven.

Father Andrei follows this moving scriptural story with the sacrament of reconciliation, allowing Nathaniel to confess his own sins, while granting him also the peace of God's forgiveness. For the first time in the novel, "as the dawn breaks," Nathaniel's journal records: "I am at peace. There is no guilt, and no guilt feelings. No fear, no anger. Just clarity."[33] Soon after, Father Andrei leaves; another apparently curious, irrational decision, but he explains that he goes to seek Maya, Nathaniel's estranged wife, and their son Arrow, for Father Andrei fears they are in "spiritual danger." We don't hear more of this trip in this novel, but by this point in *Plague Journal* we understand Father Andrei's intent and methods. Though one might call him a "minor" character, his presence and spiritual ministry substantially alters Nathaniel's heart, a very important change because, as Andrei teaches Nathaniel just before leaving, the human heart is the "only indestructible sanctuary" in which the peace of our Lord can live despite the despair induced by evil in the world.[34]

---

33. O'Brien, *Plague Journal*, 239.
34. O'Brien, *Plague Journal*, 251.

The complex nature of this evil is depicted, in the final part of the novel, through Dr. Wooley. Ostensibly Nathaniel's one true friend in a town frequently fickle about *The Echo*, in most ways Wooley seems like a good person. As a doctor he spent time in the Third World, fighting the deadly combination of disease and political corruption that plagues those countries. He also dissents, in many ways, from the assumptions of his own culture, knowing from his own experience in medicine how large corporations and powerful governments have colluded to create an inhumane world. It is perhaps for those reasons that Wooley took a liking to Nathaniel's iconoclastic editorials in *The Echo*, and the two developed a steady friendship that frequently included both a game of chess and some strongly alcoholic spirits. There does not seem to have been, however, the spirit of truth.

For although highly educated, wealthy, and seemingly a friend to Nathaniel, Dr. Wooley does not prove to be "a true man" in any sense comparable to Matthew, the Vietnamese refugee who earlier shared "home-brew" beer on the deck of the Christmas boat that is the "last homely house" in the novel. Readers can't initially understand or expect Dr. Wooley's infidelity, any more than Nathaniel does, until a scene key not only to this novel but to O'Brien's entire oeuvre. Nathaniel has heard that Dr. Wooley does not perform the abortions or euthanasias that are becoming common in Swiftcreek, as they are common in most Western societies, but Wooley insists that his choice "is not a matter of morality"; rather, he says, he simply "lost [his] taste for death." Nathaniel wants to hear more, but Wooley is reluctant, asking him, "Are you my friend?" and "How much honesty can you take?" before repeating the strange phrase that starts this conversation with a summary question: "Would you like to know how I lost my taste for death?"[35] Wooley then narrates the path of his career, which began with humanitarian, "idealist" motives, but soon turned to "scientific" research on human brains that required human tissue. As the narrative becomes progressively darker, Nathaniel often feels he has heard enough, but Wooley mocks the young editor as "a true journalist." Yet what kind of doctor is here advising occupational ethics?

In our culture, the apparent answer to this question is "a highly respected one." In the recent past, Wooley was "a professor of neurosurgery

---

35. O'Brien, *Plague Journal*, 223.

at a brain research laboratory."[36] Human brains were needed, though, so young women intending to abort their children were paid to remain pregnant to full term. Through a now common procedure used in full-term abortions, the babies' brains were saved while their bodies were killed. Wooley describes the procedure in gruesome detail, and Nathaniel is repulsed: "For an instant, I wanted to kill Wooley with scissors." Wooley anticipates this emotion and admits his own self-loathing, "In recent years I have felt all that you feel and more, a hundred times more."[37]

The full reason for Wooley's self-loathing is revealed when he tells the story of one of the full-term "procedures" that did not go smoothly:

> One day there was a birth that didn't come off as planned. The baby slipped out too fast and slid round in my hands before I knew what was happening. Its eyes opened. It gasped and it cried. The mother heard it and jerked her head up and saw it. She began to struggle. You could tell she was having doubt. A nurse sedated her while I clapped my hand around the child's mouth. I pinched off its air with my thumb. It wriggled mightily. It looked at me as it died. It looked at me.[38]

Wooley's language here betrays the deceptions inherent in abortion. One can hardly avoid using ironic italics to comment on the contradictions, for Wooley can't help but beginning by calling it "a birth" and "the baby." Even these impersonal words quickly become third-person neuter, "it," as Wooley evades the question of whether he committed murder. The key question, however, of whether the foetus is a human being, was for Wooley here definitively answered, "It *looked* at me." In the following paragraph, Wooley admits that the one who looked at him was "a child, a person." Without saying so directly, surely the questions on Wooley's heart, and the novel's readers, inevitably follow: How is the choking of this baby different from any other murder? And if the baby was capable of "looking" back, while Wooley looked also, on what empirical or scientific basis does one then claim that this baby is not a human being? Perhaps the most damning question, given the number of abortions performed each year in North America, is: What is the difference between this murder outside the womb and the abortion of those inside the womb?

---

36. O'Brien, *Plague Journal*, 225.
37. O'Brien, *Plague Journal*, 226.
38. O'Brien, *Plague Journal*, 227.

As literature typically does, *Plague Journal* here gives a concrete, personal illustration of a broad and apparently abstract question. Abortion and most significant ethical questions are concrete in life, affecting individual people, and perhaps this literary text helps us to see the reality of abortion in a more effective way than theoretical ethical argument. Serious ethical issues can be evaded by the "rational" mind cynically biased towards material gain and all the other "gifts" offered "legally" by Western culture, but perhaps the truth about abortion stays in the human heart even if it is evaded by our rational mind. As the representative Western man of the novel, Nathaniel is initially disgusted by the narrative, angrily leaving and not seeing Wooley again for several months. Yet, then, their "friendship" resumed as if nothing had happened, and they returned to chess, drink, and the ironic humor allowed by their mutual cynicism. In what seems almost an allegorical representation of the average "professional males" of Western culture, Wooley and Nathaniel are well aware of what John Paul II famously called the "culture of death," but they are fully capable of ignoring this reality around them and enjoying the rest of what our culture has to offer.

Faced with much harsher elements of this culture, and Anthony's bleeding, bullet-riddled body, Nathaniel forgets Wooley's ethical errors and sends a message asking the doctor to come to Thaddeus's shack and treat Anthony. A message comes back clearly saying no, as Wooley reminds Nathaniel that "I resigned from our civilization a long time ago," and that the "collapse of an age produces numerous sacrificial lambs."[39] Nathaniel naïvely interprets this, however, as a coded message saying to bring the wounded Anthony to his house. Tragically, just after arriving there, Anthony dies. Nathaniel reveals himself to Wooley, who initially seems sympathetic, but then calls the government police. Nathaniel knows he has been betrayed. As Nathaniel is arrested, Wooley voices the nihilism underlying his isolationist hedonism: "The mistake you made was in thinking that anything matters."[40]

Nathaniel's reply, "Everything matters. Everything!" can sound like more naïve, angry idealism.[41] However, this attitude allows him to avoid return to the fear that Father Andrei had delivered him from, and the emotional strength to write a final note to Wooley. From prison, Nathaniel sends these words:

39. O'Brien, *Plague Journal*, 229.
40. O'Brien, *Plague Journal*, 265.
41. O'Brien, *Plague Journal*, 265.

> Dear Wooley,
> I believe in the man you once were, and may be again.
> I forgive you. Check,
> Mate,
> Nathaniel Delaney[42]

The playful reference to their chess games can sound triumphalist, but competitiveness even here is an unsurprising element of their very male friendship. The much more surprising point of the note is that there remains any friendship at all between the two men, after how Wooley betrayed Nathaniel. Only the clear, concise word of forgiveness in the note can allow this, and open the way to future hope for Wooley's soul. As for Nathaniel, the note shows that Father Andrei's ministry to him has changed his soul. Though imprisoned, Nathaniel's heart is free, awake.

There are two "extra" sections after the proper conclusion of the novel. The first is a note from the RCMP officer who saw Nathaniel imprisoned at novel's end, explaining how he has acquired the journal we have just read. Though minor, this note adds to the realism developed throughout the *Children of the Last Days* series. More significant, and moving, is a final note from Nathaniel's daughter, Zöe. From a fragment "in child's handwriting" found in the manuscript of her father's journal, the novel's final word is a nod to Tolkien, and note of hope for the future. Zöe wrote:

> Daddy,
> Don't be sad. Don't be scared.
> Remember Frodo and Sam.
> Love,
> Zöe[43]

The concluding section of *Plague Journal* also includes some flashbacks that help us understand the separation of Nathaniel and his wife Maya. Not enough is given to give the reader a full sense of her problems, or of the real troubles of their marriage. This "flaw" is perhaps inherent in a novel dependent upon the gradual revelation of Nathaniel's inner life. Although Nathaniel suffers due to Maurice L'Oraison, the "hell-cops," and even Wooley himself, the novel does not give us anything like an objective diagnosis of the "plague" afflicting Western culture. For that, we have the much longer *Eclipse of the Sun*. *Plague Journal* stands, however,

---

42. O'Brien, *Plague Journal*, 268.
43. O'Brien, *Plague Journal*, 273.

as one of the clearest and most accessible statements of O'Brien's aesthetic vision. Of all his works, it might be the easiest to approach biographically; O'Brien did work as a journalist highly critical of Western culture, did raise children within that culture by offering them imaginative alternatives to this culture, and the novel is dedicated to his wife. A much more universal note of hope closes the novel, however, as Nathaniel has discovered a way to remain human within our culture while also working towards a better time. He affirms: "In spite of everything there are people out there. Something in them can still hear a word that shatters a lie."[44]

---

44. O'Brien, *Plague Journal*, 269.

"Arrow and Nick" from *Eclipse of the Sun*

"Seeing the Form": *Eclipse of the Sun*

> You have made an eclipse of the Sun, Maurice.... Never can it destroy the light of the sun. The sun bides its time, but when it comes, the shadows will flee.... When he comes, there shall never again be eclipses. When he comes, it will be for us as if the shadows never existed. They will be remembered no more.
> —Father Andrei, in O'Brien, *Eclipse of the Sun*, 710

THE NEXT NOVEL IN the *Children of the Last Days* series, *Eclipse of the Sun*, picks up chronologically precisely when *Plague Journal* ends, and according to the summary outlines included at the end of each novel, covers the year after the five-day crisis that leads to Nathaniel Delaney's arrest. This chronology, and the detailed material and spiritual realism to which O'Brien's aesthetic is committed, makes *Eclipse of the Sun* one of the longest novels in the series, totaling 854 pages. Hardly a sequel, then, to *Plague Journal*, it might rather be taken as the culminating epic of the entire series. As such, it is tempting to see *Eclipse of the Sun* as a dystopian novel, as a dark vision of how even a prosperous democracy like Canada could become a totalitarian state. Yet though the political elements of the novel are easy to caricature, they are not its real subject.

Rather, evil in O'Brien's vision, as is normative in Christian art, is met by the reality of God's holiness such that we see how much stronger is God's goodness than anything which would oppose it. The novel's title alludes, as in the key passage just cited as an epigraph, to the eclipse of the sun that occurred during Christ's crucifixion. This scriptural source makes the sun/Son pun the most commonplace figure of speech in Christian literature, but O'Brien's novel as a whole enacts the greater theological point: in the midst of darkness, in what appears to be the triumph of evil, God does his most important, eternally significant acts to reestablish communion with those who love him.

In the midst of a world that often appears engulfed in suffering and sorrow, it is not easy to see this. It is thus essential to O'Brien's aesthetic that his novel offers not simply an epic confrontation of evil vs. good, but rather helps us to "see the form," to recognize the pattern, of how spiritual apocalypse could unfold even in our own country. "Seeing the form" is a repeated phrase and motif in the novel, so while O'Brien's art might seem to have little in common with the densely philosophical tomes of Hans Urs von Balthasar (often described as the high point of twentieth-century Roman Catholic theology), it is probably no coincidence that the first and most well known of this pioneering theologian's multivolume attempt to rehabilitate the role of aesthetics in theology is titled *Seeing the Form*. O'Brien's and Balthasar's fundamental point is the same: Christians must learn to see how the essential forms of reality, most of all the form of the living, triune God who creates, redeems, and comforts us even in the midst of sin and death—is the real form, the lasting metaphysical structure, of our own lives as well.

One way to "see the form" of this central point is to compare the most obvious representations of good and evil in the novel, Father Andrei and Maurice L'Oraison, the latter now fully transformed into an anti-Christian minister of the national government, and being groomed for even greater things on the globalist world stage. *Eclipse of the Sun* begins with Father Andrei undertaking the mission he had promised Nathaniel Delaney in *Plague Journal*, searching for his wife Maya and son Arrow.

Father Andrei cannot prevent Maya from being killed in the genocide of a drug commune which, along with a similar deployment of the murderous black helicopters seen in *Plague Journal*, wipes out a small convent of nuns. These crimes serve as the early and shocking evidence of the rise of a secret police force within the Canadian government. Much more important than this evil within the novel, however, is the work Father Andrei begins with Arrow. By novel's end, readers can glimpse some of the eternal consequence of Father Andrei's faith not only in Arrow, but in many other people as well. If Father Elijah shows the role of a priest called to the most sublime Christian service, Father Andrei shows that the humble work of a backwoods priest, even in a backwater country like Canada, is equally valued by the Lord.

Maurice often appears in *Eclipse of the Sun* as the opposite of Father Andrei's priestly *in persona Christi*, but his evil never appears as a comparable opponent of Father Andrei's good. Rather, implicit in O'Brien's presentation is St. Augustine's famous definition of evil having no lasting substance or reality, existing briefly only as the absence of good, a notion dependent on the good having the eternal reality that only God can provide. Some might critique *Eclipse of the Sun* for not providing enough detail on the societal factors that allow a secret police to arise in Canada, but O'Brien's concern is showing the individual form of this evil, how it rises in the heart, mind, and soul of one man who, we will recall from *Strangers and Sojourners*, was once a young poet who loved Anne Delaney and appreciated her enough to risk his own career by warning Nathaniel Delaney, at the start of *Plague Journal*, of the nightmare about to arise.

So *Eclipse of the Sun* is not a dystopian novel depicting the epic conflict of equally powerful forces of good and evil, but rather contrasts the vital spiritual life offered by the Lord to the dismal grab for temporal power typical of princes of this world. The eternal prince of darkness, still masquerading as Lucifer the angel of light, has deceived Maurice, but this novel follows the Gospel of John in proclaiming that God's light still shines bright amid the darkness of this world.

The essential optimism or, from a Christian viewpoint, the spiritual realism of the novel allows its two central characters to emerge as being not Father Andrei or Maurice, important as both are to O'Brien's intentions, but rather Arrow and Nick. The latter, Nick, is a "hydrocephalic" (a child whose brain is swollen by fluid), literally picked from the junk heap by another of the novel's great individuals, and great characters, Alice Douglas, also known as the "Queen of Junk." Nick is no piece of junk, but rather a twenty-two-year-old person who becomes Arrow's friend and teaches everyone who gets to know him about the meaning of joy.

Arrow and Nick are depicted in the iconographic painting on the cover of this novel, with Nick on Arrow's back as in the many scenes where the two play together. In this form, they will also flee from the police, and Arrow's raised hands could indicate surrender; they are also the form of Christ's crucifixion, though, and the upside-down or reversed nature of this novel's world, as compared to O'Brien's previous novels, is also shown by the placement of the symbols above them.

Whereas the good have been on the left and the evil on the right, in this novel an eclipsed sun is on the left and the old Irish stone cross of Stephen Delaney, which Father Andrei delivers to Arrow from his father Nathaniel, appears on the right. The darkness of the image is lessened, however, by the blue that suffuses the cross, and creates an almost halo-like effect around Nick's swollen head. In Catholic art, blue is traditionally the color of Mary, and her significant but almost hidden role in this novel is hinted at by the medallion around Arrow's neck. Only later can we confirm this to be a Marian medallion, when another good priest, Father Ron, tells Arrow that he serves a Lady who is protecting them both.

Before that point, however, there are many other spiritual elements that this novel presents in the most realistic of ways. As O'Brien's readers became familiar with in *Strangers and Sojourners*, this is primarily achieved through showing that even "ordinary" or "normal" people have extraordinary spiritual lives. O'Brien's Christian realism is primarily responsible for the detail and depth of his work, and those who wish for shorter, abstract novels of ideas might risk detaching aesthetics from the theology that allows this art's being. Paradoxically, this is true even of individuals whose significance does not grant them a place within the longer novel as a whole, whose lives, at least in this world, never become connected to the greater Life that unites Father Andrei, Arrow, and Nick.

Early in the novel, we meet a drug commune shaman who promiscuously makes his way to Maya's bedroom, all the while so deluded that he believes radio broadcasts of football games to be alien accounts of giants. Later we learn that this "shaman" is Ronald, wanted by the FBI for various criminal offenses, though we learn little else about him. We also meet an elderly couple, Bill and Irene, who initially shelter Father Andrei and first hear his story of the black helicopters. Yet they almost cannot really believe totalitarianism could be rising in Canada, and even if they could they would not have the energy or willpower to substantially alter the comfortable, middle-class life they have grown accustomed to, however much their affection for Father Andrei and the murdered nuns reminds them of an eternal world in which they intellectually believe.

A much deeper and more complex story is told by O'Brien through the lives of Julie, Bill and Irene's daughter, and her husband Colin. Julie has the passionate faith of a heart awake, and her deep Catholic faith and love for Father Andrei are evident throughout the novel. In her husband, Colin, O'Brien explores how disillusionment with our natural spiritual desires can lead to strictly empirical rationalism. Colin had become involved with an unnamed, San Francisco–based cult while he was an idealistic youth, only to discover its corruption. Colin then turns to the popular though misunderstood conception of "science" as a purely empirical approach to life in which all that is real must be observed physically by the human eye. Colin's past is presented admirably and with great detail by O'Brien, and one can certainly understand the attraction Julie feels to Colin's form of common human sanity. Colin becomes an expert sailor, and when we learn that he will lead his family on a yearlong trip around the world, on their sailboat the *Osprey*, it seems like a great adventure, a way to build a family despite the madness that the world is descending into, rather than an escape from reality.

Colin does hesitate when Julie asks their family to conceal Arrow and Father Andrei—the government now presenting both as fugitives potentially connected to the mass killings—but eventually he does consent, and develops a deep friendship with Arrow. Colin perhaps feels intuitively the isolation and alienation that plagues Arrow separated from his family, and Colin teaches Arrow how to sail, knowing that the skill will increase his self-confidence. Later in the novel, during their family's long voyage, Julie will wish for the insight of Father Andrei as Colin continues to struggle with theological questions, but by then Colin has long shown the commitment to realism that will eventually lead to his knowing the reality of God. Later in the novel, Julie will wish for Father Andrei's presence to speak to Colin's theological doubt, but the eternal significance of the *Osprey*'s early, protective voyage is a symbolic representation of the eternal conversation that Colin seems likely to continue.

A shorter route to truth is granted to Arrow when, in the first very moving spiritual moment of the novel, Father Andrei baptizes him during their voyage on the *Osprey*. Though not technically an infant baptism, for Arrow very much wants to be baptized, one certainly could make the argument that this eight-year-old fugitive does not have full free will. Thus, the theology and significance are the same "form" as infant baptism, seeing this sacrament as a gift of God which promises later, greater gifts. Naming is always an important element of baptism—hence the word "Christening" at many English baptisms—for the sacrament follows the biblical commonplace wherein people chosen by God have their name changed to reflect the new religious significance of their lives.

Clerics have also usually done this at the moment of their ordination, so it is no surprise when Father Andrei gives the boy two new names "before the throne of God: Aaron Nathaniel."[1] Typologically, this Aaron will help Father Andrei, his people's Moses, to seek the promised land, and he will continue the journey of the man who loved him, his father

---

1. O'Brien, *Eclipse of the Sun*, 198.

Nathaniel. Even his original name will be redeemed: he will be "Arrow-in-the-bow-of-the-Lord." Newly named, "the boy half-smiled, overcome by awe."[2]

O'Brien's description of the baptism then reverts to simple language, stressing how Father Andrei makes the grace of baptism meaningful to an eight-year-old boy:

> The sacrament took its simplest form. Andrei prayed over the boy, explained the death and Resurrection of Jesus in terms he could understand. He told him that baptism would cleanse him from original sin and the power of death. It would help him to resist the whisperings of the serpent. It would make him grow strong and true like a straight arrow. It would help him to hear God, to love him, and to serve him. Then he anointed the boy and laid a white stole on his shoulders.[3]

Father Andrei then speaks the biblically mandated formula of baptism—"in the name of the Father, and of the Son, and of the Holy Spirit"—a key confirmation of the centrality of the Trinity in Christian life. Aaron "closed his eye, a smile playing on his lips," and slept. For his part,

> the old priest covered him with the sleeping bag, blessed him, and went back on deck, where he watched stars until the sky in the east attested that the planet had completed another revolution.[4]

After the *Osprey* delivers Father Andrei and Arrow to the coast of Northern British Columbia, another "minor" character briefly takes center stage. Father Potempko is an old friend of Father Andrei, a priest whose weaknesses and good humor remind us of Billy in *Father Elijah*. Potempko's deeper connection to Father Andrei, and his probable importance in the novel, stem from the fact that both spent time in the concentration camps created by the mid-twentieth-century totalitarian regimes of Eastern Europe. The explicit politics of these governments is less important, O'Brien suggests, than their implicit, assumed attitude to the human person: disposable pawns less important than the proposed social and political program. "They never change," Potempko succinctly comments upon hearing Father Andrei's story; perhaps he can more

---

2. O'Brien, *Eclipse of the Sun*, 198.
3. O'Brien, *Eclipse of the Sun*, 199.
4. O'Brien, *Eclipse of the Sun*, 199.

readily believe this story than can native Canadians because he has personally seen how inhumane seemingly rational people can become when blinded by their own ego.[5] Against this evil, Potempko well knows, Enlightenment philosophy exalting human reason and culture offered no significant defense; twentieth-century Germany had suffered due to WWI, but remained among the most well educated and cultured nations on earth when the Nazis took over.

The next "minor" character important in *Eclipse of the Sun* is Charley Manyberries, one of Potempko's most faithful parishioners, whom O'Brien's narrator describes as "a man of immense dignity."[6] Charley keeps the secret of Potempko hiding the fugitives partly because he knows the mistreatment often given to his wife's mother, Cecilia, whose Catholic mysticism and work with Vancouver's street people often brings her to the door of the insane asylum. Charlie says, "She ain't crazy. She ain't drunk. She's just doing what the Lord tells her to do."[7] Far from crazy, Cecilia is one of the key spiritual characters of the novel, one who often shares Father Andrei's inner life through the great mystery that the Apostles' Creed terms "the communion of the saints."

Potempko, with some help from Charlie, enables Father Andrei and Aaron (as the novel's narrator now usually calls him) to drive to an inland town where it is hoped they will be safe. Just after they arrive, however, they are captured by two incompetent police officers, aided by the massive state media campaign to catch the "fugitives." Further incompetence allows Aaron to escape from a helicopter during a refueling stop as he was being transported to Vancouver. He then hops a freight train and returns near the area where he had lived with Maya in the commune. Disoriented and afraid, Aaron runs into the wilderness and soon reverts to thinking of himself as Arrow, but through the providence of God stumbles into the backyard of another "minor" character in the novel who will play a major role in the young boy's life. Alice Douglas is an elderly lady, in her seventies, who presents herself to the world as a cranky curmudgeon, a chain-smoking, hard-drinking "Queen of Junk" who runs her antique curiosity shop with no interference, and certainly no assistance, from the rest of the world. Yet inside Alice is a heart of gold that the Lord uses to accomplish his will.

5. O'Brien, *Eclipse of the Sun*, 205.
6. O'Brien, *Eclipse of the Sun*, 209.
7. O'Brien, *Eclipse of the Sun*, 210.

The nature of this heart, and the nature of the gifts that Alice will provide for Aaron, are shown through a key scene in which we discover how she first met Nick. Alice's defiance of convention attracted her to the makeshift junk site created on the side of a mountain by government trucks, who leave behind warning signs after dumping several large boxes buried in sand. Alice wonders, "What was in those boxes that would get you prosecuted if you saw it?"[8] Opening one, however, gives the shocking answer:

> She shrieked when she saw it. Then she threw up. It was full of small human body parts. Very small arms and legs. There were heads and faces too—that was the worst part. They smelled bad.[9]

In another box, Alice finds something perhaps even more shocking, and certainly more wonderful:

> This time she didn't scream. But it was just as shocking as the little body parts. There was a living face in this one. The eyes looked at her, blinking in the flashlight. Then they looked shyly away. Looked back. Then smiled at her. "O God," she said, "O God."[10]

Alice's extraordinary discovery of Nick gives another dimension of "seeing the form" that is both essential to the purposes of the novel and particularly, whether consciously or not, exemplary of a Balthasarian theological aesthetic. Probably the most often cited passage in Balthasar's writings is a "résumé" of his thought, given to an American Catholic magazine, to try and explain the importance of the "transcendentals," the medieval conception of how truth, beauty, and goodness unite to lead us to experience the "being" or metaphysical reality of God. To explain this sublime notion, Balthasar chose the most common of human experiences:

> The infant is brought to consciousness of himself only by love, by the smile of his mother. In that encounter the horizon of unlimited being opens itself for him, revealing four things to him: (1) that he is one in love with the mother, even in being other than his mother; therefore, all being is one; (2) that love is good; therefore, all being is good; (3) that that love is true; therefore,

---

8. O'Brien, *Eclipse of the Sun*, 264.
9. O'Brien, *Eclipse of the Sun*, 264–65.
10. O'Brien, *Eclipse of the Sun*, 265.

all being is true; and (4) that that love evokes joy; therefore, all being is beautiful.[11]

Following her own unique path to what her civilization has discarded as junk, Alice has become mother to an emotional infant (though biologically speaking, according to a label on the box, marked "termination permit," the hydrocephalic child is twenty-two years old) and through the love shared by their gaze, is experiencing the joy of knowing God. To "see the form" of this encounter, as Balthasar would put it, is to know the actual beauty of the child, despite Nick's "deformities," and it is to see the real goodness of Alice's motherly heart.

O'Brien's fiction also allows us to see, in a uniquely concrete way, the interdependence of the transcendentals. As the medievals often taught, and Balthasar reintroduced to modern theology, beauty, goodness, truth never exist independently of each other, but are all present together within the one reality who is God. This beautiful idea, however, like the logical sequence and conclusions of Balthasar's résumé, can seem too abstract. O'Brien's narrative account of Alice and Nick concretely gives form to this abstract theology. Though it is something which she herself can hardly believe and frequently denigrates, in concrete, day-to-day, and moment-to-moment terms, Alice is a mother and Nick and Arrow are her two sons, as beloved in her heart as God made mothers to be. On the way home from the junk-site, O'Brien reinforces this key insight by having Alice repeat, "O God. O God," and his narrator clarifying that this "wasn't a prayer or anything," but "it wasn't cursing, either."[12]

The depth of Alice's love for this discarded child is suggested by the name she gives him; she'd had a boyfriend who died in the war named Nick, and so she names what she calls "the li'l factory reject" by the same name. Perhaps the intensity and commitment of romantic love resurfaces as she gazes upon her child. Perhaps also the name echoes the saint whose spirit of giving is the oft-forgotten historical foundation of Christmas. Nick is a gift of God to Alice, and perhaps she dimly recognizes this "form" by the name she gives him. Yet she cannot see the form of redemption which Father Andrei has already begun in Arrow, or grasp the motherly form of Mary that she herself has begun to enact. As Alice looks at Arrow:

---

11. Balthasar, "Résumé of My Thought," 470.
12. O'Brien, *Eclipse of the Sun*, 226.

The stuffed animals crushed under the boy's arms stared back at her. Button eyes. Goofy little smiles. They almost got to her. Then she saw that there was a silver chain around his neck, an oval medallion hung on it. It was a picture of a lady with her arms open wide and what looked like rivers flowing out of her hands. There was also a tiny crucifix on the chain. She raised her eyebrows at that.[13]

Whatever Alice's limitations, it is the quality of every human person that O'Brien stresses in his portrayal of Nick. More than a friend to Arrow, more even than a brother, Nick becomes perhaps the most important human being in Arrow's life after Alice finally reveals the secret she has long concealed from him: Nathaniel and Maya, the parents whom Arrow had hoped to have been reunited with, have both been killed by government forces. This devastating news at first sends Arrow into shock, as he curls up and cries in a ball for hours at a time. Nick is the one who returns to Arrow the basic human desire to live, but O'Brien never suggests this is due to some sentimental "inspiration" by which Arrow seeks to follow the example of this handicapped child who has gone on living much longer than medical and government authorities expected. Rather, Nick helps Arrow because of a much more realistic, commonplace human motivation: the need to be needed. When Arrow definitely decides to go on living, O'Brien shows him going to Nick's crib and telling him, "It's okay, Nicolo . . . Everything's going to be okay."[14]

As with Balthasar's transcendental Thomism, one can see that the form of O'Brien's art here enacts a famous idea in twentieth-century Catholic theology: *disponibilité* (availability) as being the essence of the human person, as taught by French Catholic philosopher Gabriel Marcel.[15] This idea is a key foundation of the phenomenology that John Paul II follows through to the philosophical school of personalism. As befits a novelist, though, O'Brien gives concrete illustrations rather than lengthy discourse on these ideas.

For Arrow, Nick becomes "Nicolo Piccolo," a nickname suggestive not of some sentimental affection, but rather of the fellow traveller and great friend that Nick becomes for Arrow. Nick learns to communicate beyond the air "whistle" that Alice first hears from the junkyard box, and even learns to speak Arrow's name, pronouncing it as "Awo, Awo," but

13. O'Brien, *Eclipse of the Sun*, 267.
14. O'Brien, *Eclipse of the Sun*, 302.
15. See Marcel, *Mystery of Being*.

this wonder is preceded by something even more fundamental. Being with Arrow allows Nick to learn to laugh, a wonder Alice also witnesses:

> Her *two boys* (she snorted every time she thought of it) spent a lot of time nose to nose, making sounds at each other that only a mother could love. In the second week Nick did something that knocked her for a loop. Arrow was making funny faces at him and whistling bird noises. Nick laughed. He had never laughed before. It was really something special.[16]

When Arrow finally leaves Alice's home, many months later, he carries Nick on his back, as in the novel's cover icon. But by that point the cumbersome arranging of handicapped bodies seem much less important than the unity of the boys' souls. As brothers, as friends, Nick and Arrow need each other, and this extraordinary love—not only the love they have for each other but also that which they have received from Father Andrei and Alice, icons of Christ and Mary—"bears all things" (1 Cor 13:7) in the concrete way in which St. Paul's famous chapter on the theological virtues promises.

If the love of Arrow and Nick allows us to see the form of divine love, its polar opposite, satanic hate, next appears in the novel when Maurice visits Nathaniel in prison. The narrative order might give a reader hope. However, the scene is a flashback, as Maurice recalls how Nathaniel died. Readers must have an attitude of skepticism when Maurice first speaks to Nathaniel as an old family friend. Maurice does seem to have sincere admiration for Anne Ashton, and it remains puzzling to him (and to Nathaniel and the novel's readers) as to why he called, as recounted at the beginning of *Plague Journal*, to warn Nathaniel of the coming police raid. Yet these hints of friendship pale beside the human community we have just seen in the novel, of Alice, Arrow, and Nick.

It should come as no great surprise to readers that Nathaniel realizes too late that he is not being given sedatives to endure the pain of prison, as Maurice falsely claims, but rather drugs intended to sedate him during the injection of a lethal poison. As a journalist, Nathaniel wondered whether his "controversial stands in the public arena" could be dangerous, but he had "never considered the possibility" that this threat could come from "an old friend of his family, and in such a matter-of-fact

---

16. O'Brien, *Eclipse of the Sun*, 276.

manner."¹⁷ Yet as he revives and realizes he is being murdered with the injection, Nathaniel reaches out his arm: "I forgive you, Maurice."¹⁸

Maurice's response, "Don't say that!" indicates not merely disbelief, but rather the cry of an anguished, conflicted soul. O'Brien depicts Maurice as not just the cold, cruel hand of barbaric totalitarianism, nor even as the senior politician firmly convinced of the moral goodness of his party's totalitarianism, blithely unaware that this Canadian fascism might reproduce the totalitarianism so destructive in the middle of the twentieth century. Whereas these political movements were largely atheistic, the warning given in *Eclipse of the Sun*, as in the earlier *Children of the Last Days* series, is of a spiritual, New Age totalitarianism that is at its core satanic, and ushers in the traumatic events of the book of Revelation. In this narrative, Maurice is important precisely because he comes from such a strong Catholic upbringing, but has shed this supposedly dying faith's beliefs in order to become open to a new kind of spiritual transcendence.

After murdering Nathaniel, Maurice reflects on his own life, and thinks, "It had taken years to shed the indoctrination of his childhood." But after a 1990 trip to Russia, he had discovered that the "transcendent" did exist, "populated by spirits who loved mankind and who desired above all to bring the reign of peace to this wounded planet."¹⁹ Barbara, one of the leaders of the movement, had taught him the "courage" necessary to achieve this change; however, though one quarter of humanity is open to transcendence, another quarter is locked in old beliefs. A "cleansing" period is thus required in which some self-destructive humans are "eliminated" in order to allow others to transcend. Perhaps unconsciously, Barbara signals this work as a prelude to the coming of the antichrist in the book of Revelation, telling Maurice, "We are the riders of the pale horse, Death."²⁰ As he becomes more aware of and guided by the "spirit masters," Maurice gains his own personal guide, who comes to him in darkness and "stood before him like a blade of fire," showing him "the Christ of this Age" who is already "ascending rapidly in global affairs."²¹ This, of course, is the President of *Father Elijah*, so readers familiar with the *Last Days* series can readily see that Maurice has been indoctrinated

17. O'Brien, *Eclipse of the Sun*, 340.
18. O'Brien, *Eclipse of the Sun*, 341.
19. O'Brien, *Eclipse of the Sun*, 341.
20. O'Brien, *Eclipse of the Sun*, 345.
21. O'Brien, *Eclipse of the Sun*, 346.

into believing in the great moral mission of this new world order, and experiencing the directly satanic spiritual push to commit acts of great evil, such as the murder of Nathaniel.

It continues to bother Maurice, though, that he made the initial call of warning to Nathaniel in *Plague Journal*. Perhaps O'Brien intends to remind us, as Tolkien does with Smeagol (the original hobbit identity of Gollum), that evil cannot completely obliterate the spiritual reality of the soul created by God. This key point is certainly further suggested by Maurice's end in the novel, but it appears earlier as well. The grace-filled reality of the human soul is joyfully depicted in Alice, Arrow, and Nick, and more painfully through the faithful resistance of Father Andrei to the "new world order," even when he has been captured and physically tortured by this regime. Technology created drugs that mechanically retrieved memories from sedated patients, but even in this state Father Andrei's soul resisted.

As the government interrogator reached inside his induced coma, with "a voice like a pale rider upon its pale horse," Father Andrei's soul internally rebuked it: "You are but a chimera that will fade with the dawn."[22] Father Andrei is also given a consoling vision of "He Who is Faithful and True," who in turn shows him "a priest climbing a mountain in Italy who like himself bore the blood of the Old and the New Covenants in his veins." The name of this priest, as readers of the Last Days series certainly know, is Father Elijah. In prison, Father Andrei gained spiritual freedom, coming to understand that "whatever he had to suffer must be offered for this Elijah, to assist in the accomplishment of his mission, hidden in the mysterious designs of God."[23]

Consoling visions of this kind are supernatural graces, and they occur frequently in *Eclipse of the Sun* as a reminder that even as satanic evil seems to control the human political world, God remains alive, active, and present to those who love him. Though Father Andrei has never met Cecilia, the mother of Charlie Manyberries's wife, Father Andrei had a vision of her as she "pulled a wagon of grace through the cold city"; despite the interrogator's drugs, Father Andrei

> turned the eyes of his soul across the spiritual chart of the west in search of her. And when he found her, he fell back in shock at the radiance of her, for she was a very great saint, though she

---

22. O'Brien, *Eclipse of the Sun*, 313.
23. O'Brien, *Eclipse of the Sun*, 314.

> was only a fool in the eyes of the world. He suddenly knew her perfectly, and she knew him too, for she was in a tiny room in a cabin at Bella Coola, prostrate on the floor before a crucifix, weeping and fasting for him.[24]

O'Brien is vividly depicting here what Catholicism, in the Apostles' Creed, calls the "communion of the saints," the union of believers through the Holy Spirit. This concept is also central, one must realize, to the Catholic conception of the church itself. For Roman Catholicism, the church is not essentially a building, a source of law, or a human institution. The Catholic Church's substance is an eternal reality formed by the union of God with human souls. This transcendent church, sometimes called the "church triumphant," is a grace-filled, spiritual reality that Father Andrei participates in, regardless of the suffering that he physically endures.

Though the transcendent, eternal church is essential to any Catholic vision of reality, *Eclipse of the Sun* is also strongly concerned with the revival of the church in our world, particularly in O'Brien's home country of Canada. The theme is important enough to pursue through several characters whose lives interconnect as O'Brien artfully weaves a suspenseful narrative in the second half of the novel. The transcendent reality of the church known by Father Andrei and Cecilia is unchanging, but O'Brien is also concerned enough with the concrete reality of the Canadian church to depict its revival, its awakening, from the slothful slumbers that have allowed men like Maurice to become leaders of a nation whose national anthem prayerfully asks that "God keep our land glorious and free."[25]

Revival on this level requires many to turn towards God, but O'Brien begins with a figure surely fundamental to Catholicism's revival: a parish priest. Father Ron at first seems too typical a parish priest to become the leader of any revival. He is not an evil man friendly with any mortal sin, but he numbs any serious religious angst—like many in our culture—by nightly escape to the violent but entertaining world of American television, whose drama enacts the tragedy and joy of human life in an "ersatz" transcendence that both mocks and reminds us of the moral and spiritual stability that our society has largely lost. Like most, though, Father Ron does not think of such matters as he slumps at night into an easy chair,

---

24. O'Brien, *Eclipse of the Sun*, 315.
25. "O Canada," refrain, line 1.

tired from a long day that had contained two meetings, three Masses, a visit to sick parishioners at the hospital, three confessions (one of which tested his knowledge of moral theology), a catechism class for the kids preparing for First Confession and Communion, and about a dozen telephone calls.[26]

It is in this state, "desperate for distraction," that Father Ron begins to watch a film of a pseudo-hero. As he drifts off to sleep, though, a dream comes to him with a very different voice and vision:

> "Son of man," cried the voice, "these are the bones of the whole house of God. They have been saying all hope is lost, our life is dried up, and we are cut off. Therefore you must say to them, "O my people, I will open your graves and have you rise from them and bring you back to your true home. Thus will you know that I am the Lord who saves you, I will do it. I have promised, and I will do it."[27]

This is the voice of the Lord, giving Father Ron, despite all the priest's flaws, the same mission, to rebuild his house, that was given to St. Francis of Assisi in medieval Italy. As then, as always, the key work of this revival is done by the Lord himself, faithful and hoping to save his people from sin.

The effect of the dream on Father Ron's ministry becomes manifest first through a Sunday sermon that begins with words designed to get the people's attention: "Awake, my people!" he roared. Then Father Ron recalls them to the basic realities that one must always be aware of:

> "There is a God!" he cried. "There is a Saviour. There is a Holy Spirit, and they love you with an everlasting love. Our God is a consuming fire! Our God is coming to cleanse the earth, to end the things of death and to bring to life what is called to eternal life!"[28]

Many in the crowd are embarrassed, and some call Father Ron's archbishop to complain, but at least one member of the congregation approves. Theophane Nguyen, an adolescent boy whose family has faced the same trials under atheistic Marxism as the Thu family of *Plague Journal*, comments, "Faddah real hot today. Hot stuff!"[29] These words are

26. O'Brien, *Eclipse of the Sun*, 381.
27. O'Brien, *Eclipse of the Sun*, 385.
28. O'Brien, *Eclipse of the Sun*, 389.
29. O'Brien, *Eclipse of the Sun*, 393.

prelude to further dramatic action. After Mass, Father Ron goes into his apartment, grabs his television, and smashes its screen with a hammer, explaining to the crowd: "If you're able to keep one of these things in your homes and not let it take over, more power to you. . . . As for me, I'm a weak guy, and it's time for me to get a life."[30] Put in this humble way while radically attacking the sin in his own life, Father Ron prophetically calls his people towards the abundant, joyful life that God wants for them.

Eclipse of the Sun further depicts the revival of the church and resistance to the spirit of the antichrist as an ecumenical challenge that could draw together both Roman Catholics and like-minded Christians of diverse denominations. Primarily this is suggested through Beth Potter, an evangelical Christian who befriends Alice and comes to her aid in the most difficult of circumstances, when Arrow becomes ill and needs professional medical attention. Beth, against all of her conservative and moral biases, offers Arrow the official identification of her own son Noah, thus making herself and her family a target of the same government forces that have terrorized the people of Father Andrei. There is also some ecumenical response to Father Ron's assault upon televisions, as similar actions spring up in many places, in response to the same cultural pressures. As O'Brien's narrator puts it:

> The phenomenon had erupted from no identifiable source, like a subterranean root fire springing up in all sectors of the Christian community. Evangelicals, Catholics, and Pentecostals were involved throughout the country and abroad, and incidents had occurred even in that most reasonable of reasonable circles, the liberal mainline Protestant denominations. The Catholics and the Evangelicals were the largest statistical group, the liberal Protestants the smallest, and everyone else was somewhere in between.[31]

For O'Brien, however, as for any Roman Catholic, revival of the church cannot occur in just laity or ministers, important as both are, but also must affect the hierarchy of the church, the bishops who lead the people. *Eclipse of the Sun* depicts this struggle, and hope for the church, through the distancing and perhaps maturing lens of literature. Through the archbishop of the church in Vancouver, BC's largest city, O'Brien shows empathy to the many challenges faced by the church's shepherds

---

30. O'Brien, *Eclipse of the Sun*, 396.
31. O'Brien, *Eclipse of the Sun*, 494.

in a time when so many wolves run free. Most of all, as in the novel as a whole, through the archbishop we see how God works in and through his people, in ways beyond what any human could ask for or imagine, in order to bring good out of the evil whose existence seems so implacable.

O'Brien's sensitivity to the challenges faced by the church hierarchy is suggested by the archbishop's words to Father Ron as the parking lot fires, which have expanded to include pornography and birth control devices, are being investigated: "I wonder if anyone realizes the complicated webs we bishops have to maneuver these days."[32] Cynics of the church, especially after the sexual abuse scandals, might reply harshly, but Father Ron's response is both more diplomatic and practical: "Maybe when faced with a spider's web we should just cut through it."[33] The simplicity of this approach cannot be accepted as simple wisdom, however, for the archbishop must lead and govern both the sanely pious and insanely radical within his diocese. In colloquial language that only the readers of the novel can interpret archetypally, in relation to the "two" Noahs being cared for by Alice and Beth, the archbishop tells Father Ron: "My problem is, Father, are you Noah or Chicken Little?"[34]

This question is not unanswerable, for the archbishop is sufficiently well versed in Jesus' teaching on knowing the value of trees by their fruits. He comes to recognize the real faith of Father Ron, and even to begin a reform program to strengthen the faith of his entire diocese. His own sermons also become more evangelical, "as he proclaimed in a strong, steady voice, and in the clearest language possible, the end of the era of compromise."[35] Instead, he exhorts his people to become "signs of contradiction" against the decadent culture. The archbishop does not become authoritarian, rather inviting his director of religious education: "Would she work with him to implement programs that were consistent with the mind of Christ?"[36] When she resigns, the archbishop firmly continues on his path of reform, strengthened by mystical vision and supernatural promptings, just as Father Ron had been. In a dream, an angel of God speaks to him about the mission an archbishop has; but, as often in the *Children of the Last Days*, the italics here represent an eternal, divine voice speaking directly to the soul of the archbishop:

32. O'Brien, *Eclipse of the Sun*, 498.
33. O'Brien, *Eclipse of the Sun*, 499.
34. O'Brien, *Eclipse of the Sun*, 493.
35. O'Brien, *Eclipse of the Sun*, 535.
36. O'Brien, *Eclipse of the Sun*, 527.

> *Here is one who has defended his flock amidst many trials*, cried the angel with a voice like a trumpet. *All of his labors are seen and recorded, his sacrifices, his suffering, and his courage. Yet I have this to say to you: Too readily did you falter and not trust. Too much did you rely upon yourself, your strength, and your own mind. Too much did you expect from the City of Man. Too little did you trust the heart of the Father. Too easily have the deceivers played upon your kindness and bent you to their ends. Even so, they have bent you but a small measure. Stand up now, be firm, and strengthen the flock that remains.*[37]

The element of rebuke and discipline inherent in this message must, O'Brien always stresses, be understood as the voice of a Father who shows love to a son by disciplining him. Lovingly exhorted, the archbishop of *Eclipse of the Sun* does join in the "strengthening what remains" motif of the entire *Children of the Last Days* series. He even begins a process of substantive resistance to government after he receives a call reporting a sighting of Father Andrei (after Maurice had taken the holy man into the desert of urban Canadian life, seeking to tempt him). In so doing, the archbishop leads his flock with words and actions, fulfilling the authentic role that bishops must play in God's church.

The archbishop's public attempt to use legal means to obtain the release of Father Andrei introduces two other "reform movements" within the novel that offer some future hope against the growing cultural darkness that the novel so vividly describes. First is the reform of government itself. After officials discover the use of her son's identification to obtain medical services for Arrow, Beth Potter is arrested and then disappears into thin air, much like Nathaniel Delaney and Father Andrei before her. Her husband Ted cannot be aware of the recurrent nature of such disappearances in this Canadian "brave new world," but he is shocked by the inability to obtain any answers about what, if any, legal process is being offered to Beth. Desperate, Ted eventually enlists the aid of his local Member of Parliament, Ed Burgess. Though a low-ranking member of the Opposition, Ed uses a combination of grassroots town hall meetings and strategic statements in the media and the parliament's regular question period to bring public attention to the case. Against major odds, Ed succeeds in creating even international news bites for a simple question that soon many are asking: "Where is Beth Potter?"

---

37. O'Brien, *Eclipse of the Sun*, 502.

The work of MP Burgess is certainly hopeful and suggests that popular reform is still possible within Canadian democracy. Through another character, a friend of Burgess, O'Brien suggests the even greater complexity of reforming another element of society essential to any democracy, journalism. Peter Stanford has been a lifelong journalist, a newspaper man always on the lookout for important stories, but when he begins to notice and report on the political and social movements that will raise up the President of *Father Elijah*, he is surprised to find his writing on this topic suddenly unpublishable, even in newspapers where he has had a long working relationship with the editor. More ominously, at least from his own point of view, is that after one such editor transfers him to report on troubled regions of Africa, Stanford narrowly misses boarding a plane that is mysteriously blown up in flight.

Stanford cannot quite put together all the pieces of the story he is following—readers of the *Children of the Last Days* series have a broader perspective than this global journalist—but all his experience has left him very cynical about any freedom of the press, even in the democratic West. He tells Burgess:

> Look, Ed, there's no such thing as an independent press any more. There's not one of us hacks who'd dare to write a no-holds-barred article about the sacred cows, and if we did, it would never appear in print.[38]

Despite Stanford's seemingly justified cynicism, Burgess's pressure does eventually cause the government to release Beth Potter. She is let go in the woods of interior BC, still heavily drugged from government interrogation, a circumstance that allows the creation of a media pseudo-story about her running off into nature and escaping into drugs. So while Beth is released and eventually recovers her basic faculties, the meaning of this "good news" in the novel is unclear. Readers never find out, for example, how much if anything she remembers of her time in captivity. Moreover, will her ordeal, or even Ed Burgess's good work, have any long-term effect on the political or ecumenical ethos of the Canadian evangelical church?

After Beth's release, O'Brien gives a survey of all the minor characters of the novel, showing where they are at that point; for many, the events of the novel have not made much difference. Stanford, for example, has been transferred to Asia where he dies of "a pulmonary embolism."[39] Julie

---

38. O'Brien, *Eclipse of the Sun*, 642.
39. O'Brien, *Eclipse of the Sun*, 696.

and Colin are on their sailboat in the Pacific, Colin still struggling with "unanswerable theological questions—his spiritual hunger disguised as philosophical musing."[40] Julie's parents, Bill and Irene, are "arm in arm in the Winnebago," sleeping peacefully after Irene has won back some of the money that Bill lost gambling in Las Vegas. The Potter family moves to Alberta, and finds the economic means to live, but their children "began to complain about being forced to go to church."[41] Whenever she turns towards BC's Rocky Mountains, Beth's "mouth tightened a little and she shivered and turned east."[42]

The traditional Christian hope in the rising sun of the East is then vividly portrayed in perhaps the most important chapter of the novel, Father Andrei's final meeting with Maurice, "The Altar of Sacrifice." It begins quietly, with the still-imprisoned Father Andrei saying by memory the office that he has said for fifty years as a priest. Yet the words of Ps 102 now have a special resonance, and the psalm is quoted at length:

> Lord, hear my prayer;
> Let my cry come unto you . . . .
> I lie awake and moan
> Like a sparrow on the roof . . . .
> May the children of Your servants live on
> May their descendants live in Your presence.[43]

The last two lines cited here—two of the more than forty scriptural verses that O'Brien's full chapter includes—are repeated by Father Andrei, perhaps because near death he is very conscious of the meaning of his legacy as a priest. He has no biological children, but many spiritual children, and it is to their eternal souls that his life has been dedicated. Psalm 102 thus provides a thematic prelude to the main point of the chapter, which dramatically shows how Father Andrei, much like Father Elijah, is a priest *in persona Christi*, ready to imitate Christ even by the sacrifice of his own life.

Maurice soon arrives speaking the same friendly babble that preceded his murder of Nathaniel Delaney, but here offering a "deal" which faithful readers know Father Andrei can never accept. The old priest's life will be spared, Maurice claims, if he just goes before a camera and says, "I

---

40. O'Brien, *Eclipse of the Sun*, 700.
41. O'Brien, *Eclipse of the Sun*, 702.
42. O'Brien, *Eclipse of the Sun*, 703.
43. O'Brien, *Eclipse of the Sun*, 704.

wish to apologize to the people of this country for the many mistakes the institutional Roman Catholic Church has made."[44] Not an entirely false statement—John Paul II will give official apologies for Catholic errors at the start of the new millennium—but one here designed to appeal to anti-Catholic bias rather than true reconciliation. Knowing who alone can offer that, Father Andrei looks into the camera and says, "Praised be to Jesus Christ, the King of Glory. . . . He is coming soon to judge the whole earth. My children, do not believe the lies told to you by the government and the media."[45] At these words, Maurice goes berserk and begins bludgeoning the old man over the head until both are soaked in blood. Recalling the final earthly moments of Nathaniel Delaney, and of Christ himself, Father Andrei yet has a word for Maurice: "I forgive you."[46] Maurice's reaction is predictable, "You can't forgive me," but again faithful readers know that these words are lies. We cannot know, however, what seeds are planted in Maurice's soul by Father Andrei's dying words. Against all hope, in the humanly impossible love of enemies that Christ modeled on the cross, Father Andrei yet hopes for a better life for Maurice.

On the night of Father Andrei's death, in the section of the novel just after his murder, O'Brien again surveys the minor characters of the novel, solely focused now on those closest to Father Andrei. All feel something of his death. O'Brien is appealing to the traditional Catholic concept by which Father Andrei continues to influence those united with him in divine love. Death for a holy person can only make this unity stronger, and the influence of Father Andrei seems obvious upon Colin, for example, who though attending Mass many times with Julie now comprehends spiritually more of what is going on: "At the Consecration his eyes widened and filled with tears."[47] The full meaning of the communion of saints, however, is given in the chapter's final words, which focus again upon Cecilia Manyberries:

> She alone, of all those who had known Father Andrei, understood what had happened. She saw it all. Shortly before the sun burst over the coastal range, he appeared before her. His face was radiant, and he smiled at her with great love.[48]

44. O'Brien, *Eclipse of the Sun*, 720.
45. O'Brien, *Eclipse of the Sun*, 721.
46. O'Brien, *Eclipse of the Sun*, 722.
47. O'Brien, *Eclipse of the Sun*, 741.
48. O'Brien, *Eclipse of the Sun*, 744.

After this climactic chapter, in which the centrality of Father Andrei to the novel is so clear, the remainder of the story, focused upon the eventual fate of Arrow and Nick, feels a bit slow. Still, O'Brien achieves at least two important things in these chapters. Perhaps most important is what occurs when Maurice returns to Alice's store one last time, intending to finally arrest her and Arrow. At the last minute, after taking Arrow in his car, Maurice is given a vision of the human fall, and a message that Arrow says is from his father, Nathaniel. Without understanding that he is with his father's murderer, Arrow tells Maurice, "My father says, forgive."[49] It seems too late for Maurice to confess, but he does allow, even urge, Arrow's escape out of the car. We cannot know how to view this last-minute repentance, but perhaps Maurice is right when he explains:

> I don't know if there is any hope for me. But perhaps, somewhere in the universe, maybe somewhere beyond it, my one small act will be noted. It will say that I was not completely evil.[50]

We later learn, from the new OIS men who return to arrest Alice and Arrow two weeks later, that soon after releasing Arrow, Maurice was arrested and killed after suffering the same drug-induced invasion of his memory previously suffered by Father Andrei and Beth. However, illustrating his interior repentance, Maurice did not give up the location of Alice's store. As with Maurice's original call to Nathaniel at the start of *Plague Journal*, the source and strain of goodness in Maurice seem as mysterious as the "mystery of iniquity" in his soul, the obvious evil that governs so many of his actions.

The novel's final chapters again show the importance of seemingly unimportant people in the kingdom of God. This theme, a favorite of O'Brien's, is suggested first when the car of Mrs. Nguyen blocks the road, first slowing down Maurice on his way to Alice's. We don't know what effect this alteration of timing creates, nor can we know the effect of the spiritual message that could be given Mrs. Nguyen only through the supernatural medium of the Holy Spirit: "They forgave you!" she cries, "The man forgave you! The Faddah forgave you! Missus Pottah forgave you!"[51] What effect does this supernatural message have upon Maurice's eventual repentance? Then there is Murph, an RCMP officer who calls to warn Alice when the two new OIS men arrive. His call is against protocol,

---

49. O'Brien, *Eclipse of the Sun*, 762.
50. O'Brien, *Eclipse of the Sun*, 763.
51. O'Brien, *Eclipse of the Sun*, 754.

but reminds us of Maurice calling Nathaniel; perhaps conscience can and should trump the demands of our occupations, for perhaps this is a means by which the Holy Spirit can speak to our souls and affect our actions.

In the final chapter, after Alice is given the sweet release of passing from this life via a heart attack, Father Ron leads Arrow and Nick to the refuge in interior BC which has been mystically seen earlier in the novel. "The Camp of the Saints," as O'Brien's chapter title terms it, is the place that Grandpa Thaddeus has led the other Delaney children, who are now joyfully reunited with their brother. O'Brien not only depicts the joyful reunion, but also the long life that the Delaney children enjoy, thus fulfilling Father Andrei's prayer that his descendants will live in the presence of the Lord. There, Arrow becomes finally known as Aaron, while Nick lives until his thirty-third year. The obvious link to Christ, though, has long been known more by his life than his death. As Arrow puts it, taking over narration of the novel's final pages, to him Nick was always "Nicolo Piccolo . . . for his heart was a high and beautiful instrument, a reed of God, infecting us with his peculiar joy."[52] In his farewell to the reader, Aaron's voice seems to merge with O'Brien's, suggesting again that what has been important in the novel is not the details of how the terror of totalitarianism in Canada has been transcended, but rather how the reader was shown "the form" of how the remnant has been preserved:

> What can I tell you about the dark years? What can I say that would be of use to you? I have told you my story. That is the way it was. In those days we could not see the true shape of things, for we were covered by the great shadow that lay over the end of time. We had delayed our battle with it, century after century. When it came at last, we did not recognize it, for we were inside it.
>
> The shadow has now passed. The eclipse of the sun is finished. We have lived through the end of things and come to a new beginning.[53]

How finally should we see the achievement of this voluminous novel, *Eclipse of the Sun*? Over twenty years since its publication, it is easy to claim that its dark prophecies were exaggerated and that Canada has not yet become a totalitarian state. To dismiss the novel in this way, however, misses entirely the point of a dystopian novel. Did we stop reading *1984*,

---

52. O'Brien, *Eclipse of the Sun*, 852.
53. O'Brien, *Eclipse of the Sun*, 853.

for example, when, by 1985, society wasn't exactly as Orwell depicted it? Rather, we continue reading *1984* because it vividly reminds us of how a Big Brother state could be created; in the age of social media, this warning is all the more important.

Eclipse of the Sun remains a relevant warning in at least two important ways: first it shows how the public means of totalitarian control are already available; as David Jeffrey said on the back cover when the novel was first published, "the instruments of coercion" that O'Brien describes "are already largely in place."[54] Second, the critique of contemporary journalism in *Eclipse of the Sun* seems especially relevant. In 2018, *Time* magazine awarded its famed Person of the Year award to a compound rather than individual person, the endangered journalist, focusing on the many journalists around the world who have been killed because of their pursuit of truth.[55] The broader aesthetic point is made by O'Brien himself, in an "author's afterword" that was published with the novel in 1997. If a novelist "selects well," O'Brien argues, "he enables his reader to focus and thus to see more clearly the shape of reality—as one of my character says, 'seeing the form.'"[56]

Even the secular world now knows that honest journalism is essential to democracy, so perhaps it is also possible that the Western world might regain a sense of the need to develop the human consciousness that makes the apprehension of truth possible. The traditional religious term for such is conscience, the development of heart written about so well early in the twentieth century by C. S. Lewis in his *Abolition of Man*, and later by John Paul II in his *Redemptor Hominis*. Such authors are given voice by the clear, rational archbishop of *Eclipse of the Sun*, who midway through the novel articulates this key point:

> The foundation of democracy is conscience—personal responsibility. The society that abandons moral absolutes must eventually degenerate into a police state. Well, this nation has abandoned morality. Is it realistic to think we can avoid the consequences?[57]

The point here, though spoken in and clearly relevant to the twentieth century, is not temporal or historical. Conscience and its development

---

54. David Lyle Jeffrey, back cover endorsement of O'Brien, *Eclipse of the Sun*.
55. Felsenthal, "Choice."
56. O'Brien, *Eclipse of the Sun*, 855.
57. O'Brien, *Eclipse of the Sun*, 491.

are relevant to humans always and everywhere. Divine grace is "always now," as Canadian poet Margaret Avison put it,[58] and this basic religious claim the secular world may someday again take seriously. O'Brien's warning, however, is that there are both evil and good spirits loose in the world, and that New Age spirituality does not help us to know the difference. O'Brien's further consoling witness, though, is that Christ himself not only remains alive, but is actively using holy men and women in his church to preserve a remnant through even the darkest periods of human history.

O'Brien's thesis is hardly new. Christians have been children of the last days since the time of Christ. As the apostle John seems to be telling us in the book of Revelation, perhaps we can appreciate the meaning of the apocalypse best, perhaps merely glimpse its significance, only through symbol and paradox. To conclude with the lines from Chesterton that O'Brien uses as an epigraph for the novel:

> For the end of the world was long ago,
> And all we dwell today
> As children of some second birth,
> Like strange people left on earth
> After a judgement day.[59]

---

58. Avison, *Always Now*.
59. Chesterton, *Ballad of the White Horse*, 1.

"Creation" from *A Cry of Stone*

"Words-without-Words": *A Cry of Stone*

> She fell-into-seeing inside herself and found the quiet place in her heart where Jesus was. —Rose, in O'Brien, *A Cry of Stone*, 30

A Cry of Stone was the first novel that O'Brien wrote. Like many first works by prolific creative writers, the novel's form is easily criticized as primitive, but tells us much about the kind of writer developing. The novel's main character, Rose Wâbos, is a native, female artist, raised in poverty in an isolated village in Northern Ontario. Rose's journey illustrates how spiritual life can transcend earthly troubles, and how this transcendence can be presented through the medium of painting. Of course, that sounds like O'Brien himself, and certainly one could read *A Cry of Stone* as a semi-autobiographical bildungsroman, or novel about the growth of an artist. Yet as one begins to understand this novel's primary concerns, its literary genre seems less important than its historical and spiritual inspiration.

The opening dedication of the novel is to "the unknown martyrs of North America," a category that includes both natives and white missionaries.[1] An afterword to the novel also thanks the inspiration of a particular native woman, "Rose Prince, a woman of the Carrier people of northern British Columbia who died in 1949."[2] This novel "is not her tale," O'Brien clarifies, but she also was "a suffering servant of God," whose dead body, like many saints, remained incorrupt many years after her death, according to "native witnesses and the priests and nuns who were also present."[3] Rather than being the enemies commonly portrayed in Canada today, historically Catholicism and native culture have often

---

1. O'Brien, *Cry of Stone*, 5.
2. O'Brien, *Cry of Stone*, 849.
3. O'Brien, *Cry of Stone*, 849.

been mutually friendly and deeply intertwined. O'Brien's afterword further credits the influence of the much better-known Kateri, a canonized Canadian saint who is also an important figure in the novel itself.

The cover art of *A Cry of Stone* is iconographic, employing the physical to draw us into the spiritual. On first glance, given a clearly female figure embracing a small child, we might take the cover painting to be Rose embraced by her grandmother. Yet the name of this novel's painting, *Creation*, given inside the front cover, suggests a far broader significance. There are multiple meanings suggested by this title. First, there is the literal, physical creation of babies. "First," the novel's opening sentence tells us, "she was small." She "was very, very small . . . a seed inside a pod."[4] At the moment of birth,

> She was swept down a river of fire, heard screams, and fell through space pulling her twisting cord after her, until she landed in wrinkled brown hands, and a face with eyes as old as God pressed against her unknown face and kissed her and cried.[5]

This old face is not her birth mother, but the person who will bring God to her in this world: Oldmary Wâbos, so called to distinguish her from the physical mother, Youngmary Wâbos, who is not present in Rose's life. As a spiritual mother, Oldmary typologically embodies the Catholic tradition of Mary as mother of the church, which has its origins in Jesus' words to John and Mary at the foot of his cross (John 19: 25–27), and allows further layers of meaning to the cover painting: Oldmary is aiding the formation of Rose's eternal soul, as Mary cooperated with God to create an eternal church whose cornerstone is Jesus Christ.

The role of stone in the cover painting is especially striking. The stone at the top of the cover sits above the iconic figures, seemingly at rest after rolling along a gold fissure. On the novel's first page, Oldmary is described as "a rock that could not be moved," marking her as a follower of the "solid rock" who is the Lord and a member of the church built upon the rock who is Peter, but also recalling the many depictions in Catholic art of Mary's aid to those shipwrecked amid the rocks of this world. Soon, other stones in the novel become associated with key characters. Together with the closest friend of her youth, a young boy named Binemin, Rose finds a quartz stone that the two make the centerpiece of a natural garden that, in a complex fashion, symbolizes eternal beauty. Later, to express his

4. O'Brien, *Cry of Stone*, 7.
5. O'Brien, *Cry of Stone*, 7.

own devotion to Rose, Binemin gives her a "partridge" stone, "a flat green oval with a small beak at one end." "It *is* a partridge," Rose exclaims with delight, "a *binemin*"—the Ojibway word for bird. Oldmary describes this in O'Brien's terms: "He puts a word of himself in your hand."[6] Later, but less happily, Rose will paint a black pearl inside the heart of another dear friend, a teacher named Euphrasia Gorrel, to symbolize the pain of a life without God.

The novel later alludes clearly to other scriptural passages related to stones, such as Jesus' entrance to Jerusalem the first Sunday of Holy Week, when "all the stones cry out" (Luke 19:40) to lament his passion. The most famous stone of the Bible, though, is the stone rolled away at the resurrection of Christ. In an important sense, this is the most significant moment of "creation" in all of history. It is at the resurrection that God's plan for the redemption of humanity becomes clear: Christ's defeat of sin and death on the cross allow a new form of humanity to be created, for all who follow Christ themselves become "children of God" (John 1:12).

The resurrection, as with all elements of Christ's incarnation and ministry, affects both future and past time because it is part of the timeless reality of eternity. Hence Jesus' passion and resurrection provide the model for the power of martyrdom to be evidenced in Peter's life, and open the way for the re-creation of humanity explicit in the Catholic doctrine of the immaculate conception, which asserts that Mary is born without the stain of original sin and is made free by God to accept or reject his plan of salvation.

The most sublime doctrines of Catholicism are thus evoked by the painting on the cover of *A Cry of Stone*, but this is also the first novel—*The Father's Tale* is a notable later example—in which O'Brien supplements the painting on the cover with a realistic photograph. Facing the title page inside the book cover is a photo of a young native girl, taken from the National Museum of Canada's photos of Quebec, in which a girl is playing with old cans in a muddy puddle. Apparently much less sublime than the cover painting, and with no obvious connection to O'Brien's life, the obvious question is: Why does O'Brien include this photo? Perhaps it is due to the almost inevitable reaction of the typical North American viewer: here is a photo of someone unimportant, doing something that is clearly a waste of time. Through Rose Wâbos, O'Brien iconoclastically attacks both of these false, pejorative assumptions. We cannot see the inner

---

6. O'Brien, *Cry of Stone*, 122.

life of the girl in the photograph by looking only at her outward form, nor can we know how the Holy Spirit is shaping her creativity through the most mundane elements. *A Cry of Stone* cries out for us to look again.

The novel opens by sensitively portraying Indigenous culture, but also suggests its difficulty in coexisting with the more affluent white culture around it. O'Brien often gives the Ojibway word along with the English term, especially for significant cultural markers such as names. Rose's native name, for example, is *Oginiwabigon*, the "name of the wild roses that grew behind the outhouse." Grandma's English name means Oldmary Rabbit, which "some white peoples thought was funny" because "they did not know how beautiful it sounded in the Ojibway tongue: Mari-Wâbos."[7] Some have questioned O'Brien's knowledge of the Ojibway language, but an early Christmas shared by Rose and Oldmary gives a key response:

> At the end of Mass they all sang the "Huron Carol," which contained words that were close to the Objibway tongue, though they said *Gitchi-Manitou* instead of *Kije-Manitou*, which is the proper way for the Ojibway. But it did not matter, because all people were as one at Christmas.[8]

There are two key points here: first, an oral language like Ojibway has many dialectical variants, so it is simply unrealistic to insist on any "official" spelling or pronunciation. Second, important as language is, its technical details are not as important as the cultural meaning offered at an event like a Christmas Mass. O'Brien is clearly knowledgeable about native culture, but this also causes him to distinguish native spirituality and the spiritual reality of the Christian faith. As Rose gets older, the difference becomes increasingly important, but this conflict is there from the start. Oldmary, like many Canadian natives, carries a soul touched by the living Christian God inside a head aware of spiritual conflicts around her.

The grandmother uses native myth to shield Rose from painful information about her physical mother. Rose began as a bird lit by Gissis the Moon, and brought to Oldmary by Mang the Loon, from whose necklace fall the diamonds that make the *tchibekana* (river of stars). Binemin, the young boy soon to become important in Rose's life, is so named because he is a small bird delivered from the *tchibekana*; in this world,

---

7. O'Brien, *Cry of Stone*, 7.
8. O'Brien, *Cry of Stone*, 120.

human mythology and the divine art that is nature illuminate each other. As O'Brien's narrator puts it later in the novel:

> Names were poems. All words—except evil words—contained the many poems, as the deep ice of lakes contained masses of water waiting for the swelling sun. The deepest word was in the heart, where the sun always throbbed as pulsing blood, the words thawing and running like the many waters overflowing from rainwater pools.[9]

Despite the evident richness of her native culture and its peaceful integration with Catholic spiritual life, Oldmary cannot stop Rose from fantasizing that she is Marleena, a white girl whom Rose met in hospital. "Sometimes," Rose explains, "*there* is more real than *here*," and Oldmary can only "put her face in her hands" and weep.[10]

Rose fantasizes about Marleena by "falling-into-seeing," a term that is used throughout the rest of the novel to describe the practice of Rose's aesthetic imagination. Yet it is the reality of the Holy Spirit that becomes the prime comforter of Rose's interior life. Thus Catholicism blends with native culture in the novel not in a syncretic way that blurs or diminishes either, but rather by allowing the essential good of both to shine forth. Oldmary reads to Rose from the Bible, telling her of Jesus, "who came from a place far beyond the loon's necklace"; after his resurrection he "sent a white bird" that spoke "tongues of fire," named "Winijishid-Manito, Holy Ghost God in the white people's tongue." Father Andrei, a central character in the trilogy of the Delaney family, is also ministering among these natives, and he is "a *mekatewikwanaia*, a priest of Jesus."[11] At Mass, Rose can "hear words which Jesus sent by the messenger bird," and feel "the opening petals of fire that does not hurt."[12]

It is in this Spirit that Rose dreams of "a white bird, delicate and strong, formed in the current of blood, yet spotless," who appears to her and suggests she make one request and ask for "what your heart desires."[13] She requests "a brother I could love," and soon there appears in her village a small boy named Binemin Edzo. He hardly appears lovable, however, for when Rose greets him with a whisper, he "snarled—a long, low

---

9. O'Brien, *Cry of Stone*, 254.
10. O'Brien, *Cry of Stone*, 27.
11. O'Brien, *Cry of Stone*, 15.
12. O'Brien, *Cry of Stone*, 16.
13. O'Brien, *Cry of Stone*, 25.

gargling in the back of his throat," and "mouthed a word that was evil."[14] Next time at Mass, "the fire-song" speaks within Rose, "*I ask a sacrifice of you*," and Oldmary must explain this difficult new word:

> "A sacrifice," Oldmary whispered, "is when you take a heavy load on your back, like a hurt or a not-fairness. You give it to God and he puts it on the Cross of Jesus, the Big Sacrifice, and the Mass which is also the Big Sacrifice. Then you have a part in it."[15]

"What kind of part?" Rose reasonably asks, and again Oldmary has the answer: "Part mending," she explains. Gradually Rose understands:

> As she grew older, month by month, followed by another year, she began to see the pattern. When she hurt most and poured it into the wounds of Jesus, he poured it into Binemin. And soon after, Binemin would make another step, and another, and another.[16]

Sharing in the sacrifice of Christ or, as it's often popularly called, "offering it up," is strongly associated with Catholicism but often denigrated as sadistic self-flagellation, or seen by Protestants as one more evidence of "works-based" theology by which Catholics are vainly trying to earn their way to heaven. As with any doctrine it could be abused, but in its sanctified form, as in the life of Rose, it might instead be seen as a response to Christ's call: "Take up your cross" and come, "follow me" (Matt 16:24). One might see it as human participation in the divine response to the problem of evil: as Christ comes to suffer with us, finally on the cross, so we suffer with him so that the effect of the cross in our world is concretely seen.

The effects of Rose's participation in the sacrifice of Christ are then distinguished from what Binemin gains from three months in the hospital; he returns and "did whatever people told him to," and he "ate," and "grew" but, "he never smiled" and "he never talked."[17] The "life" desired for him by Rose and the Holy Spirit begins with art, as he responds to Rose drawing the small bird of fire with his own drawing, a "crude manshape." Then, he takes a symbolic stick of fire and "pressed the stick" into the drawing of his face and "began to twist" as he "pitched forward into

---

14. O'Brien, *Cry of Stone*, 28.
15. O'Brien, *Cry of Stone*, 29.
16. O'Brien, *Cry of Stone*, 45.
17. O'Brien, *Cry of Stone*, 31.

his own falling-into-seeing"; when Rose whispers, "Did this happen to you?" A "complete madness possessed" Binemin, and he ran "howling into the forest."[18]

Binemin is clearly a long-term project, but Rose makes gradual strides in friendship over the next few summers through minor sacrifices, such as swallowing the minnows that he would pluck from streams. After one hike for blueberries, Rose "made a silly face at him showing her blue teeth" and "his facial muscles contracted into a trembling smile"; this might seem insignificant, but Rose knew it "was a great victory."[19] The real breakthrough comes, though, after Binemin finds "a nearly perfect orb of white quartz,"[20] which Rose places at the center of a group of other white and pink stones, "so that gradually the whole began to emerge as a corona of roses." Bineman's quartz, she tells him, "is a speckle that fell from the *tchibenka*, the necklace, the river of souls."[21] The myth and resultant garden also create a new name that Rose gives to Binemin: Tchibi. This poetic name, she explains later, means this:

> Tchibi is from the *tchibenka*, the river of souls, the river of stars, which our people call the loon's necklace. He is like a star to me, because he is like the loon. He does not speak, and he likes to be alone. But his song is sweet.[22]

Unconsciously, but spiritually aware of how love unites souls eternally, O'Brien sees the garden of Tchibi and Rose as creating a natural representation of the mystic rose that Dante depicts at the height of *Paradiso* in *The Divine Comedy*. Of course such literary allusions are meaningless to them at this youthful stage, but the purity of their prepubescent love does recall Dante and Beatrice, both of whom grew up to marry another. Rose and Binemin never have romantic love, but long afterwards Rose is affected by the great lesson she learns from him: "She could at least offer the word of her presence, and this she now realized was no small thing."[23] The two share a friendship formed in the Holy Spirit, as O'Brien's narrator

---

18. O'Brien, *Cry of Stone*, 33.
19. O'Brien, *Cry of Stone*, 37.
20. O'Brien, *Cry of Stone*, 38.
21. O'Brien, *Cry of Stone*, 39.
22. O'Brien, *Cry of Stone*, 89.
23. O'Brien, *Cry of Stone*, 35.

makes clear: "It was so beautiful the fire in her heart grew very strong as they laughed and laughed and laughed together."[24]

Rose's friendship and art, through the Holy Spirit, affect many other people as she grows up. One relationship important to the novel as a whole is with Euphrasia Gorrel, a teacher who comes to Rose's community. She is a sort of early sketch of the young Anne in *Strangers and Sojourners*, and in most ways she seems the polar opposite of Binemin. Sophisticated, learned, a world traveller, Euphrasia has abandoned both romantic love and any belief in divine presence. Ironically, at the very moment when she remembers herself closest to the former, she may actually have been in the presence of the latter. As we have seen in other novels, the appearance of angels in O'Brien's fiction is not an uncommon occurrence, and such might also have happened when Euphrasia was in Scotland, on a remote moor, when out of the fog an attractive shepherd emerged. To her amazement and delight, he recites from memory Euphrasia's favorite passage in *A Midsummer Night's Dream*, Theseus's famous act 5 speech on the imagination, which concludes:

> And as imagination bodies forth
> The forms of things unknown, the poet's pen
> Turns them to shapes, and gives to airy nothing
> A local habitation and a name.[25]

Euphrasia gives the lines a reasonable intellectual interpretation, one based on the "fuller context" of the plays, which show Shakespeare's "belief that drama gives to invisible realities a local habitation and a name." To this the shepherd can only laugh, causing Euphrasia to laugh too; she recalls, "it lasted a few seconds only, but there are seconds which stretch into infinity."[26] He does not give a name, Euphrasia sadly laments, "to keep in the sanctuary of the heart," but perhaps his is an angel's name hidden in the invisible reality of heaven. Such is strongly suggested in his parting words to Euphrasia: "Your way lies there (he pointed back down the path) and mine there (pointing up into the cloud). Though all paths eventually join at the gate."[27]

---

24. O'Brien, *Cry of Stone*, 43.

25. Shakespeare, *Midsummer Night's Dream*, 5.1.14–17, quoted in O'Brien, *Cry of Stone*, 71.

26. O'Brien, *Cry of Stone*, 72.

27. O'Brien, *Cry of Stone*, 73.

Not even the magnificent reality of Canadian nature can alter Euphrasia's disbelief in an invisible Creator, but she does recognize Rose's creative gifts and is moved to give the young artist her first coloring tools. Observing the rapt Rose then at work, the well-travelled teacher sees the similarity with other cultures, "the exteriorizing of the interior icon," but she is unsure if this suggests theism:

> She was not sure which was correct: either the unknowable which lay beyond the frontiers of infinity was an impersonal nothingness or it breathed and had a name.[28]

Rose's drawing of her, however, suggests the divine lover trying to reach Euphrasia:

> Beneath the double sun of her spherical breasts, in the hollow where the heart should be, her two hands gripped fiercely an ugly black stone.... A large bird with unfurled wings enveloped the top half of the image, surrounding the sleeping woman, protecting her like two enfolding hands.[29]

Readers familiar with O'Brien's art can recognize this as an apocalyptic icon revealing the choice facing Euphrasia, and all human beings, but the motivation of the young artist Rose is much simpler. Understandably shaken, Euphrasia demands to know why Rose has painted the icon; "Because you are beautiful!" the child blurted out. "Because I love you."[30]

Euphrasia is no more aware than most modern people, sadly, of the meaning of these "three radioactive words."[31] She dismisses beauty as "an accident," and sees love as "a game at best . . . at worst a devouring, around which we spin the rituals."[32] Euphrasia's words become sad, self-fulfilling prophecy after she becomes engaged in the ritual of long-distance courtship, only to have her hopes dashed by mysterious forces of cruelty in human nature. Romantic love is also denied to Rose, due in part to her small stature, as she never grows past about four feet tall, but more so due to her increasingly deformed spine. From Rose's suffering springs the mystery, however, that she can ease the pain of others through offering up her own sacrifice to the universal sacrifice for all, consummated by

---

28. O'Brien, *Cry of Stone*, 56.
29. O'Brien, *Cry of Stone*, 78.
30. O'Brien, *Cry of Stone*, 79.
31. O'Brien, *Cry of Stone*, 79.
32. O'Brien, *Cry of Stone*, 93.

Jesus on the cross. Is this thought a delusion or a divine mystery? On this question hinges much of the novel's meaning.

Euphrasia Gorrel soon flees the north, apparently never to be heard from again, but Rose's ability to love and mend others increases, paradoxically, even after she is sent south to a residential school in Thunder Bay. To do so, she must learn to accept how the beauty of her art can cause suffering to others, as it did to Euphrasia, and to her own soul, which can see both great joy and extreme pain. For a time, she gives up drawing, but then is helped by Father Andrei, who tells her, regarding the images that arise in her mind:

> The pictures can come from God, or from your own feelings and imaginings. And sometimes they can be false, sent by the matchi-manito, the evil one, to lead you from the safe part. . . . Pray, and do not cease to pray. Then, if the picture is bad it will go away. If it is good, it will be very simple, to guide your prayer and nothing more.[33]

Art for Rose is thus both an aesthetic and a spiritual practice. Rose regains joy in drawing through the art classes offered by the nuns of the school, and after such classes "her heart was full of the old joy," and even her spine feels better: "She fell asleep without an ache in her heart or her body."[34] From these French nuns, Rose will learn that "*le Bon Dieu* is a potter" and "a singer" and a "poem maker," "the maker . . . the *Artiste*, the Maker of all this." Yet when Rose concludes, "the world is beautiful," the nun with her "cast a worried look," aware of Rose's unawareness of sin and evil also in the world.[35]

The school in Thunder Bay gives ample evidence of the sad reality of these latter elements, especially for Binemin Edzo, who goes there hoping to be with Rose. The key character in O'Brien's approach to the still-sensitive issues raised by the "residential schools" is Mr. McKenna, supervisor of the boys at the school. In some ways, McKenna is a stereotypical abuser, a man who screams at the boys to be pure and clean in shower lines, then secretly abuses them later. O'Brien's depiction of this monster, however, strikes one as realistic rather than simply caricature.[36] First, for

---

33. O'Brien, *Cry of Stone*, 131.
34. O'Brien, *Cry of Stone*, 169.
35. O'Brien, *Cry of Stone*, 255.
36. Much of Binemin's experience at residential school was also experienced by O'Brien himself, as he makes clear in a recently published essay ("Scandals and Shepherds").

example, the power McKenna wields comes in part from six young men whom he controls through a combination of intimidation and reward-giving so that McKenna always has ready servants and, if need be, an alibi, if he were ever to be charged. It is one of the six, normally, whom the "frog"—as all the boys call McKenna—sends when he selects a sexual victim. The details of such abuse are never depicted by O'Brien, but the implication is very clear when his narrator tells us:

> There were times when the frog was hungry and ate a fly, usually very late at night. These incidents were known only to the initiated, the six who were bound to him by guilt as well as by their desire for comfort.[37]

Binemin avoids the direct pain of such encounters by saying no when one of the six call. While some might view this simple refusal as naïve, within O'Brien's narrative it could be quite realistic. Binemin's past prepares him, and gives him the strength of will, to be prepared to die rather than submit to more abuse. McKenna does cease to bother Binemin, but this is no surprise given more easily obtainable victims. McKenna does damage further any hope that Binemin might develop faith, however, for he sees that "the supervisor took the sacraments, and they did not make him better."[38]

Also realistic, in my judgment, is O'Brien's depiction of how the Roman Catholic Church allowed such horror to occur within its institutions. Certainly there were some evil clerics involved, but more common is the administrator of the school depicted by O'Brien in *A Cry of Stone*, Father Morin, who is overworked, incompetent, and unwilling to engage in any direct confrontation of McKenna. No wonder the "supervisor" is "pleased by the temperament of the new rector."[39] Father Morin is not without blame, of course, but his crime is negligence rather than willful compliance. A similar but different problem is shown by a nun to whom Binemin reveals the truth; her response, "We must pray for him," is to be expected, but it is clearly inadequate to the problem. Eventually, McKenna is reported to the police and arrested, but long after damaging many young men for the rest of their lives.

What kind of reconciliation is possible between such victims and men such as McKenna? This is one of the many hard questions in which

---

37. O'Brien, *Cry of Stone*, 191.
38. O'Brien, *Cry of Stone*, 197.
39. O'Brien, *Cry of Stone*, 183.

this scandal remains mired, and no easy solution exists. O'Brien points the way towards a Catholic response when his Rose "falls-into-seeing" McKenna's past, and sees how he himself is a soul damaged by pain, poverty, and abuse. Rose sees McKenna's absolute need for the healing fire of the Holy Spirit, so her response is not only the words of human prayer, but also the word of divine presence. This response might seem ineffective in historical context, but at least it persuades Binemin not to murder McKenna and endanger his own soul through mortal sin. Again, Rose's supernatural sight here will strike some as unrealistic, but as with Father Andrei in *Strangers and Sojourners* her vision is a gift, a word, given by the eternal reality of the communion of saints, one of the core doctrines of Christianity as expressed in the Apostles' Creed. The arrest of McKenna is of course just and moral, but Rose's prayers, like those of the nun whom Binemin first speaks with, hope to take McKenna to the divine throne of perfect mercy and justice.

Other aspects of these troubling schools are suggested by how both Binemin and Rose leave Thunder Bay. Upon arriving back in his home town, Binemin is taken in by Kinoje and his wife, a native couple usually shown in the novel as engaged in shamanism, the attempt to manipulate primitive spirits. They don't take Binemin for spiritual reasons, however, but simply to get foster care money. Father Andrei objects that this couple "is not suitable," for religious reasons,"[40] but his probably valid objection is ignored. The sad tendency of the late twentieth-century Catholic Church to undercut its own authority, however, is shown when Rose must also leave the school, though she wants to stay and applies to become a nun after graduating from high school. The order's Mother Superior, writing from France, rejects her because "she believes we must have novices who are strong, strong enough to meet the demands of the coming times." Ironically, Rose's immense spiritual strength is discarded in a time when the church seems most in need of it. Rose accepts that "it is the will of *le Bon Dieu*," however obvious the mistake seems from a human point of view.[41] Yet Rose would probably not have continued her prolific religious art if she had become a nun. The Mother Superior's decision sends Rose on to an art school in the big city of Toronto.

This setting allows O'Brien to compare the natural world of the north to the urban world of the south, and to contrast the professional

---

40. O'Brien, *Cry of Stone*, 221.
41. O'Brien, *Cry of Stone*, 259.

technique typically taught at art school with the spiritual aesthetic practiced by Rose. In a downtown Toronto park, for example, Rose is observed drawing by two men, one old and grizzled, the other young and handsome. Clearly allegorical, and never to be heard from again in the novel, the younger praises Rose as someone who "will become great" and "rise steadily" in the art world. The old man, though, perceives that Rose's "eye regards all wounded, untamed things and reverences them," and he believes she will be judged by criteria often unvalued in the world: "She will desire what is true and beautiful and good . . . She will be great, but by a different measure."[42]

Rose's experience of these distinct audiences prompts her to ask perhaps the most fundamental question that must be considered by any serious painter:

> Did not the appearances of things reveal their inner condition? Rose asked herself. Was not the golden-haired man a visible form of the beauty of life and its ever renewed powers? Was not the old man an image of weakness and decay? As Rose pondered these questions, she realized that appearances both revealed and misled. She reminded herself that the surface images of her many beloveds were not beautiful. They were lovely in her eyes because something within them had quickened her heart.
>
> "What is beauty?" she asked in great perplexity.[43]

Rose's eventual answer to this great question is practical, lived, rather than simply theoretical, but the art school does pose questions that clarify her Catholic aesthetic. *Eclipse of the Sun*, we recall, does much with Balthasar's conception of "seeing the form," but what is "form"? At the art school in Toronto, Rose studies "a thing called 'form,'" defined as "the outer shapes of objects and their masses and the spaces that they displaced."[44] Yet when forced to paint the outer form of a naked body, Rose cannot ignore the human person inside the skin. With the first nude model, a woman, Rose realizes, "I am ashamed, for I do not love this woman."[45] Rose's objection is not moral, in a narrow sense, and she later realizes that art depicting evil can be "a word of warning,"[46] but she

---

42. O'Brien, *Cry of Stone*, 292.
43. O'Brien, *Cry of Stone*, 292.
44. O'Brien, *Cry of Stone*, 317.
45. O'Brien, *Cry of Stone*, 322.
46. O'Brien, *Cry of Stone*, 333.

objects to a purely materialistic conception of art. "Only love creates,"[47] Rose insists, refusing to paint the nude woman.

When a clearly uncomfortable black male model takes the woman's place, Rose does pity him and approaches to speak with him and share some of her lunch. She falls-into-seeing, sees that he has come to Toronto to feed his family back in Jamaica, and gives him two hundred dollars, telling him that she gives the money so that he "will know you are not a thing, you are not a no-thing, you are a good man, a father, a husband, a man who went naked for his babies." Faced with Rose's simplicity, many readers might share the model's reply to her, "You crazy girl," but Rose has an immediate response: "I am not crazy. You know who gives this to you." "In a child's voice" the man replies, "I know him. I know him."[48]

This expression of the unity of souls in Christ is repeated many times in the novel. Sadly, it does not protect Rose from Deirdre, a confused fellow art student and supposed friend to whom Rose naively lends money before Deirdre and a boyfriend steal all of Rose's remaining money. Desperate, Rose resolves to follow the "suffering way," the "darkness-way, where all treasures but him are dropped,"[49] by walking home to Northern Ontario. Providentially, she is picked up by a kind Catholic woman on her way home to Ottawa. In a dream, Rose is given the consolation so important to O'Brien's theological aesthetic. Our Lord tells her: "A life is a word. Its meaning and its shape are the answer you seek. It must be lived in order to be spoken."[50]

In Ottawa, Rose briefly meets Wolfie, another of O'Brien's portraits of the pseudo-artist who beneath all appearances is a nihilist. Wolfie makes a brief attempt to seduce Rose, but fortunately she flees via a bus ticket to Montreal. Rose has heard that Mt. Royal is "the place where God touched the earth in this land,"[51] and she happily finds what she is looking for in St. Joseph's Oratory. This famous church, sanctified by the healing miracles of Brother André in the early twentieth century, is beautifully described by O'Brien. There Rose feels

> the infusion of presence that was thick in the air—that she inhaled and exhaled. Joy burst upon her like a wave, and washed

---

47. O'Brien, *Cry of Stone*, 322.
48. O'Brien, *Cry of Stone*, 330.
49. O'Brien, *Cry of Stone*, 366.
50. O'Brien, *Cry of Stone*, 389.
51. O'Brien, *Cry of Stone*, 393.

through her, and carried her deeper into the radiance hidden within the church. Slowly the light of her eyes increased, and everywhere she looked were glowing wood, and marble floors, and gold. Then she saw a giant statue of St. Joseph above the altar and the tabernacle, where the Beating Heart pounded with a love so great that Rose fell to her knees and pressed her face to the floor.[52]

Within the typological iconography common in *A Cry of Stone*, it is not inaccurate to say that Father Andrei is a type of brother, now Saint André, founder of the famous oratory of St. Joseph in Montreal. The key thing they share is that both are touched by the living, eternal God. Rose rests in the rich presence of the Holy Spirit in the Oratory, and prays that St. Joseph can become a father for her.

God certainly hears her prayer, but answers it in a highly unexpected way. She is about to begin acting a minor part in a troupe performing *A Midsummer Night's Dream*, when suddenly the voice of the set painter resounds behind her; he is highly critical of the actors, saying, "See how they take the genius of the bard and make themselves superior to it, bending it to their purpose."[53] He is Hugo Dyson, whose strong views on art have been cultivated within a long marriage to another painter, Esther. Survivors of the Holocaust, both now believe solely "in Peace and in Art."[54] Neither is thus formally Jewish, but both have histories "touched by God," and both have a very significant effect upon Rose's development as a painter, and arguably an even more profound effect on her eternal soul.

Esther met Hugo when he was a British pacifist or "conscience-objector," though Esther had a different name for him when they first met, as she was recovering from the horrors of the concentration camps: "imbecile."[55] From this unlikely beginning blossomed a lifelong friendship based on honesty and serious artistic expression. The couple is long used to each other by this stage in their lives, but in the occasional rancor of their relationship we see one of O'Brien's gifts as a writer: the capacity to take clichéd, stereotypical figures, such as a cantankerous older couple, and depict them as real people with eternal souls that make them unique individuals highly valued by the living God.

52. O'Brien, *Cry of Stone*, 394.
53. O'Brien, *Cry of Stone*, 413.
54. O'Brien, *Cry of Stone*, 495.
55. O'Brien, *Cry of Stone*, 495.

Rose hesitates to stay with the old couple, but then receives interior confirmation from the Lord, which O'Brien conveys through his characteristic italics; inside, Rose hears Christ say: "*Though they do not know me, they are within my eye and within my own suffering.*" With them, the Lord assures Rose, she can pursue her "*great gift*"; Rose asks, "Do you speak of the seeing which is for the offering way?" The Lord replies: "'*This also,*' said the word, '*And with it the pictures that you make, which are words for the blind to see and understand.*'"[56]

The years in which Rose stays with Esther and Hugo can seem uneventful to many readers, especially those uninterested in aesthetic theory, but in many ways this seems to me the heart of this novel, as O'Brien depicts how real people create serious, spiritual art. It is perhaps easiest to see this with Esther, who has painted to express the immense pain that must be felt by a survivor who lost most of her family in the Holocaust. She shares Hugo's view of the *Midsummer Night's Dream* troupe, and after seeing the live performance, Esther rebukes its director: "It was not about Shakespeare at all," but rather about the director's own ego.[57] The episode is not important because of Shakespeare, but rather because of how Rose grows in her understanding of the difference between true and false art.

At the party after the play, Rose is goaded to give an "Indian song,"[58] and eventually she consents, but sings a song that must defy all stereotypical expectations. Offering her own "poetry of thawed ice," she seems to sing of Oldmary, "an old woman's memory / in a casket sitting on the stones,"[59] from whose "silent speech" she learned to sing "her spirit / in sacred, fragile, / summer." This sublime poetry is not understood by the play's drunken director, who stands up and praises how Rose has "entertained us with the story of a coffin full of bones."[60] "Here's to death," he shouts, raising his glass. Rose and Esther flee, both aware of the difference between the culture of death and the culture of life that authentic art helps to create.

Many of the other aesthetic issues considered in the chapters with Hugo and Esther are not solely theoretical but also existential. Much of the debate is between realistic and abstract art. Esther strongly favors the former; amid the pseudo-art and stunted humanity of the theatrical

---

56. O'Brien, *Cry of Stone*, 442.
57. O'Brien, *Cry of Stone*, 463.
58. O'Brien, *Cry of Stone*, 471.
59. O'Brien, *Cry of Stone*, 472.
60. O'Brien, *Cry of Stone*, 475.

troupe, Esther insists, "As you know, my Rose, faces have texture and forms and content because human beings are not abstractions. "They are real. . . . We are real," she corrected, "You and I."[61] Paradoxically, like some other characters in O'Brien's fiction who come to know God while living under totalitarian regimes, Esther has learned about the dignity of humanity amid the horror that was the Holocaust. Suffering does not disprove God's existence and is not unrelated to art, but part of it; after Esther has recalled saying the Shema, the foundational prayer of Jewish theism, at the concentration camp, she tells Rose, "To suffer is to live. To live is to suffer. This I have accepted. This is the price of the paintings."[62] Realism is thus at the core of the aesthetic that produced Esther's most famous wartime painting, *Birds in Wartime*. Perhaps this painting, and her current realistic practice, allows Esther to appreciate Rose's aesthetic, despite not accepting the metaphysic that lies behind it.

Hugo's case is more complex. Esther tells Rose that "once he was a gifted realist," but, after a nervous breakdown, he "embraced abstraction as therapy"; Esther's own aesthetic, though, rebukes abstract art as a lie: "Absurdity and darkness and destruction dissolving into one lie—that there is nothing but death."[63] Hugo himself explains to Rose that his change of artistic practice was not unrelated to his development of a nihilistic metaphysic. Though he believes "in painting" and in "Esther's love," he is even more certain of the "selfishness of human nature," and that there are no "ascensions" from this world; as he puts it, "the souls of the just do not fly up like little birds. The world is all there is."[64] There is, of course, a realistic cynicism behind this nihilism, if one has any awareness of twentieth-century history. As Hugo tells Esther: "I'm not doing anything but telling this girl the facts of life. It isn't just millions who have perished since the turn of the century. It is hundreds of millions."[65] Counting the dead produced by the culture of death is a tautological rather than compelling argument, but the sheer numbers involved are surely depressing.

Esther and Hugo do combine to convince Rose that she must learn to paint evil as well as good. Esther teaches her that depicting evil within a good story can be part of how a symbolic image affects its audience, for as

61. O'Brien, *Cry of Stone*, 468.
62. O'Brien, *Cry of Stone*, 462.
63. O'Brien, *Cry of Stone*, 505.
64. O'Brien, *Cry of Stone*, 428.
65. O'Brien, *Cry of Stone*, 433.

she puts it, in language close to O'Brien's own aesthetic, "The story would shift the balance of the world, if it were known. Even if only a little. As does every true word."[66] Then, she teaches, the painting becomes "a story and an icon all together."[67] Yet on the whole, Rose's aesthetic has greater influence upon Esther and Hugo than vice versa, for Christian realism has been central to her identity as artist and person for a long time. Long ago she became aware that art "was not, in fact, a falling into nothingness, for the speaking of words sent waves throughout the world."[68] She has painted many pictures of "the many faces where Christ hides."[69]

Rose further learns, in holy fear, of what Tolkien called sub-creation, the sharing in creation possible because we are made in God's image.[70] On this view, artistic creation is an exercise in the fundamental freedom which God calls us to share in:

> The bare palette was terrifying. If she chose one path it eliminated paths. And if she added a second color—burnt umber for instance, or red oxide—this also changed the course of things. But you must choose, she admonished herself. God chose first, she explained. You are not making yourself into God, no, if you are placing your little choosing within his great choosing. Has he not put a little of himself in you, a reflection of the light, in order to share the power of his love?[71]

As O'Brien's narrator then summarizes: "*Yes*, so the choosing is love, it is creating *with* God, and it is good!"[72]

Rose's aesthetic has been, she realizes, neither a materialistic realism nor a spiritual abstraction, but rather what she comes to call "figurative." The meaning of this aesthetic is perhaps best revealed in a conversation with Hugo; he laments time spent on abstract art, "painting the surface of closed doors . . . ignoring whatever it is that breathes softly behind closed doors."[73] When Rose probes, inquiring "what it is that breathes behind the closed doors," Hugo retreats to agnosticism, "Don't know. Don't presume to know." When Rose recalls a time Hugo had told her about, when "a

---

66. O'Brien, *Cry of Stone*, 523.
67. O'Brien, *Cry of Stone*, 524.
68. O'Brien, *Cry of Stone*, 311.
69. O'Brien, *Cry of Stone*, 312.
70. See use of "sub-creator" in Tolkien, "Mythopoeia."
71. O'Brien, *Cry of Stone*, 515.
72. O'Brien, *Cry of Stone*, 515.
73. O'Brien, *Cry of Stone*, 519.

king appeared in a window" and spoke to him, Hugo himself can guess, if not speak, the identity of the man who spoke. Hugo never acknowledges the king whom Rose knows, but soon he is painting symbolic horses, and Rose is "pleased to see that he had shifted toward the world of the figurative," and that "her prayers for him had not gone unanswered."[74]

The effect on Esther is perhaps even more profound, as she returns to the theme of her famous wartime painting. She herself suddenly dies, but that only confirms further the figurative meaning of the painting found after her death; in her room

> There was a new painting on the easel, a depiction of a woman selling crated pigeons. Similar to the earlier work, it was different in that the woman gazed at the birds with great love, her hand resting on the open doorway of the cages. The birds, ruffling their wings, took flight.[75]

Rose is also engaged in a struggle, throughout this time, over what "native" art should mean or, more broadly, what should be the relationship of the Christian faith to native culture? As a prolific young female artist, Rose is easily typecast and expected to express what has become a familiar narrative: Christianity suppressed native religion so that White Europeans could colonize and control native culture. The abuses of the residential schools have made this narrative almost unchallengeable today, but O'Brien, through Rose, offers another viewpoint.

As is often the case with African Christians who have lived experience of spiritual conflict, Rose sees in some native art the depiction of the shamanism by which men like Kinoje had, in her youth, terrorized and sought to control her people; pointing to one painting, Rose says:

> Here, in this one, for example, is a shaking tent, which my grandmother warned me against, for it is the shaman-way, the way of opening to the demon spirits which the magicians say are good. They are not good. For it is the realm of the people who frightened me when I was a child.[76]

Rose is especially disturbed by the paintings of a native artist called Thunder-Eagle; his painting *Windigo Dancing*, for example, "portrayed

---

74. O'Brien, *Cry of Stone*, 508.
75. O'Brien, *Cry of Stone*, 540.
76. O'Brien, *Cry of Stone*, 530.

a crazed man-beast holding human captives in its claws," and "a small church burned at the Windigo's feet."[77]

Rose's concern becomes much more personal after Hugo gives her an article to read in which she learns that Thunder-Eagle was born Binemin Edzo, in a small Northern Ontario trapping village. The article tells her that he was "arrested last week," in Thunder Bay, Ontario, and "charged with malicious destruction of public property." In her spirit, though, comes a message directly from Tchibi: "*Come to me. I am dying.*"[78] Travelling immediately to Thunder Bay, Rose learns that Binemin is near death in hospital, suffering from burn wounds after he set his own cabin on fire during a night of drinking. On first seeing him, Rose feels despair not so much because of his horrible physical condition, but

> beneath this was an undertow of deeper horror—the realization that the brother she had loved throughout all these many years had not remained the image in her mind. . . . Over no part of him, it seemed, had her prayers and offerings exercised an influence. Perhaps a little at the beginning, but if his art and his accident indicated anything, it was that her endless sacrifice had been futile.[79]

Here is the temptation to despair that must often be faced by any holy person in our vale of tears: the apparent certainty that good action, prayer, a faith-filled life, produces no definite consequences and leads merely to the same futile tragedy suffered by everyone else, death. Binemin does soon die, but not before interior vision that acts as a great consolation to Rose's spiritual life.

In one of the most eloquent, moving passages in O'Brien's work—comparable in this novel to Father Elijah's confrontation with the President in *Father Elijah* or Father Andrei's final meeting with Maurice in *Eclipse of the Sun*—the Lord makes clear that he is doing much more within Binemin's soul than can be discerned simply by looking at his body:

> Then there came to her suddenly, as a word is sometimes read on the wide extended firmament of the sky, a promise. A promise that only his flesh was falling . . . the man-spirit of Binemin Edzo was washed clean of the false names that clung to him,

---

77. O'Brien, *Cry of Stone*, 533.
78. O'Brien, *Cry of Stone*, 552.
79. O'Brien, *Cry of Stone*, 556.

entangling his heart and mind, the serpents were pried from him and cast down, he was cleansed in the waters of the Great Mercy and bathed in the waters of her tears flowing as creeks flow to rivers, and rivers to lakes, and lakes by many waters into the sea. And then she knew that his spirit was becoming as silver as *atikameg*, though the washing was like a purification, it was a terrible burning yet within the burning was joy, for he was going up, up, up into the hands of God. And one day, too, his flesh would rise with the rising of all flesh and be restored and the last of the enemies would be hurled into the Lake of Fire.[80]

O'Brien follows this long paragraph with one of his shortest paragraphs, three sentences which remind us that Binemin is a living stone, Christ the cornerstone is at work within him, and the stone rolled away at the resurrection means that spiritual reality, not physical death, is ultimately true: "Then the stone exhaled slowly. After that, it did not inhale. It was still."[81] Rose's grief cannot allow her to know what transpired through her prayers for him dying, in this moment of pain, but the presence of Christ in Tchibi is reaffirmed by what remains by his bedside, recovered after the fire: "a spherical soot-blackened stone . . . and a scorched aluminum medallion."[82]

After her moving farewell to Tchibi, Rose returns to Montreal. The novel's stone imagery again becomes crucial, but not before Rose is further immersed in the issues raised by new native art. Rose remains "disturbed" by its pagan themes, and asks the key question: "Where was it leading her people?"[83] Amazingly, Hugo helps Rose get her own show, and, after Esther's death, he even more clearly than before becomes "the father she had never known."[84] The exhibition sells well, but is not critically acclaimed, with most critics lamenting the presence of clear Christian themes in Rose's work. At the exhibition, the curator, Favio Ontolli, describes Rose as a native artist who acts "as channel of the earth spirits," but Rose corrects him in a way that not only rejects paganism, but reminds us of the sub-creating, religious aesthetic consistently practiced by O'Brien:

---

80. O'Brien, *Cry of Stone*, 562.
81. O'Brien, *Cry of Stone*, 562.
82. O'Brien, *Cry of Stone*, 563.
83. O'Brien, *Cry of Stone*, 566.
84. O'Brien, *Cry of Stone*, 567.

> "Actually, no, Mr. Ontolli," Rose spoke up. "I am not a channel. The shaman is a channel or a hollow tube through which the wicked spirits speak. My way is to be a beloved twig in the hands of the Creator. We make the pictures together."[85]

Far more important than critics, however, is the presence at the exhibition of an elderly native woman named Elizabeth. Her name suggests typological relationship with the cousin of Mary whose unborn babe (John the Baptist) leaps in the womb upon hearing the annunciation. This modern Elizabeth has also been led by the Spirit to travel north to the exhibition, to deliver some messages from the Lord. She tells Rose: "He says that you must not cease to trust him in all that is about to happen. Do not be afraid."[86] Again recalling the biblical Elizabeth, she also tells Rose of a mysterious family relationship: "Your sister awaits you, across the river. She who is the firstborn of the Lord among our peoples."[87] Educated readers might guess that Elizabeth speaks of Kateri, the first native North American to be canonized, and imagine that the "river" spoken of here is the division between time and eternity that is death. Either from holy simplicity or intellectual naivete, Rose interprets Elizabeth literally and begins planning her trip "across the river."

With the aid of Hugo, Rose travels to the native reserve of Kahnawake, Quebec, immediately across the river from Montreal, and there begins searching, in a literal, childlike way, for her sister. Kind strangers soon direct her to the shrine to Kateri found in that town, and there Rose experiences extraordinary new graces:

> Of the many churches and shrines where Rose had prayed during her life, this was the one that seemed most saturated in holiness. Older than the shrine of St. Joseph, poorer than any church she had ever seen, save for the chapel at Three Finger Lake, yet it was the richest. The air was thick with the presence of the Holy Spirit.[88]

As eloquent as this paragraph is, more moving within Rose's heart are the words directly spoken to her at the shrine by Christ himself:

> *Soon, he said to her, you will go farther. You will go very far, but first you must be purified. Three journeys do I give you. Three*

---

85. O'Brien, *Cry of Stone*, 588.
86. O'Brien, *Cry of Stone*, 593.
87. O'Brien, *Cry of Stone*, 594.
88. O'Brien, *Cry of Stone*, 605.

> *journeys lie before you, for the good of many souls and for the good of your own soul.*[89]

The "three journeys" structure the rest of the novel, but there are many "side journeys" in the story of this saint's life. Returning to Montreal from Kahnawake, Rose has a crucial meeting with a woman who, for some time in the novel, has hovered around the life shared by Rose, Esther, and Hugo. Estelle Morgan is a wealthy woman who seems to support all the arts of Montreal—including the tragicomic theatrical troupe—and was a friend of Esther, though for some inexplicable reason Rose dislikes her. Estelle's identity as a "mysterious friend" is an important part of Rose's experience of the Montreal art world, but it takes a painful turn when Estelle visits and, while looking at her recent painting, asks Rose to give her the quartz stone and the partridge stone given her by Tchibi. Though it is very difficult to part with what Rose regards as her two most valued possessions, she does; when Estelle leaves, Rose "went up to her bedroom, threw herself onto her cot, and wept as she had not done since Tchibi's death."[90] Soon after comes a letter from Estelle that is full of surprises.

First, Estelle shows a rare degree of self-knowledge, especially for a wealthy person shielded in so many ways from the reality of life; grateful for Rose's real friendship, Estelle reflects:

> With our success we are given a lethal dose of insecurity. Ever after we doubt the motives of all. Never again can we assume that we are being valued or disvalued for ourselves. It is always a case of are we useful or not useful, and in this manner we rich are degraded into the world of objects.[91]

Further, Estelle values the realism in Rose's art, and urges her to continue aesthetic creation that helps the blind see; humbly, she admits that she is the very kind of person who most needs this art:

> You must paint what you see, Rose, and you must not hold back your honesty. Our times are ill. Indeed, I am ill. We all are infected with the desire to see only what we want to see.[92]

---

89. O'Brien, *Cry of Stone*, 607.
90. O'Brien, *Cry of Stone*, 620.
91. O'Brien, *Cry of Stone*, 623.
92. O'Brien, *Cry of Stone*, 625.

Most surprising of all, however, is the letter's revelation that Estelle is actually Euphrasia Gorrel, the teacher whom Rose has felt abandoned by all these years. Estelle/Euphrasia now claims to have been watching over Rose in various ways, ready to help Hugo and Esther if need be. It turns out that her recent visit for the stones had been a way of testing Rose—the reader wonders if this is part of the "purification" that the Lord had promised—but again Estelle shows self-knowledge by saying: "I know what it cost you to give those two precious stones to a strange, wealthy woman who you believed could never treasure them." Promising to return the stones soon, Estelle/Euphrasia concludes the letter in a vulnerable tone that again suggests her own humility and penance for sins past: "Please do not abandon me, as I abandoned you." Inside a small box in the envelope, Rose finds another stone: "a small black pearl."[93] Painful as Rose's original painting of Euphrasia was, it was true, and has affected Euphrasia's entire adult life.

The first of the three journeys promised by the Lord then occurs, as Hugo helps Rose go to Europe to experience great works of art. This journey has two distinct parts, first in England then in France, though in neither place does O'Brien describe in detail the art galleries and museums that Rose visits in London and Paris. Rather, his interest is outside the city, as in England the Lord leads Rose to the home of her grandfather, Kyle Bradon, who around the time of WWI had travelled to Canada, met, and married Oldmary. Confirmation of identity between Rose and the present-day Bradons understandably takes time, but genealogy is not the reason the Lord has brought her here. As described by the current Mrs. Brady, who married into the family, the Bradons have long suffered under "a curse"; though outwardly Christian, they have no real heart for outsiders, or even deep love within their own family. As Mrs. Bradon tells her husband, diagnosing the problem, "There's a dungeon in your minds—all you Bradons, so harsh and proud."[94]

Rose's deep love for the grandfather she never personally knew moves both Mr. and Mrs. Bradon, who know only the pain caused by the trauma of WWI. One Bradon son was killed, while Rose's grandfather was treated as an outcast after he immigrated to Canada. Mrs. Bradon angrily accuses her husband's grandparents of treating others as "disposable people," but Rose counsels mercy. "How can we know what they felt,"

---

93. O'Brien, *Cry of Stone*, 626.
94. O'Brien, *Cry of Stone*, 646.

she says, for she "knew that the merciless were the ones in greatest need of mercy." However, the Bradon husband, Ned, admits that "it was pride" that caused his parents to reject his great-uncle; "that hard thing in them," he says, before having the crucial insight for which the Lord has brought Rose: "And in me."[95]

Yet the meeting with the Bradon parents is not the bulk of the English story. Rose stays with them long enough to become close to their son; like her grandfather, his name is Kyle Bradon. Rose and this Kyle bond mainly because Rose is the first person in the Bradon family to take seriously Kyle's claim that there was a medieval knight in the Bradon ancestry. This claim begins to seem much less fantastic, however, after Kyle shows Rose his extraordinary discovery on the Bradon family grounds: the remains of what appears to be medieval artifacts beneath a grassy hill. From this unlikely narrative, O'Brien weaves one of the most suspenseful sections of the novel, as Kyle and Rose work together to discover the truth about the Bradon medieval ancestry.

With the help of an old parish priest who can read medieval Latin and Middle English, Kyle and Rose become fairly certain that the remains found on the Bradon land were the last stand of an aristocratic medieval knight, Karolus le Breton, killed in 1485 during the last part of the Wars of the Roses. The novel's "stone" imagery reappears when inside the medieval remains Kyle and Rose find stones with these Latin inscriptions: *Abscondita ab Oculis* and *Lapides Clamabunt*, along with citation of a specific source: *Evangelium S Lucam XIX*.[96] Not knowing even enough Latin to translate these simple phrases as "hidden from the eyes" and "the stones cry out," Kyle and Rose go to Luke 19, open to the spiritual meaning they find there. The exact phrases are in this chapter of Luke, as part of the Palm Sunday narrative in which the Pharisees try to silence worshippers of Christ. There, Jesus prophesies that even the stones will cry out in witness of the paradoxical peace that the imminent Passion will bring.

Rose begins to suspect at least part of the reason that the Lord might have brought her here: "she now began to wonder if *the great wounding*" which the present-day Bradon family traces only to WWI, "had its root farther back than she supposed."[97] Kyle is especially pleased when documents show that the medieval remains were once an entire castle, and

---

95. O'Brien, *Cry of Stone*, 651.
96. O'Brien, *Cry of Stone*, 665.
97. O'Brien, *Cry of Stone*, 671.

that he and Rose—as well as all of the present-day Bradon family—have now inherited both the property and all the aristocratic titles associated with it. In the more spiritual language of the novel's iconography, the stones' ability to convey meaning, to send a word, across the centuries speaks of the power of faith—both the medieval faith of our fathers and the gospel—to survive violence and continue to bear fruit. The concrete reality of faith spoken of by the stones gives concrete reality to the familiar cliché, the presence of the past. As Rose sums it up for Kyle: "Remember what was, because it's a part of us—you and me—and because when you forget the past there are holes in your mind and you're walking blind."[98]

Rose soon leaves England and continues her European journey in France, where her education in the spiritual meaning of great art continues. Soon she is out of the city again, though, off to the country to visit the nuns who had encouraged and developed her artistic gifts in the residential school. On this visit she again meets Sister Madeleine, who first taught her to use paints, but this particular nun has grown much more in physical size than spiritual strength. She symbolizes, perhaps, the state of her vocation since Vatican II, as the numbers of nuns, and their spiritual influence, sharply decline though their worldly activity increases. The visit reawakens the question of Rose's own vocation, since she would still be young among these aging nuns. The most spiritual of them, however, is the Mother Superior who had long ago rejected Rose's application to join the nuns and has had recent supernatural messages that Rose will soon visit. Upon Rose's arrival, Sister Brigitte boldly claims: "It was the Lord's will." The novel's readers could reject this message as an authoritarian confirmation of senility, but Rose simply assents, "Yes, it was the Lord's will."[99]

Why it was the Lord's will for Rose to take the path she has in life rather than become a nun could be understood via the value of her work as a serious artist, but O'Brien does not encourage this interpretation. Rather, Rose then goes to meet with Mère Jean, who had first conveyed the decision on vocation many years ago. Mère Jean here teaches Rose in a way that clearly follows the Lord's plan for these journeys in that it purifies and is for the good of Rose's soul. Mère Jean tells Rose that "what pleases" Christ "is seeing me love my weakness." "Love your weakness?" Rose questions, and Jean replies:

---

98. O'Brien, *Cry of Stone*, 685.
99. O'Brien, *Cry of Stone*, 720.

> Yes, love my weakness, Rose. Love it—all of it, my littleness, my poverty, my blind hope in his mercy. Do not think this is a sad thing. No, it is a joyful thing—to consent always to remain without strength.[100]

In the loss of Rose, whom Mère Jean regarded as "a daughter," Mère Jean believes that Christ

> taught me the greatest and most scandalous lesson a soul can learn: that in losing everything, we find everything. In the dying I was reborn. In place of the great Theresa he gave me his Little Therese, and he gave me you.[101]

Jean's reference here to two famous European saints, St. Teresa of Avila, and St. Thérèse of Lisieux, is especially apt; the former was a pillar of the powerful nunneries of Catholic Christendom in Spain, while the latter French child became, in the much less powerful post-Vatican II Catholic world, one of the "doctors" who teach the church the most essential divine wisdom.

Nor are Mère Jean's words meant to diminish the artist whom God has made in Rose. Even from her commercial failure may come great good, Mère Jean sees,

> For in your failure you may bring about a greater harvest for souls than if your work is praised throughout your nation and beyond. Perhaps the failure is a necessary sacrifice.[102]

When Rose returns to Montreal, she is forced to face the sad human spectacle of Hugo having a nervous breakdown and even burning some of his paintings. Rose is naturally upset, and again doubts the value of her vocation after visits to Hugo in hospital show him incoherent and despondent. He eventually dies and, as with Tchibi, Rose's prayers go up to God with no apparent immediate effect. After his death, though, comes a final letter which suggests, despite the fact that Hugo dies a confirmed agnostic wallowing in nihilism, that there were lucid moments in his soul:

> In the home stretch I am willing to reconsider. Perhaps you are right. Maybe it is supposed to be this way, this inexplicable fragility of being, the not-knowingness of life, the beauty that can break your heart. Without it we would soon enough make

---

100. O'Brien, *Cry of Stone*, 723.
101. O'Brien, *Cry of Stone*, 725.
102. O'Brien, *Cry of Stone*, 724.

ourselves into gods . . . if death is the last horizon, then we are in no way betrayed. I shall see my wife again. I shall take her hand and we shall spar, for old time's sake. Then together we shall fly.[103]

Rose's second journey is given divine direction by the appearance of another obviously angelic being. When Rose sees "an old street person" late one night, she says a prayer for him. "Not necessary," he says, then also refuses food and a bus ticket while reassuring Rose that he does, in fact, have "a home."[104] He then gives Rose a newspaper, in which she reads of two doll makers, Winnifred and Minnifred McCaul, who live in St. Peter's-by-the-Sea, a small Acadian village in Cape Breton, Nova Scotia. Rose knows, in her soul, that she is meant to visit them, and doing so she discovers a pair of delightfully considerate sisters even smaller than she is; they are, to use the pejorative term common in our world, midgets. The two live together in a home specially designed and built for them by their now-deceased father; never having married, despite one potential suitor, the two yet tell Rose, "we do have our own children."[105]

Rose "supposed that they were referring to their dolls,"[106] but in fact their "children" live in a large institution for the handicapped near their village. These handicaps are of various kinds, mental and physical, but when Rose goes with the sisters it is not their peculiar appearance that strikes her; rather, as she looks upon them excitedly greeting their "mothers":

> Her eyes changed focus, and she saw each and every one of these people as an incarnation of a word. Theirs was physical poverty of the most abject and permanent kind. Yet within the flawed forms and limited minds there was something so eternal, so beautiful and holy, that at certain moments Rose was struck immobile with the wonder of it all. They lived daily in their crucified flesh, and within their deprivation were the marks of crucified hearts. But they were free to love in their pain.[107]

Nevertheless, the deformity in some cases is so great that even Rose cannot help questioning God, asking the age-old problem of human

---

103. O'Brien, *Cry of Stone*, 762.
104. O'Brien, *Cry of Stone*, 767.
105. O'Brien, *Cry of Stone*, 778.
106. O'Brien, *Cry of Stone*, 778.
107. O'Brien, *Cry of Stone*, 788.

suffering: "Why had God, the creator of all things, allowed it?"[108] One of O'Brien's most profound answers to this question then appears in the form of Jimmy, a young boy confined to a crib because "the right side of the cranium was caved in."[109] As Rose looks at him, purification of her soul begins to happen. Rose understood that, despite all of her sacrifices and faithfulness over the year, "she had retained a filament of resentment." Jimmy, despite his far more damaging handicap, "slept in peace, and dreamed."[110]

When Jimmy awoke, he "blinked, and smiled." Rose smiles back, but it is her interior movement that is more significant; she is "flying up the heights of the river of souls with him."[111] Then he says to her the "three radioactive words" once so painful in Rose's heart due to Euphrasia Gorrel, but which now fill her soul with an extraordinary energy. "I love you," says Jimmy, curling his fingers around Rose's hand; for her,

> The entire *tchibekana* exploded into song, the sweet-green fire blazed throughout the wide-extended firmament, the ten million times ten million times ten million stars rang with the holy laughter of measureless joy, all wild flowers opened their petals and poured out their perfumes, whales in the deep sported, all birds flew up into the skies, and for a single moment—the pause between one breath and another—light burst into every soul in the world.[112]

Rose feels such joy with the McCaul sisters that she strongly considers their offer to move in with them permanently, and even as she returns to Montreal she is planning to return and become a physically present mother to Jimmy, whom spiritually she renames "'John'—Beloved of God."[113] When Rose is stricken by cancer and given just two to six months to live, however, readers might expect that her third journey will be death, like all humans.

The Lord has another idea, however, directing her third journey back to Ottawa. Ill, on the streets, sleeping again amid Christmas nativity scenes, Rose is taken in by Jack Tobac, of the BC Tobac family in *Strangers and Sojourners*. Rose will spend her last days with them, but not

108. O'Brien, *Cry of Stone*, 794.
109. O'Brien, *Cry of Stone*, 795.
110. O'Brien, *Cry of Stone*, 798.
111. O'Brien, *Cry of Stone*, 797.
112. O'Brien, *Cry of Stone*, 798.
113. O'Brien, *Cry of Stone*, 811.

before completing the circle of the novel by becoming a mother to Jack's daughter, Kateri. When Rose arrives at the Tobac apartment, the young girl "smiled" at Rose "as if she had been waiting for her."[114]

Kateri is of course named for the native saint, at whose shrine in Kahnawake, Quebec, Jack and his wife Mari had seen Rose praying. Rose tells this young Kateri the tale of Mang the Loon and the *tchibekana* that has been so important to her own spiritual journey. She also gives Kateri a polished stone in the shape of an artist's palette, this one retrieved from a shipwreck off the coast of St. Peter's-by-the-Sea. For Rose this stone had symbolized the colors of a painter's art, but in giving it away she now sees in it something of the living, figurative art that her life and art together has made. As O'Brien's narrator describes it, "then [Rose] understood":

> If God could patiently create this stone over thousands of years, seeing ahead to the woman who would one day walk on the beach with discouragement in her soul, he could do anything. If he could send her a message like this, he could bring a harvest from barren soil. He could bring dead things to life, and even a life that seemed a failure might become fruitful.[115]

As she leaves this life, Rose becomes aware of other "words the Beating Heart sends." Though only the young Kateri seems to see her, finally Rose is enfolded in the arms of a woman "with stars all around her," suggesting the heavenly Mary, but also reminding readers of how Oldmary held her beloved Rose at the novel's beginning. Finally, readers are not meant to distinguish the two, for as in heaven they are one in Christ Jesus. Finally "the woman pulled a blanket of peace over Rose's body," and there is no lament, only Rose's acceptance at last of how the fragility of humanity allows divine love; in italics, the final line of the novel signifies the peace in Rose's soul: "*Small, Io! We are so small! Rose sighed. But this is how it must be.*"[116]

Finishing at 847 pages, *A Cry of Stone* is not a small novel. Had the novel been accepted by mainstream or literary Canadian publishers, it seems likely to me that at best they might have demanded that O'Brien divide the book into two parts, with the first focused on Tchibi and the controversial nature of the residential schools, while the second (assuming the first part sold) could have been about Rose's maturation as an

---

114. O'Brien, *Cry of Stone*, 839.
115. O'Brien, *Cry of Stone*, 845.
116. O'Brien, *Cry of Stone*, 847.

artist from the time she moves in with Hugo and Esther Dyson. What would have been lost, though, is any unified sense of how the growth of Rose as an artist is directly connected to the sanctification of her soul as a saint.

Because of its intensity and integrity of vision, it is possible to regard *A Cry of Stone* as O'Brien's greatest novel. Clearly it is very directly about the two subjects that most interest him as a writer—the nature of God and the role of art in human spiritual life. Despite the novel's simple structure, I would not hesitate to recommend it as an introduction to O'Brien's work, or even to what is most essential in any Catholic theological aesthetic. Rose Wâbos may be O'Brien's single greatest character, in that she enacts so many of the trials and themes that most concern his fiction. However one "ranks" her, Rose is undoubtedly memorable. It is instructive to consider, as their hump-backed bodies might cause us to compare, why Shakespeare's Richard III, a paragon of evil, more naturally stays in the human imagination than this believable example of holiness. For those spiritually open and willing to read the entire novel, however, Rose lives on as a "word" who can speak to our soul long after we have ceased reading.

"The Rescuer" from *Sophia House*

"Love?" *Sophia House*

> What was love? Every question led inexorably back to that.
> —Pawel Tarnowski, in O'Brien, *Sophia House*, 258

IF ROSE WÂBOS MOST perfectly embodies O'Brien's theological aesthetic, the final two novels of the *Children of the Last Days* series return to the character largely responsible for O'Brien's widest readership: Father Elijah. Yet it would be not only unfair but wholly inaccurate to see in this move a commercial aim in this phase of O'Brien's career. Neither of these two later novels presents Elijah in a manner that can easily attract casual "fans" of the by-now-famous priest. *Sophia House* is a prequel, fully depicting the time period briefly alluded to in the original novel, when Father Elijah was a young Jew and survived the Holocaust in Warsaw, Poland, in no small part because of the protection of Pawel Tarnowski, a Catholic bookseller. Like most prequels and sequels that are worth writing, *Sophia House* clarifies readers' understanding of crucial questions raised by the original story; the most obvious of these questions is: What formed Father Elijah?

What makes *Sophia House* well worth reading is the wisdom of its answer, at once simple and complex. The two obvious answers are a) God, or b) Pawel, the man who saved Elijah's life during the Holocaust, but both answers further evoke foundational definitions of wisdom. In Prov 8, Wisdom plays with God to create the world, while Pawel names his bookstore Sophia House, substituting the older Greek term for wisdom—Sophia—for the vernacular Polish term, *madrosc*; in this house of wisdom will not only be books but what he learns from his relationship with David. Other answers lie in the multiple interactions of God and mankind. According to Catholicism, the Christian God typically mediates his will through many persons and moments of salvation history, and Pawel's wide experience of good and evil, and David's, create the novel's complexity.

What also makes *Sophia House* especially powerful is its unflinching exploration of other questions that continue to haunt humanity today. First, how could God allow the horror that was Nazi Germany and the Holocaust? Where was God while so many innocents were killed, burned in organized hells of suffering and death? The second issue might seem much less important, but anyone aware of late twentieth- and twenty-first-century culture must recognize it as an issue which divides and causes intense suffering in both the Christian church and its people: the meaning of homosexuality. *Sophia House* was published long before the legalization of "gay" marriage in both Canada and the United States but, as with native issues in *A Cry of Stone*, O'Brien's writing can be seen as socially prophetic. The slogan for the legalization of homosexual marriage in the US was "love wins," but of course the slogan and legal campaign begged the question long central to our culture: "What is love?" *Sophia House* is a sophisticated exploration of this question, with Pawel telling us at one point that "every question led inexorably back" to that one. Ultimately, the central characters of the novel understand that this key element of wisdom must lead back to God.

The cover icon seems straightforward but, like the title, is quite complex. Entitled *The Rescuer*, the painting depicts a man releasing a bird to flight, as Pawel will free David.[1] Yet there are many other elements if we look closely at the icon. Beneath the central bird are many other birds, perhaps other souls also freed, or perhaps the movement of the Holy Spirit, often depicted as a bird in Scripture. These birds fly up above flames that could represent the Holocaust; from black they fly towards a gold corner clear on the painting's left-hand corner. Above the fiery hell of the Holocaust, the painting seems to say, the soul finds a way to heaven. Perhaps most striking of all is the man himself in the painting.

He is "bent," a term that could apply to Pawel's own soul, yet his face reminds one very much of the face of Christ in O'Brien's great painting, *Creation of the Birds*. There Christ's eyes are also closed, but his inner life is dreaming of freedom and creativity for the birds being created, just as Pawel dreams of a future for David. A very short, two-paragraph foreword for the novel gives advice that should help the reader see spiritual meaning both in the cover icon and the novel itself:

---

1. O'Brien, *Sophia House*, 4.

Stand back, find proportion, locate the range of vision, and the portrait emerges. It is my hope that through the lives depicted here the face of Christ will be visible.[2]

In addition to the short foreword, the initial pieces of the novel provide a number of other intimations of its meaning. The title page includes a long quotation from Greek drama, Euripides's *Suppliants*, the cry of one without a family, both "childless, childless" and "bereft of my poor father," suggesting that the themes of the novel will be relevant to the human condition, beyond the horribly unique setting that is the Holocaust.[3] The novel's dedication is also quite general: "For those whose sacrifice is hidden in the heart of God, those whose 'small' choices shift the balance of the world."[4] Finally, the preface thanks some real people—such as the Russian filmmaker Andrei Tarkovsky and the French painter Georges Rouault, whose artistic vision have helped O'Brien. This is another novel that reflects on the nature and meaning of art.

The novel opens with three short chapters that rapidly change time and setting. First, we are in 1963, which we know from *Father Elijah* is a time when David Schäfer had taken a new name and become a high ranking Israeli politician. A mysterious woman arrives in his offices, claiming to have been guided by an angel, and tells him, "I know your real name."[5] Initially he rebuffs her. She explains, "I bring you a letter and a gift from one who loved you," but he cynically replies, "Love is an illusion."[6] Readers remember the loss of Ruth and hear pain in this reply, but it is a common middle-aged human response to the great question of the novel. When Eva tells the politician his original name, saying, "You are David Schäfer," he is reduced to tears and cannot comprehend how this woman has found him.[7]

No explanation is given to the reader, either, as O'Brien begins *Sanctuary*, the first section of the novel, with a chapter that shifts to 1942 and tells the story, in Warsaw, of Pawel opening the bookstore, inherited from his Uncle Tadeuz, and then taking in David. The short chapter ends with a suspenseful but rhetorical question, readers knowing the answer from

2. O'Brien, *Sophia House*, 9.
3. Euripides, *Suppliants*, quoted in O'Brien, *Sophia House*, 3.
4. O'Brien, *Sophia House*, 5.
5. O'Brien, *Sophia House*, 12.
6. O'Brien, *Sophia House*, 13.
7. O'Brien, *Sophia House*, 14.

Father Elijah; David asks, "Will you please hide me for a few days while I think?"[8] The next chapter flashes back further, to Pawel's childhood in Poland. About one hundred pages of the most depressing prose in all of O'Brien's fiction then follows, as the focus shifts to the inner demons against which Pawel Tarnowski must fight throughout the novel. These times of suffering also make Pawel the man who gives sanctuary to David in 1942, so to understand how God aids him it is necessary to first understand the struggle.

Foremost among these demons is the inclination towards homosexual feelings. *Sophia House* traces the origin of these feelings in Pawel to two primary sources. The first is Pawel's troubled relationship with his great-uncle Nicholas, an odd figure about whom the older family members seem to know some dark secret; when he dies, for example, Pawel's mother says, "It is for the best," while his father says, "He was not always like this."[9] After swimming in a pond on a hot day, Pawel comes out, and then suddenly, "From behind, two furry arms grabbed him around the ribs and lifted him high." Pawel is "confused and uneasy" with his uncle's actions, but "let himself be undressed."[10] O'Brien never describes any sexual interaction in physical detail, but it is clear that this is a painful experience for Pawel. "I don't like it!" Pawel wailed, but Great-Uncle replies, "'It's just playing,' said Great-Uncle, 'Don't you like to play? Let's play.'"[11]

The ominous meaning of this common childhood term becomes almost clear that night. O'Brien realistically positions the experience deep in Pawel's subconscious, in an interior wound that cannot be entirely healed or ignored. Pawel remembers the night as "a bad dream," and "always thought of it as a dream, though in later years it seemed to him it was something that might have happened in the strange country between waking and dreaming." For many possible reasons, "of this he could never be sure,"[12] but readers of the *Children of the Last Days* series familiar with satanic imagery of bears and other dark monsters cannot help but feel that physical assault is symbolically described in the chapter's final paragraph; in the night,

---

8. O'Brien, *Sophia House*, 29.
9. O'Brien, *Sophia House*, 47–48.
10. O'Brien, *Sophia House*, 42.
11. O'Brien, *Sophia House*, 43.
12. O'Brien, *Sophia House*, 43.

the hands resumed their play, and then he felt lips touching his chest. He tried to cry out, but a bear loomed in the darkness, a roaring beast, its jaws open wide to devour him, though it was a bear like no other, for its single eye glared red at him. The cry froze in his throat. He thrashed, but the bear pinned his limbs to the cloud. Once again he began to scream, but a hairy paw clamped over his mouth, cut off his breath. Immobile now, he could do nothing to resist the paws that played and played until finally the weight of the bear fell upon him totally and he was crushed out of existence.[13]

The second source of homosexual feelings in Pawel is more common and less dramatic, but it is a fairly common psychological theory, despite being rejected a priori by those convinced that homosexuality is perfectly normal and good. This is the theory of the "absent father," whose lack of presence in a child's life leaves them longing for male affection and unsure of their own potential to become a physical father. Pawel experiences this in two ways in the novel: while very young, his father is away, at war, and then imprisoned by the Russians. Even after being freed and brought home, however, he is a shell of his former self, hardly capable of physical interaction or emotional intimacy with his family.

One could respond to O'Brien's narrative by pointing out that there are happily practicing homosexuals who were not abused as children nor had absent fathers. Would this argument really invalidate O'Brien's viewpoint, however? There may be other examples where such wounds did cause homosexual orientation, and the "normalization" of homosexuality in culture could cause its acceptance in those who might otherwise reject it. While there are those who claim sexual feelings are out of their control, there are others who change "orientation," and in many cases behavior, after a key turning point in their life. The normalization of homosexuality in O'Brien's own country, Canada, makes this among the most controversial elements of O'Brien's fiction. Even if one disagrees with it, it should not be condemned, let alone criminalized as "hate" speech, though that is exactly what would be demanded by those who would replace public debate or free art with state coercion and propaganda. For centuries, due to clear statements in scriptural revelation, the common Christian view was that homosexual behavior was intrinsically disordered, so it cannot be surprising that the Catholic Church still officially holds this position today. The sexual revolution has normalized many forms of sexual behavior

13. O'Brien, *Sophia House*, 44.

that are clearly destructive, while also making far less common the kind of love that leads to long-term stability within families. Before God as judge, apart from the judgment of all the kingdoms of this world, can one affirm sexual license without accepting the many painful consequences of these sins?

For Pawel, the pain of home leads to a period of wandering and exile. He travels to Paris in search of becoming a painter. In exile, with its alienation and pain, Pawel denies the existence of his Heavenly Father, thus universalizing the theme of an "absent father." Many in the modern world do not feel any closeness to either an earthly or Heavenly Father, and so it should be no surprise that they lack authoritative spiritual direction. In this crucial sense, the "absent father" refers to the commonplace modern alienation from God which causes us to doubt or feel unsure of how to use any of our natural gifts, including sexuality. Homosexuality could be linked to DNA (as typically claimed by those with faith in biology) or brain chemicals (a more recent claim caused by the growth of interest in neurobiology), but given the absence of definitive empirical evidence in either field, belief in this particular causation is driven more by desire than science. Is it not possible, as many world religions claim, that sexuality is integrally linked to spirituality?

This apparently extratextual question is very relevant to the novel because it is a "sub-question" within the broader, central question of what formed David Schäfer's identity; in the opening part of the novel, we ask: What formed Pawel Tarnowski? The journey to France introduces Pawel to different responses to these questions, through key figures that we can designate as historical (actual people in twentieth-century Paris), or purely fictional (invented for this novel), but also a third category in which we meet characters familiar to us from other novels in the *Children of the Last Days* series.

The most famous figure portrayed is Pablo Picasso. We recall from *A Cry of Stone* the largely negative view that Rose and the Dysons had of Picasso's immense influence on the growth of abstract twentieth-century art; when we first meet him in *Sophia House* he is touting the political power of art, claiming, "Art is war . . . an instrument for attack and defense."[14] O'Brien's brief preface to the novel notes that Picasso's statements within it "are extracts from his manifestos on art,"[15] but this

---

14. O'Brien, *Sophia House*, 58.
15. O'Brien, *Sophia House*, 9.

initial selection seems especially ironic, given the failure of art to alter the course of either the Spanish Civil War or WWII. Whatever the effectiveness of Picasso's art, in this novel he is surrounded by would-be apprentices; what is most striking is Picasso's dismissal of Pawel as a person. Pawel is awed by Picasso's presence, but when Pawel stutters greetings "the Spaniard snorted" and acted "as if he had not heard."[16]

O'Brien next realistically depicts a fictional character who is a far more commonplace figure in human life. Achille Goudron, a middle-aged writer, takes Pawel into his home when the Polish youth is on the verge of starvation, unable to find work and living on the streets. Goudron mentors Pawel artistically, and the young man at first seems to find much more of what he is looking for:

> The relationship grew steadily into one of unexpressed love. Pawel thought he had found the guidance of a true father, one who would unlock the greatness within him. He believed that in return he was giving to Goudron the companionship of a son—a blessing the man sorely missed because he was divorced from his wife, who lived with their children in South America.[17]

Pawel's hopes are cruelly dashed, however, when after a night out drinking Goudron attempts to seduce him. Unaware of his own youthful attractiveness, Pawel suddenly sees the truth:

> He saw in an instant Goudron's whole strategy during the previous year. He had built up Pawel's immense respect and love for him, his dependence upon him, only to reveal it all in the end as a calculated sexual seduction.[18]

One good thing occurs, however, while Pawel lives within the security of Goudron's false love: he discovers the art of Georges Rouault. One of Rouault's paintings is in a small gallery that Pawel stumbles upon, "an image of Christ in agony, nailed to the Cross."[19] For some "inexplicable" reason this moves Pawel, and he writes to the famous French painter. In stark contrast to the dismissive attitude of Picasso, Rouault writes back thoughtful letters that not only reveal but also try to teach a Christian aesthetic. "A man can create only with the material of what he loves," Rouault writes, reminding us of Rose Wâbos, but Pawel has a bitter

16. O'Brien, *Sophia House*, 58.
17. O'Brien, *Sophia House*, 77.
18. O'Brien, *Sophia House*, 100.
19. O'Brien, *Sophia House*, 91–92.

rejoinder: "What if he loves nothing?"[20] Rouault does not dismiss this as a rhetorical question reflective of simplistic nihilism; instead, he sends an answer that hints at the essence of the painting of icons:

> The man who does not love does not yet know himself. Inside every heart is an image of love—however buried it might be. He must seek it, and find for himself his own language, the words that will unlock the hidden icon.[21]

Pawel's response is again dismissive, but this seed of wisdom is but the first that Rouault plants deep within Pawel's soul. For Rouault, "the rejected Christ" is the most "difficult to paint," but also perhaps the most important; if the human artist's "eyes are clear," then "he can see the majesty of a God who suffers with us and in us."[22] In turn, this allows the painter to depict the full reality of humanity, even the depraved. With fatherly affection, Rouault writes:

> Cher Paul,
>
> the artist must always ask himself, am I painting the surface only, or am I revealing the eternal soul of my subjects? Without this, we only add to the agony. We too would be merely using the prostitutes—and worse, for we do not pay them.[23]

More than the wit, what Rouault teaches Pawel is the Christian personalism that O'Brien fully learns from his spiritual father, John Paul II. This teaching does not find fertile soil in Pawel's soul until the devastating end of his "love" with Goudron, but travelling back to Poland through Vienna both the philosophical and aesthetic meaning of this teaching is enacted. Pawel sees what he thinks is a nineteenth-century depiction of the last judgment; in it,

> people staggered about the desolate landscape, unable to look up to the light. They could no longer see; they could no longer believe. They thought that ruin was the sum total of reality. He could see it in their faces, their despair, their terrible loneliness. The loneliness of the apocalypse. And in those faces he saw his own face.[24]

---

20. O'Brien, *Sophia House*, 92.
21. O'Brien, *Sophia House*, 92.
22. O'Brien, *Sophia House*, 95.
23. O'Brien, *Sophia House*, 97.
24. O'Brien, *Sophia House*, 102.

Pawel begins to weep, telling an old man who happens on the scene, "If I could meet the man who painted this, I would thank him.... He has left a message for all who have been where he once was."[25] The old man consoles Pawel, and invites him to a restaurant for dinner; with his wife recently passed away, he could use some company. After dinner, the man leads Pawel to a cab, and leaves him with another word:

> My friend,
>
> I thank you for weeping over my painting. I have waited more than fifty years for such a compliment. I painted it when I was young as you, during a period of darkness, a time when I believed there was no love in the world. From then on I could paint nothing. God speed you on your journey. There is love in the world. You will find it.[26]

Again, the effect of this moving word in Pawel's soul is not immediately apparent, for back in Poland he falls back into old cycles of worry and despair. Breakthrough comes, though, when his brothers Jan and Bronek convince him to "make a pilgrimage to the shrine of the Mother of God at Czestochowa."[27] At this famous shrine, so important to the spiritual life of John Paul II, Pawel kneels before the icon of the Black Madonna, and hears another word: "I too have received blows," she said, "and a sword pierced my heart."[28] The effect on Pawel cannot properly be described as theological, or as a biblical reference to Mary before Simeon or at the foot of the cross, but rather as existential. Mary, through divine grace, reawakens Pawel's inner life:

> At that moment, inexplicably, a rush of feeling returned to his inner world. He longed to weep. To cry out. It hurt terribly, like blood beginning to move in a frozen limb, yet there was a harsh exuberance in it that promised the return of life. And in this state, he was struck by the possibility that whatever was happening to him might have come from a source beyond the limits of his enclosed self. He staggered into a confessional.[29]

There, Pawel meets a figure familiar to readers of the *Children of the Last Days* series: Father Andrei. Younger than earlier in the series,

25. O'Brien, *Sophia House*, 103.
26. O'Brien, *Sophia House*, 105.
27. O'Brien, *Sophia House*, 112.
28. O'Brien, *Sophia House*, 113.
29. O'Brien, *Sophia House*, 113.

Andrei's already serious faith respects the solace of the confessional, but his real care for the troubled young man he hears causes him to ask Pawel to meet him outside the church. There, Father Andrei asks a simple question: "Who are you most angry at?" Readers might assume Great-Uncle, but Pawel answers, "Photosphoros," a Russian priest who had treated him cruelly during his wandering days. Because he is a true priest, aware both of his own sinfulness and being *in persona Christi*, Father Andrei understands the problem. For when a priest "proves himself less than God, as he inevitably must, it is as if an icon has been defaced."[30] Anger, Andrei explains, causes unforgiveness, and a cycle of despair: "Unforgiveness locks us into unbelief, and unbelief deepens the unforgiveness."[31] The key to ending the cycle, Andrei teaches, is forgiveness, and a "poverty that opens one to the life of God."[32] Pawel finds this complicated, but Father Andrei corrects him with a crucial teaching about the nature of God's love: "God has saved us, but He will not force salvation upon us. Love never forces. Love thrives only in freedom. We must choose to accept what He offers."[33]

Father Andrei further speaks of the "singular grace" that he received when just eight years old, after being beaten by classmates:

> I looked up to the cross suspended over the city and world, and I saw Jesus nailed to it. Then He spoke into my heart, spoke without words. It was not rational thought, you understand; it was rather a perception. He told me that no human love would ever fill the hunger within me. Though every genuine love is from God, it is an incarnation, a reflection. In this world it will always be imperfect. His love is perfection. It contains everything. For the first time in my life I saw this love not as a theological abstraction. It was a real . . . aach . . . our poor words![34]

Father Andrei shares this crucial personal story with Pawel because, as he puts it later, he feels that "your path and mine are curiously entwined."[35] But he already knew this, in the confessional, because there Jesus sent a very clear spiritual word about the young man across from him in darkness: "*Here is My little son whom I love greatly. He has been*

---

30. O'Brien, *Sophia House*, 115.
31. O'Brien, *Sophia House*, 116.
32. O'Brien, *Sophia House*, 116–17.
33. O'Brien, *Sophia House*, 117.
34. O'Brien, *Sophia House*, 119.
35. O'Brien, *Sophia House*, 122.

broken. He will do a unique good in the world, but first he will be tested by fire."[36] This mysterious message is short on specific detail, and sent to a lesser man it might merely provoke curiosity. But Father Andrei knows that he is called to a different path, another fire, and he can peacefully part from Pawel with just one final key teaching: "It is necessary to know only one thing: God is with you. Trust Him. Do not be afraid."[37] Father Andrei's wisdom completes the formation that prepares Pawel to provide the hiding place, though Pawel remains, like all men in this world, a mixture of divine grace and the wounds caused by human sin.

O'Brien's narrative then jumps ahead again in time, back to 1942, back to the place of sanctuary for David Schäfer. Given that David spends several months in this "hiding place," the central question of the novel takes on a new form: what allows this place, this bookstore, to become a house of wisdom that ultimately aids in the formation of Father Elijah? Part of the answer must be the formation just recounted in the opening part of this novel, as it is a mature Pawel that enters into dialogue—on such topics as language, religion, and art—with the young but precocious lad, who has been formed by the wisdom of the Jewish tradition. Some books clearly have more wisdom than others, and part of Pawel's and David's conversation is how to tell the difference. Valuable writing often inspires literature, and Pawel in particular will explore the questions that must occur to any writer: What is worth writing about? How should one do so? All of these questions, in this bookstore, are made much more difficult by the horrific tension and reality of the Nazi occupation, here given concrete focus through the present danger to both Pawel and David. Suspense naturally accompanies the sanctuary, but it also becomes a place where the interior hearts of both can grow in wisdom, guided by God despite horrific evil.

As we return to 1942 in the narrative, the date introduces a letter that Pawel is writing to Kahlia. One might first imagine it to be a love letter, but the letter contains little more than narrative information, and no sign that Pawel is in any sort of romantic love affair. There is a sense in which he is writing to a real female, Elzbieta, a concert pianist whom he sees and hears briefly, deeply moved by her music. Pawel never even attempts to meet with this real woman, however, and as the novel progresses it becomes clear that Kahlia is a muse to help Pawel become the man and

---

36. O'Brien, *Sophia House*, 119.
37. O'Brien, *Sophia House*, 124.

the writer that God intends him to be. Kahlia is a feminine name in Polish, just as Sophia commonly is in multiple languages, but here and in the novel the word "Kahlia" functions as a synonym for "beauty." Can a man learn to love both Kahlia and Sophia? This philosophical and aesthetic question, also a concrete existential question in many men's lives, is for Pawel part of a much more painful struggle.

It becomes clear, in several passages, that despite the graces which have brought Pawel back to belief in God, he remains haunted by homosexual desire and terrified that he might use David in the same way he was abused by Great-Uncle. "I want to love," his heart cries, but he cannot answer these questions: "To love? To love whom?" Instead he can only babble, "rotten cherries," and recall the "lust-maddened bear" that marred his youth; "he tried to throw off the bear, but it was locked within him."[38] Prayer clarifies the subconscious pain:

> O God, how can I love with the pure love you demand when this weight is in me, pulling me daily toward disaster? I am becoming drawn to him, I tell you, and I cannot break the hold that it has on me.[39]

Pawel "cannot break the hold," but he is always well aware that any sexual relationship with the boy now in his care would be a continuation of the pattern of abuse that he first experienced through Great-Uncle and then saw again with Goudron. Pawel never gives in to his sexual desires, but the realistic portrayal of these desires gives us one of the most moving and currently relevant topics in O'Brien's fiction. Because homosexual orientation is so often accepted today as normal, even within sectors of Christianity, O'Brien's portrayal here is bound to be controversial. Christians who wish to faithfully consider this issue, though, should consider O'Brien's point of view, for it is the viewpoint widely accepted by almost all Christians for almost two millennia. Should Christian advocates of homosexuality really be so confident that all of Christendom had been misled?

O'Brien's approach to sexual desire, it is important to understand, is not presented as a single-issue argument, but rather as part of Pawel's quest to become both an authentic human being and a faithful writer. What kind of writing helps the human race? This simple but profound question is raised a number of times throughout the novel, beginning

---

38. O'Brien, *Sophia House*, 165.
39. O'Brien, *Sophia House*, 166.

with David recording basic bibliographical information for the many large lots of books that Pawel has received since the war began. David's classification system soon becomes explicitly value laden, or ethical, and he sharply distinguishes the value of books. Eventually he labels the best as "celestial language," which later he calls the "realm of gold," some from a middle "borderland" divided between "righteous gentiles" and "clever fools," with a third realm from the "sitra haru" or demonic spiritual world.[40] This division, traditional among the Jewish Hasidim who have raised David, is admired by Pawel, who wonders how one "so young, so vital," can pursue wisdom.[41] Pawel is especially struck by David's words on his father; a tailor, he had "wisdom," and though taken by the Germans (while his young son hid in the sewers), David is certain that "he now rests on the breast of Abraham."[42] Here, too, we learn how Father Elijah was formed.

David's rational faith seems to inspire Pawel, whose "mind tells" him "that God is present, even in the midst of the war," yet he believes "with my mind but not with my emotions." He recognizes himself as "a split man" akin to Haftmann, a "very odd Nazi" who before the war was an English professor but now makes at least an outward show of enforcing the cultural policies of the Third Reich. Speaking of both Haftmann and himself, Pawel asks, "Can one ever trust such a man?"[43] This question also echoes the haunting rebuke of his brothers. Bronek is actively working for the Polish underground, and comes to ask for paper to print pamphlets. Pawel does give him paper, but keeps one hundred sheets for himself, saying, "It's my hope that what I write on my paper will help as many people as what you write on yours." Bronek's rhetorical question stings, "What are you going to do to help people?"[44] The wife and daughter of another brother, Jan, are taken by the Nazis, and he is disgusted that Pawel sells books to the Germans; "What kind of man are you?" he angrily asks.[45] Pawel is haunted by such questions, but eventually has enough self-knowledge to ask of himself, "Why should I trust this box of contradictions, this dossier of futile tales that I presume to call

---

40. O'Brien, *Sophia House*, 146–49.
41. O'Brien, *Sophia House*, 159.
42. O'Brien, *Sophia House*, 151.
43. O'Brien, *Sophia House*, 152.
44. O'Brien, *Sophia House*, 157.
45. O'Brien, *Sophia House*, 161.

myself?"[46] Can his interior life ever become whole? Will he ever be able to write tales not futile but truly beautiful?

Such questions lead him back to a book on Andrei Rublev, a medieval Russian painter, whose icons had earlier impressed him as deep "as wells"; their eyes, especially, "were silently, eloquently full." Later, in front of icons inherited from his Uncle Tadeuz, Pawel now seems to repudiate his earlier faith; out loud, he says, "I do not believe in you."[47] The icons, O'Brien's narrator comically reports, "did not reply." Pawel, though, is in the mood for a conversation, replying:

> You will not talk to me. Then I will talk to you. I will talk to you as if you are real, though you are just a story. Yes, a folktale about God. I will say my part and I will make up yours.[48]

What follows is clearly fictional, subjective, a "dialogue" that "flowed effortlessly from some source of creativity within himself."[49] But it is more. The "supernatural character he created seemed unpredictable," but its insights eventually came from beyond any horizon known to Pawel.[50] The "fiction" deals with something very real, for the "stone in Pawel's heart was simply there . . . it was real," O'Brien's narrator records again, but the real questions to be revealed in the dialogue are these: "But was anything else real? Was he, Pawel, no more than a rat in a maze? Or a character in some demented playwright's imagination?"[51] The dialogue and play that follow form one of the most inspired passages of theological aesthetics in O'Brien's fiction.

As in other supernatural passages in O'Brien's fiction, italics mark a spiritual voice. Pawel begins:

> "I am alone," he seethed. "Why am I alone?"
> *You feel alone, my son.*
> "Am I a son? I do not feel like a son."
> *You are a son.*
> The bitterness swelled into vehemence. "I have no father," he cried angrily.
> *You have a father.*[52]

---

46. O'Brien, *Sophia House*, 152.
47. O'Brien, *Sophia House*, 170.
48. O'Brien, *Sophia House*, 170.
49. O'Brien, *Sophia House*, 170.
50. O'Brien, *Sophia House*, 170.
51. O'Brien, *Sophia House*, 171.
52. O'Brien, *Sophia House*, 171.

The dialogue continues, but even to this point, the reader and perhaps even Pawel himself might think the spiritual voice is talking about God the Father, the supernatural caregiver that any orphan most needs. Soon comes the vision of an old priest who "groaned in agony for the destruction of all that was true and beautiful and good in the world."[53] Pawel hears "a woman clothed with the sun," Mary of Rev 12, softly say to the old man, Elijah, and Pawel must ask, "Who is Elijah?"[54] Again, there is a comical, ironic tone in the narrator's reply, "The folktale did not answer."[55] Clearly Pawel's imagination in 1942 could not invent the character of Father Elijah, but the supernatural voice does attempt some explanation; Pawel begins,

> "This has no meaning for me."
> *You are part of it. It is real, and yet it will not come to pass if you turn towards the shadows.*
> "You have not answered my question."
> *What seems an accident to you is wholly within the plans of God. A great blessing has come to you."*
> "A blessing? That is absurd."
> *You cannot see the whole. You are only a part. The greater part of the battle is waged in realms above you.*[56]

There is one other key question, and answer, that Pawel here receives from the consoling Spirit leading him into truth:

> And what of love? . . . The problem remains: there is no love for me.
>
> *The man you seek is within you. The image of the son, and the image of the father.*[57]

The Spirit speaks, it seems, not just of God the Father, but of the deeper pattern of Christian typology and paradox revealed by the incarnation: a stranger is revealed as a beloved son and in turn allows us to see our Heavenly Father. This pattern, it seems, is being repeated in Pawel's life through the presence of David.

After this extraordinary dialogue, Pawel returns to the book on Andrei Rublev. "Within me," he asked of the eyes of Christ, "Where within

---

53. O'Brien, *Sophia House*, 174.
54. O'Brien, *Sophia House*, 174–75.
55. O'Brien, *Sophia House*, 175.
56. O'Brien, *Sophia House*, 175.
57. O'Brien, *Sophia House*, 175.

me?" The "eyes of Christ did not answer," O'Brien's narrator reiterates, but the voice of the spirit is remembered; Christ's eyes now tell Pawel "that he must go within and see." And so he takes the hundred pages of paper that he had earlier counted out in front of Bronek and says, "A hundred pieces.... That is all. Everything must be contained within its borders."[58] The narrative of O'Brien's novel then changes radically as we are given a complete, one-hundred-page play on the life of Andrei Rublev, written by Pawel Tarnowski.

The play-within-the-novel could be a medieval allegory, with various female figures representing modes of life among which the twelfth-century Rublev has to choose. Further, though, the play explores the mystery of Christian vocation, of how God calls an individual's soul to be in a particular way in the world. As poetic drama, the meanings of the events are not easily defined, but as a whole this play on Rublev offers insight into the nature of iconographic Christian art.

The play opens on the day of Rublev's planned wedding to Masha (a common feminine nickname of the Russian peasantry), but he has just finished a painting that day, of "the tree of Moses," "burning, unconsumed," with "a cross hidden in it," and from which "our Savior . . . called me," to "a holy work still hidden from my eyes."[59] He no longer feels called to marriage. Masha is understandably upset, rhetorically asking, "And is our love not holy?" Andrei explains:

> Though we are flashes of fire,
> We are but reflections of a hidden light.
> We are not the light itself.
> The way of man and woman,
> The way of soul and soul, is a sacred path;
> But there are others,
> And to another I must go.[60]

In the next scene, Andrei meets another woman, but readers of the novel can even more readily recognize her as allegorical. She is Kahlia, beauty itself, and initially calls to him in the words of the Song of Songs, most often understood by medieval readers as an allegory of the love of God for his people. Kahlia explicitly distinguishes her love from Eros and aligns herself with medieval allegory by telling Andrei:

---

58. O'Brien, *Sophia House*, 177.
59. O'Brien, *Sophia House*, 184–85.
60. O'Brien, *Sophia House*, 186.

> I come not to arouse the fires of Eros outside a holy bond.
> It is the love between being and being that I sing.
> Within the beauty of this manly form and this woman's grace,
> There is a dialogue of souls. You have not learned its language yet.
> You are asleep.[61]

The rebuke here is directly revisited at play's end, but Kahlia leaves and Andrei is left to ask, "If I am to follow, how shall I know the way?"[62]

Act 2 opens in a place where Andrei might find this way, a monastery. There the holy abbot Nikon greets him as Christ, but his young apprentice Daniil is much less welcoming. It is a chorus of monks, representative of the community devoted to listening to God, that most clearly articulates their vocation, in the form of questions that go deep into Andrei's soul:

> In all the world is there one soul who'll waste
> His life for God, who'll speak of Light?
> The Light who's born not once but over and over
> In every soul that waits.[63]

In the second scene of act 2, Nikon teaches both young men more about the meaning of the monastic vocation:

> A monk is one who gives up everything.
> Leaving the world of things and souls turned into things,
> He arrives at a secret place of the heart where he is given everything.[64]

"Even beauty?" Andrei skeptically asks, wondering if Nikon has fallen into hyperbole. But the holy man replies:

> Especially beauty.
> But not the forms of beauty that can be possessed.
> For to possess her would be to kill her. And Lady Wisdom would not
> Permit the death of her little sister.[65]

Scene 3 of act 2, the approximate center of the play, gives what might be the play's most profound theological ideas and its most suspenseful, dramatic moments. The scene opens with a child's voice reading the text

---

61. O'Brien, *Sophia House*, 192.
62. O'Brien, *Sophia House*, 194.
63. O'Brien, *Sophia House*, 199.
64. O'Brien, *Sophia House*, 203.
65. O'Brien, *Sophia House*, 204.

of Matt 17:1–8, the Gospel account of the transfiguration. The apostles followed Jesus up a mountain, when suddenly his appearance changed radically, and Old Testament prophets Moses and Elijah appear and begin talking to them. Peter, always active, begins to prepare three tents, when suddenly a voice comes to them from a bright cloud:

> "This is my Son, the Beloved on whom my favour rests. Listen to Him." When they heard this, the disciples fell on their faces. Overcome with fear. But Jesus came toward them and touched them. "Stand up," he said. "Do not be afraid." And when they raised their eyes they saw no one but Jesus.[66]

It is impossible to exaggerate the importance of this mysterious Scripture to the tradition of icon painting. Not only because it depicts so dramatically the apostles' glimpse of the Christ of eternity, to whom all sacred Artists can and must listen, but also because it depicts humanity transfigured through the presence of Moses and Elijah. Just after the vision, though, Andrei admits that "I am afraid"; he does not know who the child speaking was, and wonders, "Was it an angel, or a son who will never be?"[67] The reality of earthly mortality is then made dramatically present by the arrival of murderous Tartar barbarians. Daniil flees, but Andrei bravely greets them: "Welcome, Brother Death."[68] The Tartar laughs and mocks Andrei, closing act 2 with these words:

> I'll watch to see if this great planetary argument
> Proves you right and me the fool.
> It interests me to see if your one enormous Word,
> Shall radiate throughout all the burnt world,
> Or if my blade will have the final say.[69]

Act 3 begins to answer this question by sending Andrei and Daniil to a new teacher, Theophanes, a Greek icon painter. He preaches humility, teaching them that "he who thinks himself God's painter knows neither God nor icons."[70] He also instructs them technically in the colors of iconography; turning towards a painting of Christ he teaches,

---

66. O'Brien, *Sophia House*, 212.
67. O'Brien, *Sophia House*, 212.
68. O'Brien, *Sophia House*, 215.
69. O'Brien, *Sophia House*, 218.
70. O'Brien, *Sophia House*, 221.

Gold is glory, red is pain,
Blue is wisdom, white is pure.
All move together in the dance that's sure.
All breathe in beauty [inhales].
All breathe forth wisdom [exhales].[71]

Scene 2 of act 3 is set on the Feast of the Transfiguration, and the scene further depicts the transfiguration's theological meaning and relevance to the sacred art that Rublev hopes to paint. Reverently before an icon of Christ, Andrei both affirms his commitment and honestly describes his human limitations:

I love this face,
I love him, but I wonder, could I love him burdened
With the agony of the world, torn and ridiculed . . . broken, ugly,
    covered with vile abuse?
[passionately] Is it the ubiquitous goddess Beauty I worship?[72]

The real difficulty in answering this question is later in the scene restated by Andrei, who "must pass this inner dark / the inheritance within me of my fallen race."[73] The transfiguration directly speaks to this problem, though, as another chorus closes the scene by teaching that "through Your Transfiguration," Christ, you "returned Adam's nature / to its original splendor."[74] As the scene closes, the chorus continues to chant the meaning of the transfiguration on a darkened stage illumined only by an icon of the face of Christ.

In scene 3 of the final act, Nikon reappears, presumably transfigured in eternity. He gives a long, dire prophecy, warning of a future age whose humanity is debased because it has forgotten the face of Christ:

When the advent of the Antichrist approaches,
People's minds will be clouded by their passions.
Dishonor and lawlessness will wax strong, and the world
Will be in agony, though few will see its cause.
People's appearances will change, and it will be impossible
To distinguish men from women. . . .
And many, disturbed by this commotion,
Will turn higher the soundings of their muse,
A magic screen full of moving pictures and lies. . . .

71. O'Brien, *Sophia House*, 223.
72. O'Brien, *Sophia House*, 228.
73. O'Brien, *Sophia House*, 233.
74. O'Brien, *Sophia House*, 234.

> They will attempt to change nature.
> They will tear matter apart,
> And finding not God,
> They will say he never existed.[75]

This sounds, of course, much like the modern age. Rather than despairing, though, Andrei answers with his own manifesto of art, one that could be spoken by Pawel, Rouault, or O'Brien himself:

> Greater than a dream, greater than a reflection,
> Will be the words born from me, if I hold firm.
> Words born in silence and failure, tested by fire.
> Words that give life, luminous as the sun.
> It will come, he promised, if I choose aright,
> A word born from my poor gut, my tired eyes,
> A word to shatter chains and shout gladly down the ages
> Unto the last engagement with the foe.[76]

Andrei's medieval foes then become present again, however, as a Tartar appears and threatens Andrei's life before letting him go. Future foes are also suggested, moreover, when the Tartar promises the audience, as scene 3 closes, that he will return as "the new barbarian, dressed in fine suits / and wearing falsehood like a crown." Sounding a bit like the medieval knights who close Eliot's *Murder in the Cathedral* by rebuking the modern audience, the Tartar attempts to close the play by shouting, "Go! The play is ended. Go!"[77]

For the first time, though, this act includes a fourth scene. An unnamed woman comes forth, carrying dry sticks on her back and asking further questions of the audience:

> What? Still here? [She goes on a few steps]
> Do you think our play will end by fire?
> Should fire, the first word, also be the last?[78]

It is, she soon clarifies, of "a different fire I praise,"[79] as becomes clear when an old Andrei, now a monk, appears and begins talking with her. He takes her first to be "Masha," but no, she says, she is Kahlia, bringing another message of hope for his vocation:

75. O'Brien, *Sophia House*, 236–38.
76. O'Brien, *Sophia House*, 238.
77. O'Brien, *Sophia House*, 242.
78. O'Brien, *Sophia House*, 242.
79. O'Brien, *Sophia House*, 243.

> My little brother whom I love
> You shall be a man of prayer again.
> Hope shall be in you like bread in the mouths of children.
> You will again take up your brushes
> While all the world forges the sword.
> Beneath the Tree of Life, O dreamer.
> You shall awake;
> I shall call you forth from these brief dreams.
> And when you rise, you'll make for us
> (In an emphatic voice, with a second's pause between each of the three final words, she continues:)
> A sweet,
> holy
> fire![80]

The play's final speech, spoken by another chorus, is prefaced by further, clear stage directions that call for "three strong trumpet blasts" and for icons by Rublev to be projected. The Song of Songs in Byzantine mode is also called for, as the chorus begins:

> I hear my Beloved
> See how he comes
> Leaping on the mountains,
> Bounding over the hills.[81]

The play closes with words that, for O'Brien's readers, allude both to Rublev's development as an artist and to many other key spiritual moments in O'Brien's fiction:

> I sleep but my heart is awake. I hear my beloved knocking.
> [softly] I sleep, but my heart is awake,
> [more softly] I sleep, but my heart is awake.[82]

The effect of this moving play upon Pawel's interior life is immediately spoken of in the first sentences of the novel's final section, "Refiner's Fire." Pawel tells us: "This little tale is saving my life. To write of Kahlia and Sophia has engaged the latent powers of my mind and distracted me from the obsessions of my heart."[83] Difficult though it is to summarize without radically reducing its meaning, this play really is at the center of

---

80. O'Brien, *Sophia House*, 249–59.
81. O'Brien, *Sophia House*, 250.
82. O'Brien, *Sophia House*, 251.
83. O'Brien, *Sophia House*, 255.

the wisdom of *Sophia House*. One final, fascinating element of its meaning, though, is that Pawel seems to keep working on it throughout "Refiner's Fire," at least until he makes the mistake of giving his manuscript to Haftmann to copy. How then do readers have an apparently finished copy in the middle of the novel? This mystery is at least partially revealed at the novel's end.

We also hear the effect of the play on Pawel's interior life through the many meaningful conversations he is now able to have with his hidden guest. Though David Schäfer is young, the intellectual and spiritual foundations that shape the future Father Elijah are already strongly established. David's orthodox Judaism, formed in the Hasidic tradition, can dialogue with Pawel's developed intellect and faith—which has clearly grown through his play on Rublev—and thus give us many insights into language, meaning, and art, and how these key aspects of culture can affect one's religious viewpoint. Some of this dialogue gives ideas familiar to readers of O'Brien's fiction, but its context, in which the Holocaust makes the personal and societal stakes of such questions so high, helps to give the dialogue an added intensity.

Above all, perhaps, the dialogue's contexts ensure that its topics are, in an important sense, interdependent; the intellectual is never entirely separate from the actual, nor is the ethical—what humanity should be—ever entirely separate from the evidence invading their country, the Nazis, of what people should not become. Both Pawel and David are also aware of the evil in their own heart, though, and of the huge gap between the fall of man and the glory of God. For Pawel, Rublev's iconography reminds him that

> a God who permitted himself to be humiliated and brutally executed was demonstrating something about the nature of his love in a way so radical it could not be misconstrued.[84]

For David, sanctuary is a time to reflect silently on the wisdom of his own tradition, the wisdom kept alive, in Poland, primarily in his own soul. For him, both "spoken language and silence" are keys to communion,[85] but this is not unique to Judaism; rather, it is evidence of one Creator, the Most High, and "common to all men." We hear O'Brien's own Christian humanism when David teaches Pawel:

---

84. O'Brien, *Sophia House*, 257.
85. O'Brien, *Sophia House*, 265.

> When a man hands you a key, this has a certain meaning. A word is a key. A word is an action. Subtract the action, and the meaning is not expressed. Moreover, each man is a word. As you are a word to me.[86]

This is not a purely intellectual or artistic concept of communication; there is a key ethical element, as often stressed by Jewish or Christian writers. David explains:

> A thing is not truly said unless the speaker is willing to offer his own blood as surety for the words that come from his mouth or pen. The blood need not flow literally, but the willingness to let it flow is essential for authenticity. In the uncertainties of life, the spilling of our blood may be demanded of us, or it may not. That is not our decision. Our act of choice is to be willing.[87]

Again, as so often, O'Brien's fiction affirms Balthasar's emphasis on Christianity not being a "bloodless myth."[88] But nor is O'Brien's aesthetic ever a joyless drudgery. Again, David's spirituality is a model, for often in the middle of a busy street, even in the Jewish ghetto of Warsaw, he would "feel the great union, the great peace when speaking and listening were attuned to the voice of the Most High."[89] Divine meaning, for him as for O'Brien, is not confined to institutional religion but also found in the glory of creation. David continues:

> It is everywhere—all around us. It can be sparked by the flow through the air of wheeling pigeons; or the colors flowing across the ever-changing sky; or the flow of ideas from one's lips to the ear of another when you know that your word is spoken in the central current and heard in the central current and returned in the central current ... the current of holy fire.[90]

Despite their common theological foundation here in the living Lord, David's natural inclination is towards the ethical, while Pawel's is toward the aesthetic. Art is a kind of window for David, but one in which man "may see through his reflection to what is outside of himself—to the greatness of the world beyond himself."[91] It is in the art of dancing, David

---

86. O'Brien, *Sophia House*, 265.
87. O'Brien, *Sophia House*, 267.
88. Nichols, *No Bloodless Myth*.
89. O'Brien, *Sophia House*, 268.
90. O'Brien, *Sophia House*, 269.
91. O'Brien, *Sophia House*, 316.

says, like his famous namesake dancing before the ark of God, that "we approach paradise." For Pawel, "It is literature, the truly poetic . . . can approach mystic vision and other forms of soul-prayer."[92]

Yet literature for Pawel is never simply entertainment nor merely escape; it is always something more; as he later tells David, the writer

> observes. He reflects upon what he has seen. He suffers because of this. And from his suffering he makes a story. The soul of his listener recognizes that it is a true story, even if it is about a deer leaping on clouds or children dancing on the waves of the sea. It is not merely entertainment. It is food.[93]

In "Refiners's Fire," Pawel gives David two examples of this kind of story, one clearly fictional and one that mingles fantasy and the historical reality of his own grandfather. The significance of both stories is closely related, though, to the interior suffering within Pawel that readers have been aware of from the start of the novel, but which David cannot possibly understand. Thus "Refiner's Fire" gives further insight into Pawel's interior affliction, which always remains present despite the growth in wisdom allowed by art and theology. There are moments when Pawel is diabolically tempted:

> He began to think according to the pattern of its thoughts, and wondered if it was really such an evil thing to make an end to loneliness. In a time when men were destroying each other in the millions, why could he not burn with a desire rooted in the very sources of creation? What harm in this? Two beings, each alone, each without a family, surrounded by death?
> "Love is love," he said to the moon. "Does it matter which form it takes?"[94]

The rhetorical character of these "questions," of course, is part of their self-justifying influence. Only because Pawel has learned from Rublev to seek the face of Christ can he cry out: "Saviour of the world . . . help me";[95] another interior voice is heard:

> *Be at peace, my little one,* said a voice without compulsion, *it was necessary for you to experience this. Recognize that voice and do not again listen to it. Do not converse with it. The deceiver wishes*

---

92. O'Brien, *Sophia House*, 318.
93. O'Brien, *Sophia House*, 410.
94. O'Brien, *Sophia House*, 332.
95. O'Brien, *Sophia House*, 333.

> to shake you in his teeth. Come to me, come always to me and trust.[96]

This trusting is exactly what Pawel learns to do, and he thereby gains an understanding of his nature that allows him to resist unethical behavior. Perhaps the clearest evidence of this self-knowledge, and perhaps the most spiritually compelling portrait of sexual lust in contemporary Catholic literature, is the following long passage. Rather than employing the voice of Christ, or putting the passage in italics, O'Brien makes it part of a journal that Pawel writes for himself, thus stressing the self-knowledge that he has achieved:

> Pawel, search for the source of this pain. Try to understand it.
> The man I seek is within me. Who is this man? Is it the icon of my lost father?
> Is this, then, the source of the primal wound—the sense of fatherlessness? The wound makes one vulnerable to a lie: you have no father, there is no fatherhood, the universe is abandoned.
> The wound begets loneliness.
> Loneliness seeks relief in the theater of the imagination.
> The imagination ferments a romance.
> Then romance, impelled by the generative powers of the body, gradually degenerates into erotic fantasy.
> This in turn leaves the soul more frustrated and lonely than ever.
> Thus the primal lie begets destruction—worst of all, it does so in the name of love.[97]

The first story that Pawel tells to help heal this wound is a fairy tale, but one whose allegorical meaning is obvious to anyone aware of Pawel's interior pain. A young prince's mother dies, and when his father the king goes to search for her he is also killed by a dragon; the effect of this double tragedy gives the first key passage of the tale. As the prince

> lay upon his bed and slept, a bird flew through the window and plucked out his heart. It left a small stone in its place and flew away. In the morning, when the prince awoke, he felt nothing. Neither happiness nor sadness.[98]

The effect of this interior change within the prince is most noticeable when he grows to an age when he could marry. His people want a

---

96. O'Brien, *Sophia House*, 333.
97. O'Brien, *Sophia House*, 346–47.
98. O'Brien, *Sophia House*, 354.

queen, but the prince "had eyes for no human loves." He tells a lark who visits him, "I feel nothing." The lark's "heart is weeping" for the prince, prompting the question, "What is this thing you call a heart?"[99]

The lark offers to take the prince to a place where he can tell the answer. Near a high hill they go to a castle, and the prince commands, "Now sing me the tale." The lark's beak begins to move, but no sounds are heard. "I am singing in a key you cannot hear," the lark explains, inviting the prince to "look" through an open window at a woman lamenting some figure lying in a bed; she "fed it, sang to it, covered it with a large blue comforter upon which she had stitched a heart and a cross and the name of one who lay there."[100] At this point a dragon near the castle awoke and began to threaten the prince. "A diet of kings is my delight," it laughed. "I ate the father of her who is within, and I ate your father too. You also will I devour." When the prince heard this he cried out, "By the power of the true heart, I command you to be gone." The dragon, "taken completely by surprise," is killed suddenly as the prince falls to the earth.[101]

Then the prince awakens and finds himself in the bed he had seen, with the blue coverlet and heart and cross, but now his name is written on it. The woman that he had seen speaks to him:

> "You have awakened at last," she said, "as the lark had promised me you would." Together, the prince and the woman watched the lark fly away on the wind. As it went up over the sea, it dropped a small stone from its beak and nevermore was it seen.[102]

We never learn for sure if the prince and the woman marry, but that is not the point of the story. Rather, its clear meaning is grasped by David, even though he has no comprehension of the problem of homosexual orientation. "The prince," he said in a quiet voice. "The prince found his heart." He glanced swiftly at Pawel. "A whole heart."[103]

Readers of the whole novel can recall how Pawel's grandmother "prayed the rosary" while Pawel "slipped toward dreams under the blue quilt" that also had his name, "a heart, and a cross stitched into it."[104] It is to this memory that the second story returns, to hot summer nights

---

99. O'Brien, *Sophia House*, 355.
100. O'Brien, *Sophia House*, 356.
101. O'Brien, *Sophia House*, 358.
102. O'Brien, *Sophia House*, 359.
103. O'Brien, *Sophia House*, 359.
104. O'Brien, *Sophia House*, 32.

when his grandmother would put him in the same blue blanket.[105] But the focus of the story turns from his grandmother, nicknamed Babscia, to his grandfather, whom Pawel at first seems afraid to call by his nickname, Ja-Ja. Grandfather regains closeness with young Pawel, however, a closeness he can see has been lost with the boy's own father, by telling the story of when he fought and drove away another dragon, Wrog. Without bragging, but with appropriate suspense, Ja-Ja concludes the story:

> When the dragon did not come out, I stepped farther and farther into the tunnel. He withdrew farther and farther into it. I ran after him and he began to beat his horrible wings. He flew from me and went all the way back to his cave under Krakow. There, a few years later, a knight killed him with a sword.[106]

"This is true?" asks young Pawel.[107] Grandfather replies, yes, explaining it through the apocalyptic language of the book of Revelation that is true to any real story of the defeat of dragons, the defeat of real evil. The knight, Grandfather says, "was *He Who Is Faithful and True*," riding on a horse named "*Fearless*."[108] Domestic typology also comes into the story when the horse is said to be Pud, the old family horse still puttering around their farm. To "prove" the story true, Grandfather takes young Pawel to the place of the dragon's defeat, descending with him to the cave beneath an old well twelve meters deep. There they find, cut into the earthen wall, "a cruciform shape," a "carved stone cross."[109]

Grandfather explains: "The Knight rode back after he slew Wrog, and he put his cross here as a memorial of his deed."[110] Ja-Ja and Pawel spend many more hours in the cave, laughing and telling stories. Before bed that night, Grandfather comes to Pawel's room and shows him a big medallion on a red-and-white ribbon around his neck, promising, "When you are a grown man I will give it to you. It is the Mother of God of Czestochowa."[111]

---

105. O'Brien, *Sophia House*, 372.
106. O'Brien, *Sophia House*, 381.
107. O'Brien, *Sophia House*, 381.
108. O'Brien, *Sophia House*, 382.
109. O'Brien, *Sophia House*, 383.
110. O'Brien, *Sophia House*, 383.
111. O'Brien, *Sophia House*, 384.

Readers of the novel already know how the icon of Mary at Czestochowa helped to lead Pawel to the faithful knight who can defeat the dragon of despair, but this icon also helps Pawel, at the end of the novel, to find the healing from the childhood wounds that have so long plagued him. Rummaging with David in boxes left by Uncle Tadeuz in the bookstore, Pawel discovers old pictures that, for the first time in his life, reveal to him a startling fact: Great-Uncle Nicholas had once been a priest! Pawel had known he had spent time in prison, and had personally known his uncle only a time long after any outward sign of ministry was present, but in the old picture Pawel now "saw in stark clarity the meaning of so much that he had witnessed as a child." For "if Great-Uncle had abandoned his high calling," it was probably connected to the "secret shame" that his family had always "shrouded in cryptic references."[112]

In the old boxes, Pawel also finds his grandfather's medallion, still attached to its red-and-white ribbon. On the medal Pawel now reads the Polish words PROWADZ NAS BOZE (lead us, God) and MADROSC (wisdom). By the inscrutable path of divine providence, Grandfather's promise to young Pawel has finally been fulfilled, and Pawel's journal entry that night records this gift's incredible significance in his life:

> Last night I held my grandfather's legacy in my hand, its word purchased by countless Martyrdoms over nearly two millennia. As I held it and prayed, I offered my heart totally to God. The image of David Schäfer came before me then, and I saw his goodness, his belovedness in the eyes of God. I saw too (though I cannot explain how it came to me or in what language I understood it) that he is a word of love, though an imperfect love—as all human love is—a word spoken to me for a reason that I cannot yet comprehend.[113]

Though there is much that Pawel cannot yet comprehend, he finally gains peace. He and David share a sacred moment in the bookstore. "To be a father in the realm of the soul," Pawel says to David, "May I be this for you?" David replies, "It is a blessed gift to be a son in the realm of the soul. May I be this for you?"[114] Doubt, fear, is now gone; recalling the fairy tale, David adds, "We will remove the stone and throw it into the

---

112. O'Brien, *Sophia House*, 442.
113. O'Brien, *Sophia House*, 454.
114. O'Brien, *Sophia House*, 459.

river." Then the door of the bookstore opens and "the angle of the morning sun filled the shop with light."[115]

Into this moment of supreme spiritual bliss blasts the dark, carnal soul of Count Smokrev. He has come to buy David. After again alluding to and assuming Pawel's homosexual past with Goudron, he caustically adds, "The boy has been initiated, has he not? I ask only a share." Pawel is disgusted, but Smokrev is supremely confident: "Do not play the outraged idealist with me. Every man on this planet can be bent or bought." In response, Pawel reaches for and then raises high his Uncle Tadeuz's walking stick, and is about to smash it down when the count flees, "eyes wild with fright."[116] In no time, of course, soldiers are at the shop; as we already know from *Father Elijah*, Pawel holds them back long enough for David to escape on the store roof. When the soldiers find Pawel, he both shows solidarity with David and clearly asserts the identity he has gained throughout the novel; "Where is the Jew?" one soldier barked; in response, Pawel put the prayer shawl on his shoulders and the skullcap on his head. He stood up. "Here," he said and pointed a finger at his heart.[117]

Soon Pawel finds himself also in the "final solution" devised by the Nazis for millions of European Jews, as he is herded onto a train with thousands of others, packed like cattle, bound for the concentration death camp of Oswiecim, or Auschwitz. Even on the train, the identity he has gained by learning to see the interior icon of his heart brings some peace amid the painful horror. A grieving father mistakes Pawel for his lost, probably dead son, and Pawel understands, as he comforts the man, that "in his arms was a father, a child, a beloved, disguised in the many disguises of man."[118] It is on this train to death that Pawel writes the message to David that will help him become Father Elijah:

> My son, my friend. Never have I wanted to live as much as I do now. I go down into darkness in your place. I give you my life. I carry your image within me like an icon. This is my joy. I go down at last to sleep, but my heart is awake.[119]

---

115. O'Brien, *Sophia House*, 459.
116. O'Brien, *Sophia House*, 465.
117. O'Brien, *Sophia House*, 468.
118. O'Brien, *Sophia House*, 475.
119. O'Brien, *Sophia House*, 472.

Pawel's final word recalls his earliest memory: "Snow."[120] The word here signifies not just a return to childhood, but a reminder of God's miraculous ability to create complex beauty out of the cold reality of life.

The entire final scene does this, in an important sense, as we are reminded when the man whom Pawel first entrusts the message to David asks, "Where is God?"[121] This, of course, is the question commonly asked of the Holocaust, but O'Brien's fiction gives a further answer through an afterword that continues the scene of the novel's preface, when a Polish woman delivers Pawel's word to the now-middle-aged Israeli politician. We now see how important Pawel's message is to David Schäfer's decision to leave Israeli politics and begin the life that will lead to his becoming Father Elijah. Here, David rejects the "lure of the good he could achieve if he were to bless the earth with a philosopher-king," and instead returns to faith, to feeling "the presence of an intelligence far greater than his own."[122] In his final words in the novel, his identity is clear: "My name is David Schäfer. I wish to be poor."[123]

Again, the novel could suitably end with this line. There remains, though, the unresolved mystery of the manuscript of Pawel's play, *Andrei Rublev*. What happened to it? O'Brien adds to the afterword another short scene in which, some twenty-five years after the war, Haftmann is dying after years of presenting the play as his own and thus fraudulently maintaining a position in a German university. Dying, though, he is telling his children the truth. Why? Apparently, at the point of death, with his soul facing eternity and God, having the integrity to be an honest father was more important to him then earthly reputation. Haftmann's last words to his children remind us of the spiritual advice that Father Andrei gives when Pawel is in despair, earlier in *Sophia House*: "I beg you to forgive me. Forgive me."[124]

Despite all of these possible, apt conclusions, O'Brien chooses to add one final scene: Father Andrei wandering the wilds of North America. Readers of the *Children of the Last Days* series know well the good work he will do there, but what is the point of including this final image in this novel? Perhaps we are given one final opportunity to see, beyond the inhumane horrors of the Holocaust, that God's fatherly love continues,

---

120. O'Brien, *Sophia House*, 477.
121. O'Brien, *Sophia House*, 473.
122. O'Brien, *Sophia House*, 483.
123. O'Brien, *Sophia House*, 484.
124. O'Brien, *Sophia House*, 486.

through good men such as Father Andrei. In this long novel's final sentence, we are taken again beyond the history of WWII, and back to the ongoing conflict that has plagued the world since the fall of man. "Looking back at the earth," Father Andrei "turned and limped toward the log cabin that was his rectory, feeling only a little pain in an ancient wound."[125]

---

125. O'Brien, *Sophia House*, 488.

"Elijah Sleeping" from *Elijah in Jerusalem*

"God Is Master of Time":
Elijah in Jerusalem

> He works all things to the good of those who love him.
> —Father David, quoting Rom 8:28, in O'Brien, *Elijah in Jerusalem*, 271

ONE CANNOT EXAGGERATE THE achievement of *Sophia House*. It fulfills what every prequel to a great novel attempts—real insight into a central question raised by the original novel, in this case the fascinating question of what formed Father Elijah ... and so much more. So many of O'Brien's major themes and images are forged in the crucible of the problem of evil posed by the Holocaust, and yet the novel does present a credible, concrete response to one of the most complex questions that humanity can ask: What is wisdom?

My chapter on this novel is the longest in this book, yet *Sophia House* is significantly shorter—not quite five hundred pages—than most of the novels that came before it in the *Children of the Last Days* series. This relative concision is achieved with a one hundred page play inserted in the middle of the novel. The play could be cut, a space-conscious editor might claim, but Rublev's aesthetic is a very helpful guide to O'Brien's, and certainly illuminates both the themes of *Sophia House* and our understanding of Pawel Tarnowski's character. With this novel's strong relevance to our twenty-first-century Catholic culture, and comprehensive presentation of O'Brien's major motifs, I would not hesitate to recommend *Sophia House* as the single best introduction to O'Brien's fiction.

Of course, readers who pursue the wisdom of *Sophia House* are led forward to *Father Elijah* and then to its sequel, the final novel in the *Children of the Last Days* series, *Elijah in Jerusalem*. Given the extraordinary aesthetic skill and theological vision of the former pair of novels, expectations for the sequel, published almost twenty years after *Father Elijah*, were naturally very high. *Elijah in Jerusalem* subverts these expectations in many ways, most obviously in that Father Elijah and his fellow monk Enoch *do not* become the witnesses prophesied in the pages of Revelation, the text that concluded *Father Elijah*.

Moreover, though Father Elijah and Enoch are major characters throughout the novel, and do fulfill the mission that the Lord gives them, the novel is not really about them. Rather, over and over, we are reminded that God is the central actor in history, especially in the mysterious era of salvation history that we call the apocalypse. As was a medieval commonplace, God is the author not only of Scripture, and of nature, but of history. O'Brien, as author, seems in this novel very conscious of the need to avoid any human claim to authoritative prophecy, and of the difference between private revelation, including the insights of literature, and the public revelation authored in Scripture by God alone.

An initial indication of the contrast between this sequel and its predecessors is the preface to this novel. Like the foreword to *Father Elijah*, O'Brien educates the modern reader about the nature and certainty of an antichrist, and the need for every generation to "stay awake and watch." But the preface's second paragraph makes very clear that O'Brien does not see himself as an anointed prophet nor even as an authoritative interpreter of the book of Revelation:

> To presume that we have received in advance a precise decryption of the symbolic prophecies in the *Book of Revelation*—a route map or survivalist manual, as it were—is to weaken our faculty of discernment and our openness to the guidance of the Holy Spirit and the angels. This weakness can lead us to the tyranny of unholy fears on one hand or to self-reliance on the other, and both reactions will bring about increased vulnerability to the adversary's deceptions.[1]

Rather than relying on ourselves, or even the spiritual wisdom of so holy a man as Father Elijah, this novel continues O'Brien's vision of the "end-time" if it was to occur in our time, but fundamentally builds our faith and trust in God, author of history, united to Christ, Alpha and Omega. In union with the Holy Spirit, and the whole church, and repeating the conclusion of the book of Revelation, O'Brien's final sentence in the preface hopes that "we might cry out with renewed fervor, with the entire Church: 'Come, Lord Jesus!'"[2]

---

1. O'Brien, *Elijah in Jerusalem*, 9.
2. O'Brien, *Elijah in Jerusalem*, 13.

A second indication of the contrast between *Elijah in Jerusalem* and its predecessors is the novel's cover icon. Initially it appears to continue major motifs of the series, and perhaps also the typological technique that so often gives multidimensional meaning to O'Brien's art. For the cover could be the Old Testament prophet Elijah, sleeping in the desert and being fed by a raven. But the figure lying down can also be the Father Elijah of O'Brien's fiction, perhaps fulfilling the idea that the "two witnesses" spoken of in the book of Revelation could be Elijah and Enoch reborn, both being highly unusual in Old Testament history in that neither dies. Perhaps the modern Elijah is here shown with head on stone, listening to the church, and the cornerstone of the church, who is Christ.

Perhaps the bird in this icon is the one who took the stone from the heart of Pawel Tarnowski's sad prince, and Elijah's hand is over his heart to remind us that Pawel's faith is still awake in him. Yet whereas the closed eyes on the cover of *Sophia House* clearly signal the kind of interior creativity of the also closed-eyed Christ in O'Brien's great painting, *Creation of the Birds*, on the inside cover of *Elijah in Jerusalem* we are told the cover painting is entitled: *Elijah Sleeping*.[3] Above all, perhaps, the cover might be pointing not to typological fulfillment, but theological awareness. God is God, and we are not, as we are so often reminded by O'Brien's frequent references to Satan's original temptation in the garden of Eden. Perhaps the cover painting is another way to tell us to trust in God, and the scriptural theme it points to is: God "gives His people rest" (Ps 127:2).

Another significant distinction between *Elijah in Jerusalem* and the earlier novels is this final text's tight, very defined structure. We learn early on in the novel that the President will come to Jerusalem for a defined program of events over a seven-day period, so we are always aware of how Elijah and Enoch plan to come face to face with the President and fulfill their mission by witnessing, rebuking, and calling this human being (however depraved) away from serving Satan and back into the redemptive love of Christ. Yet within this external structure emerges the real subject of the book: how God has interacted with a very diverse cast of characters who share nothing in common except that they are all loved by God.

It is easy to quote Scripture on God's care for every hair on one's head (Luke 12:7), the "special providence in the fall of a sparrow" (to

---

3. O'Brien, *Elijah in Jerusalem*, 4.

borrow Hamlet's allusion at 5.2.165 in that play), or to note that God must be of an entirely different realm of being to be able to hear millions of prayers at once. However, it is another sure proof of divine difference from human nature if God can truly love the vast diversity of human beings, many of whom could not stand to be in the same room together.

Yet this is the God in whom Catholics believe, and thus *Elijah in Jerusalem* enacts, within a very different aesthetic, the face of Christ imaged in Rublev's icons, but now seen in the lives of sinful humanity. Some literary critics might see an episodic structure in the novel, as most characters are not developed in full, and some are seen again while others are not. Paradoxically, rather than a depiction of efficient humans scheduling time and being masters of their fate, instead, as Enoch tells Elijah, it is God who is revealed as "Master of Time" and the ultimate author of history.[4]

The novel's first chapter, "Gabriel's Sign," focuses on the racial and religious conflict that has long scarred Jerusalem, a city sacred to Jews, Christians, and Muslims. Elijah comes to the city with directions first to the apartment of a Dr. Tarek Abbas, who greets him and Enoch, then tells a story in his own first-person narrative. As a young Palestinian Muslim, Tarek had often terrorized the Palestinian Christians and other minorities of the city with abusive language and well-aimed stones, but, seemingly by chance or curiosity, he befriended a young, blind Christian youth named Gabriel. Typological meaning is never far from O'Brien's pen, and this youth eventually affects Dr. Abbas so radically that a new era in his life begins. For though Muslim, Tarek was not very devout, and in fact trusted God little more than he did the youth whom he terrorized.

That all changed through the radical act referenced by the chapter's title. Gunfire between Palestinians and police had spread out of control, as it so often does, when Gabriel made his way to the young Dr. Abbas's apartment. Wearing "a crucifix on a cord about his neck," he asks his friend to come into the streets with him, to "show them there's another way . . . an example of brotherhood."[5] Tarek's response was to slap Gabriel "hard on the cheek," not from anger, but rather to show "how worried I am about you . . . how much I love you . . . and hate you for your absurd goodness."[6] Gabriel is soon shot and killed in the street, but this is far

---

4. O'Brien, *Elijah in Jerusalem*, 174.
5. O'Brien, *Elijah in Jerusalem*, 56.
6. O'Brien, *Elijah in Jerusalem*, 57.

from the end of the sign, or guide to meaning, that he becomes for Tarek. God had another gift, as Dr. Abbas then tells Father Elijah:

> Not long after his burial I had a dream about him—about Gabriel. In it, he was walking toward me across the water, from the sea. I was on the fortress walls, reaching out my arms to him, angry at him and yet longing to see him again. When he was about ten metres away, I climbed across the stone barrier and stepped onto the water. With each step I marvelled that I was not sinking. When we stood face-to-face on top of the waves, he looked me straight in the eyes. He was seeing through his eyes. His face was totally restored, radiant, almost as bright as the sun. He said, "I am happy now, Tarek. I want you to come where I am going, and then you will be happy too." With that I woke up.[7]

In a literal as well as figurative sense, the dream started Dr. Abbas onto the path of religious faith; as the dream itself implies through its typological connection, Peter following Christ into the sea mirrors the dream. But "Gabriel's Sign" does not just explain Dr. Abbas's past. It will also inspire Elijah's immediate future, as this word from the Lord in his heart implies in closing the chapter: "*Go down without fear, my son, into the darkness of men's hearts; listen to their cries and bring them forth into the light.*"[8] Both before and after his dream, Gabriel is a great example of what one might call "transfigured humanity." Taking its name from the biblical story central to iconography, as we learned in *Sophia House*, humans such as Gabriel, Moses, the Old Testament prophet Elijah, and the Father Elijah of this fiction are *transfigured* by the Spirit of God into a form of humanity that shares in the eternal life of Christ with God.

Basic to biblical faith, though, is that Christ came to die for humanity while we were yet in our sins. In the next chapter, "The Woman Inviolate," we see the first example of humanity that is not just a bit sinful, but grotesquely so (as in the case of Smokrev), such that Elijah's Christian compassion and fatherly priesthood are severely tested. Karin is a very wealthy, very good-looking woman in her fifties who seems to live a rather sordid life, with multiple young lovers and multiple abortions, but the unusual word that the chapter title associates with her ("inviolate") is not an antonym of "immaculate," however much Karin seems an antitype of Mary. Rather "inviolate" means "untouched," a condition which Karin might use to describe her present self, which she proudly sees as being

---

7. O'Brien, *Elijah in Jerusalem*, 59–60.
8. O'Brien, *Elijah in Jerusalem*, 61.

above any emotional involvement or pain, coldly manipulating others while being amused at human folly. But Elijah suggests another way of seeing this:

> "Have you considered the possibility that you did not touch *them* 'at the core'? Did not know them?"
> "I knew them, and I touched them extensively."
> "I mean the soul."
> "That is abstract theology," she smiled indulgently.[9]

Karin knows who Father Elijah is because for years she followed the public career of David Schäfer. She did this after being "touched" in her university years by the teaching of Ruth, the wife David lost to terrorist bombs years ago. Karin recalls that Ruth listened to her differently than most teachers, indeed most people in general: "She was genuinely interested in the person hiding inside all my camouflage."[10] Even before Karin tells the further backstory that necessitated so much camouflage, Elijah begins to recognize that perhaps God has brought this woman to him for reasons greater than simply the avoidance of arrest at the security checkpoint. Elijah "knew that in a sense he was a word, as Ruth had been a word to this woman simply being herself. A word of presence . . . I am with you. I feel your suffering."[11]

The extent and real nature of Karin's suffering cannot be understood without hearing the long first-person narrative that she now gives Father Elijah. That she does so at all is a measure of her trust in him, and his integrity, for the narrative contains information that the President has said he would have her killed if she ever revealed it to another. When both were European aristocrats many years ago, Karin had known the President as a young man; both were out riding horses when she came upon him in a secluded forest. Sadistically, the future President was killing and torturing turtles, but the horror reached another level when he realized that Karin had seen him. As she now bravely tells Father Elijah,

> He dragged me kicking and whining to the edge of the pasture and threw me to the ground. He dropped the turtle, pulled out the scalpel and put it to my neck. I began to whimper. He slowly, carefully removed my clothes, and then he raped me. Throughout all of it—the rape itself, the degrading things he did, cutting

9. O'Brien, *Elijah in Jerusalem*, 79.
10. O'Brien, *Elijah in Jerusalem*, 75.
11. O'Brien, *Elijah in Jerusalem*, 79.

the turtle to pieces and sprinkling the blood on my naked body—he said not a word.[12]

For Elijah now to become a word made flesh for Karin is difficult, but it begins with her recognizing the divine image in her that cannot be defaced. "You are not indifferent to the truth," he insists, "I know you hunger for justice."[13] Though his spiritual mission to the President is something "beyond her," readers can sense if not rationally understand the providential role that not only Elijah and Karin but also Ruth play in each other's lives.

If Karin is an example of hidden interior goodness concealed by the stain of outer sin, the character referenced by the next chapter's title, "The Strategist," is the exact opposite. Met at a party hosted by Karin, the strategist is aptly nameless, perhaps because he prefers anonymity, but we do learn that he is a German archbishop, the kind of cleric who has supported Cardinal Vettore, the corrupt churchman who directly attacked the Pope in *Father Elijah*. Here, this archbishop commends Cardinal Vettore as "one of the lights in the new ecclesiology . . . a man of great vision."[14] This archbishop has clearly accepted New Age spirituality, believing "that the time for an overarching *unitas* has come, a convergence of all the spiritual streams within our histories."[15] Elijah learns of an unannounced meeting of select leaders from world religions who will meet in Jerusalem, with the President, to further plan how this new "religion," if one can call it that, will be "implemented." Elijah asks the obvious but uncomfortable question, "What deity would be worshipped?" but the archbishop simply smiles off the question and suggests the President's book *Metasynthesis* as "good news of the highest order."[16] Having heard enough, Elijah rebukes him: "I adjure you, leave the camp of the evil one immediately, return to your flock, and strengthen what remains."[17]

Also at the party, however, Father Elijah meets other souls of diverse religious belief. Karin introduces Elijah to an Israelite history professor, telling them they are "twin brothers separated at birth."[18] The two do have

12. O'Brien, *Elijah in Jerusalem*, 89.
13. O'Brien, *Elijah in Jerusalem*, 91–92.
14. O'Brien, *Elijah in Jerusalem*, 127.
15. O'Brien, *Elijah in Jerusalem*, 128.
16. O'Brien, *Elijah in Jerusalem*, 130.
17. O'Brien, *Elijah in Jerusalem*, 131.
18. O'Brien, *Elijah in Jerusalem*, 111.

much in common: Elijah's understanding of the book of Revelation parallels this Jewish believer's understanding of the book of Daniel. The Jewish professor sympathetically warns Elijah about the President, saying, "This King will not forgive," and both he and Elijah entrust their lives to "the Most High."[19] By contrast, Elijah also meets a British ambassador there for "the new revelation" that he expects from the President, "the best man humanity has ever seen."[20] Far better women are also met, however, when Elijah meets Hanna Tsukino, a Japanese cellist whose beautiful, intense, classical music recalls Elzbieta in *Sophia House*.[21] With her, Elijah experiences spiritual vision, knowing things about her life that he can possibly know only through the Holy Spirit. Between them there is a profound sense of peace and the comfort of Mary.[22]

The wide variety of worldviews met at Karin's party, and in the novel thus far, reflect the traditional image of Jerusalem as a crossroads of faith. In-depth reflection on the reality behind this image, though, comes in the next chapter, "The Pebble War." Troubled especially by "the strategist," Elijah begins by reflecting on the history of Catholicism; noting "Christ's mysterious choice to allow Judas to be in his company until the very end," Elijah further "reminded himself

> that the Church had been afflicted from the beginning by those who compromised the truth. There had never been a lack of such strategists, especially during times of crises in the Church. Whenever she had been attacked from the outside, there had arisen within her, proponents of the lesser-evil argument—make peace with her oppressors, try to save what can be saved by cooperating with their unjust demands.[23]

One must distinguish, rather, between small acts of faithfulness to the truth required by human beings, and the broader battle plan of God, which tolerates evil, for a time, to later destroy it without also crushing the reality of human freedom.

This is the basic distinction behind the chapter's title, "The Pebble War," which reminds us of the small shepherd David's initial defeat of Goliath, but which in this chapter refers to another young David,

---

19. O'Brien, *Elijah in Jerusalem*, 115.
20. O'Brien, *Elijah in Jerusalem*, 121.
21. O'Brien, *Sophia House*, 321.
22. O'Brien, *Elijah in Jerusalem*, 124.
23. O'Brien, *Elijah in Jerusalem*, 132.

ordained to the priesthood just five weeks ago. The Old Testament story is triumphant, of course, but here David is dismayed by the immensity of his task; though he sees through *unitas* and is tearing down a poster of the President when Elijah meets him, he feels: "We try to resist, but it's just throwing pebbles at a Sherman tank."[24] Father Elijah recalls "his confrontation with the President on Capri";[25] he then helps Father David to understand that his personal reading of the book of Revelation may have some objective accuracy. He can now see himself, perhaps, as part of the broader plan of God, but not because of any private or gnostic revelation. Rather, Elijah stresses, "It will be through the power of the Cross that each of us will bear witness—in the particular mission God has called us to."[26]

Fathers Elijah and David mutually bless each other. Unlike many other characters that Elijah meets in the novel, this will not be the last time that Father David plays an important role. The point O'Brien stresses, however, is that the role either will play is in the hands of God. At one point, Father David thanks Elijah and ventures to speculate that what God "wants you to do is very big," and the elder, wiser, priest replies, "I am very small, my brother. That is why I am depending on you to pray for me."[27] Reflecting on the long journey of his vocation, Elijah understands "that the path of each person in the world was known in its fullness to God alone,"[28] but he also knows what can sustain him in faithfulness: "Obedience. Simplicity. Trust. These would guide him."[29] This rational, intellectual knowledge is reinforced in an interior, spiritual way by the last words of the chapter; in italics, the voice of the Lord speaks directly to calm Elijah's heart: *My son, fulfill the task I have set before you.*[30]

The difficulty of this task is then shown in its full complexity and potentially horrific drama by the next chapter, "Cities of the Plain." In the opening of the chapter, Elijah recounts two dreams whose human meaning is not difficult to discern. Both dreams conclude with a simple imperative, but in the italics that normally suggest interior significance:

24. O'Brien, *Elijah in Jerusalem*, 139.
25. O'Brien, *Elijah in Jerusalem*, 140–41,
26. O'Brien, *Elijah in Jerusalem*, 142.
27. O'Brien, *Elijah in Jerusalem*, 144.
28. O'Brien, *Elijah in Jerusalem*, 147.
29. O'Brien, *Elijah in Jerusalem*, 149.
30. O'Brien, *Elijah in Jerusalem*, 153.

"*Look up*, said a voice."[31] "Listen to God" would be a fair translation of these lines, and in much of the rest of the chapter's opening it seems that God is directly intervening to reunite Elijah with Enoch. A ten-year-old boy arrives, "chattering in rapid-fire Arabic," directing him to go to Ramallah, a West Bank city where Elijah knows he might see Enoch; though Elijah doubts that the boy is "an angel in disguise," readers familiar with this O'Brien motif wonder otherwise.[32] In Ramallah, an interior voice becomes very insistent, "*Turn left. . . . Go inside*,"[33] until eventually he is led into a hotel restaurant where he meets a "deeply tanned" man in his late forties, "dressed in a shimmering silver suit and wearing jeweled rings and a gold wristwatch." Elijah is also given a phrase, "black fish and blue dog," which gains him admittance to the company of this strange person, along with many other details that Elijah cannot personally know.[34] Evidently, the Spirit of God has brought Elijah to this man, but for what purpose we cannot initially guess.

Victor turns out to be an Israeli crime boss who is one of O'Brien's most devotedly evil characters. Readers familiar with *Father Elijah* might liken him to Count Smokrev, who appeared in the middle of that novel and whose conversion becomes one of the most spiritually moving moments in O'Brien's fiction. Could the same happen here? Elijah's spiritual sight tells us many sordid details from the crime boss's life, and we learn his real name, Petro, but conversion never comes. Though Elijah repeatedly tells him that his "covenant with evil . . . can be broken,"[35] at the end of the chapter the crime boss binds and blindfolds Elijah and seems about to kill him, as Victor has verbally threatened. Elijah is to be shot in the head and his body disposed of in a ditch. Mercifully, there is an anticlimactic conclusion; one thug says, "Bang-bang," rather than shooting the gun, and the other laughingly adds, "Rest in peace," but one is not sure whether the mercy is divine providence or depraved prudence on the crime boss's part.[36]

Enoch soon appears, but Petro never reappears in the novel. His evil seems impervious to Elijah's appeals. So why is Petro in this novel? Perhaps the character is deliberately like Smokrev, but the outcome is so

31. O'Brien, *Elijah in Jerusalem*, 154–55.
32. O'Brien, *Elijah in Jerusalem*, 156.
33. O'Brien, *Elijah in Jerusalem*, 159.
34. O'Brien, *Elijah in Jerusalem*, 160.
35. O'Brien, *Elijah in Jerusalem*, 168–70.
36. O'Brien, *Elijah in Jerusalem*, 172.

different in order to remind us that Elijah has no supernatural power in his own person; it is only through the grace of God that any mission can bear fruit. Shortly after reuniting, as Elijah is wanting to rush to their confrontation with the President, Enoch reminds Elijah of perhaps the central theme of the novel: "*God* is Master of Time."[37] Readers expecting *Elijah in Jerusalem* to repeat and, in a human sense, complete the mission begun in *Father Elijah* are thus intentionally disappointed. O'Brien is reminding them that, just as God, not even St. John the disciple, is the source of the book of Revelation, so God will be the central author, in history, of the actual apocalypse. Humans can only wait, stay awake, and faithfully perform the small acts of faith which God encourages in us.

The ironic intent of this sequel is further stressed in the next chapter, "Riders in the Chariot," as Elijah and Enoch recuperate for a time at a diverse community of international pilgrims called the "House of Reconciliation." As a place that posts Hebrew and Arabic words together, pointing to how the historical combatants of Jerusalem can turn "to embrace each other," one might imagine that the pilgrims here are supporters of *unitas* and the President's New Age religion.[38] This is not the case, however, largely because the community is led by a spiritual mother, a laywoman named Katherine, or Katé, who shares the spiritual life within Elijah. On greeting him she affirms, "In the communion I know who you are," and we soon hear her deep faith:

> Oh, how beautiful is the heart of Jesus! How beautiful that he loves us in our foolishness, he who suffered so much for us. Now our poor world grows indifferent to what he gave, though not all. We still find many who are not blind.[39]

Katé has family that she worries about in America, but Elijah sees that here in Israel she has "many, many children," for she gives the people who come to her house real spiritual food.[40] She recognizes the Eucharist that Father Elijah can offer the community to be a "priceless gift" for "his work is in the heart of the Lord."[41] From her, Elijah also gains real peace;

---

37. O'Brien, *Elijah in Jerusalem*, 174.
38. O'Brien, *Elijah in Jerusalem*, 179.
39. O'Brien, *Elijah in Jerusalem*, 181.
40. O'Brien, *Elijah in Jerusalem*, 183.
41. O'Brien, *Elijah in Jerusalem*, 184.

knowing the extraordinary blessing of "the presence in the tabernacle," Elijah realizes that "Everything—everything—was in God's hands."[42]

Elijah meets a number of faithful pilgrims to Katé's community, and the title of the chapter refers directly to a type of sacred art—among which one might classify all of O'Brien's fiction and especially *Elijah in Jerusalem*—which is not simply scriptural but not heretical either; rather, the art builds on biblical truth to make its meaning relevant to contemporary life. On Katé's wall is a painting of the Old Testament prophet Elijah going to heaven in a fiery chariot, as in Scripture, but in this painting are also "numerous people of diverse ages and races, smiling and waving."[43] The painting is not an attempt to rewrite Scripture, but an allegorical "word" which affirms that authentic prophecy lifts up people towards the home God prepares for them in heaven. Such art can provide spiritual support provided it is received with a proper spirit of humility and obedience.

When this spirit is present, the church becomes aware, and Scripture speaks, of the faithful presence of the living and the dead as "The Cloud of Witnesses," also the title of the novel's next chapter. When this spirit becomes clouded by human pride, however, trouble ensues, a point that this chapter stresses through the negative example of a nameless Irish woman. Evidently faithful, she has created a virtual industry—books, tracts, websites, and blogs—around speculation about the apocalypse. Elijah asks her directly, "Do your books foretell the future?" and her answer implies a direct conduit to God's mind: "They give crucial information that the faithful will need in the coming days."[44] There may be self-conscious spiritual reflection on O'Brien's part here, for after the success of *Father Elijah* there was surely a danger, and an economic temptation, for O'Brien to assume a public role as apocalyptic authority or at least, a visionary. There probably is a little poke at himself, at his own stereotypical Irish gift of the gab, when Katé says of the Irish woman:

> Now, I really like Irish people, and they certainly have visions in that country, but not all of them are true. Mind you, they all know how to talk as if they are true, so it makes the weeding harder.[45]

---

42. O'Brien, *Elijah in Jerusalem*, 186.
43. O'Brien, *Elijah in Jerusalem*, 187.
44. O'Brien, *Elijah in Jerusalem*, 207.
45. O'Brien, *Elijah in Jerusalem*, 216.

Such weeding is necessary, however; the elevation of private revelation above the public revelation given by Christ to the apostles can be a serious problem. The church is bound to proclaim public revelation; furthermore, preference for private revelation by believers reveals a subtle distrust of the church. As Elijah says of the Irish woman: "On a barely conscious level she believed that God did not rule the world and the Church properly; therefore, she must do what she could to set things straight."[46]

Far from being strictly an individual or personal problem, however, Elijah notes that "false revelations" often arrive in times of crisis, "to divide and confuse us," when the church needs to be "united in prayer.... Proclaiming the truth in the face of the adversary."[47] By contrast, Katé knows an anonymous stigmatist with a much simpler message:

> We are not to put our trust in material things but to ask God for holy peace to secure our hearts. Peace that will prepare and sustain us when we are maligned and persecuted, and even killed for Christ and his Church. She emphasizes that we must forgive everything and everyone. No defending ourselves in worldly ways. Let God be God. Not enough to fill a book, you see. Not even a pamphlet.[48]

We never meet this stigmatist in *Elijah in Jerusalem*, nor do we have any concluding sense of what finally happens to the Irish woman. The lives of both are hidden in God's plans, as the public revelation that is Holy Scripture often proclaims.

Before leaving the House of Reconciliation, Father Elijah is given one final grace to prepare him for his final meeting with the President. This grace comes not in the form of doctrine, prayer, or anything overtly religious, but through a *hora*, or Jewish wedding dance, in which Katé's entire community participates. This is an earthly wedding, but on a typological level the dance symbolizes the wedding of Christ the Bridegroom and his bride the church, the joyful promise of the apocalypse. The dance inevitably reminds Elijah of his last time dancing the *hora*, though, at his wedding with Ruth; now a firmly committed priest, he accepts that this "sacrifice was now the form love took in his life," and he believes "he

---

46. O'Brien, *Elijah in Jerusalem*, 209.
47. O'Brien, *Elijah in Jerusalem*, 212.
48. O'Brien, *Elijah in Jerusalem*, 215.

would never dance again."⁴⁹ Without denigrating in any way the immense value of Elijah's priesthood, readers of O'Brien's fiction cannot help but recall the meaning of dance in *Sophia House*, where, seeing King David dancing before the ark of the covenant, the young David Schäfer saw it as his closest approach to paradise.

Father Elijah's Catholic priesthood does not abolish but fulfills scriptural typology, and in the dance of the House of Reconciliation he eventually joins in. Memories of Ruth or even Pawel no longer become so painful, for he recognizes that "their love was stronger than death," and he now feels himself supported in the dance by many kindred spirits:

> Now he saw a cloud of witnesses above him, praying for those who danced below. And he saw the guardian angels too, dancing with them—and because they were beyond time, they were also dancing for him during the long desolate years when he could not. And he saw that what he had lost was not gone forever, for he danced in a single unity of past and present and future, a stream in the great river flowing from paradise.⁵⁰

As sublime though this passage is, it does not close the chapter. Also at this dance is Ibrahim, a Palestinian Christian bound to a wheelchair. When we first see him, he is on the outskirts of the dance, where Father Elijah, perhaps recalling his Jewish traditions, offers spiritual comfort: "In paradise you will dance, Ibrahim. You will be whole again and beautiful, and you will fly as you dance."⁵¹ Then Katé comes and, professing for Ibrahim a love without guile, without mockery, she draws him and his wheelchair into the center of the dance and helps him feel its joy; he "suddenly . . . began to shake with mirth and gave a loud bark of a laugh."⁵² So after Elijah also joins in, it is Ibrahim who gives the final word of the chapter. Literally the last word here is Aramaic for "Father," a form of "Abba," the Aramaic word that Jesus often uses in the New Testament for his Father. Father Elijah *in persona Christi* was Christ for Ibrahim, particularly in a recent confession, but here Ibrahim is also Christ for Elijah, reminding him of the identity shared by all believers in Christ (John 1:12). Ibrahim simply tells Elijah, "We are little children, Abi."⁵³

49. O'Brien, *Elijah in Jerusalem*, 225.
50. O'Brien, *Elijah in Jerusalem*, 230.
51. O'Brien, *Elijah in Jerusalem*, 227.
52. O'Brien, *Elijah in Jerusalem*, 229.
53. O'Brien, *Elijah in Jerusalem*, 230.

The next chapter, "The Wall of Tears," brings Elijah and Enoch to their final confrontation with the President. Near the famous Wailing Wall of Jerusalem, the President will "usher in a new spiritual era" by presenting the world's religious leaders with *unitas*, peace, to end the religious strife that has long divided humanity. Given the significance and triumph of similarly epic moments in O'Brien's fiction, when the power and glory of the cross confronts and defeats demonic forces of evil, and given our hope that Brother Enoch and Father Elijah might be the "two witnesses" prophesied in the book of Revelation, readers understandably expect a dramatic conclusion, even though there are two remaining chapters in this novel.

Expectation is probably strengthened even more when a clearly angelic being guides Enoch and Elijah into a hiding place near where the President will address the world's religious leaders. "This is the way you must go," the angel says, "in a calm, clear voice," but, as he leaves, he also offers clear theological wisdom: "Pray to your Savior to unlock men's hearts . . . pray that the sea will be parted, that you may speak the word you bear . . . fruitfulness is in the Father's hands, and its weight and measure are known to him alone."[54] The angel's meaning becomes even clearer after the confrontation with the President, though the chapter title also prepares us; the title seems a dual allusion, both to the Wailing Wall where Jews traditionally bring their grief to God, and to the "vale of tears," the traditional English phrase for this world of suffering and woe.

The final confrontation certainly brings more of that, but the first indication of anticlimax comes when Brother Enoch and Father Elijah are given interior confirmation that "there are others" similarly called to witness to the President. The two that O'Brien's readers know best do make it onto the President's helicopter platform, but after Enoch shouts in Arabic, "May Jesus Christ rebuke you, Satan!"[55] he is shot dead by guards. Father Elijah is able to say a little more, seeming even to achieve a moment of exorcism:

> Paralyzed, terrified, his face flaming red, the President opened his mouth to make a retort, but from it there issued nothing. Through his eyes, the hidden spirit that controlled the man roared—a torrent of absolute malice, of fire without light, of

---

54. O'Brien, *Elijah in Jerusalem*, 242–43.
55. O'Brien, *Elijah in Jerusalem*, 250.

absolute hatred. Suddenly, the President convulsed, and from his mouth there erupted an unearthly scream.[56]

Father Elijah is able to remain "calm and fearless," and to rebuke Satan in the name of him "who is faithful and true, the Word of God made flesh, the King of kings and Lord of lords,"[57] but this moment is temporary, and does not seem to significantly alter the day's events. Elijah is quickly arrested, roughed up, and this and other "incidents" seem just to add to the President's *unitas* rhetoric; he tells the crowd, "A minor disturbance, my friends, a reminder for us, a symptom of all that humanity must leave behind. Be at peace, for this is a Day of Joy."[58]

Like Pontius Pilate proclaiming Jesus "King of the Jews" in his sign on the cross, the President may speak truer than he knows. As the angel prepared us to understand, the fruitfulness of Enoch and Elijah's witness is known by God alone. We can now be sure that they are not the "two witnesses" of the book of Revelation, for the bodies of this novel's Brother Enoch and Father Elijah will not lie in the streets for three days and be revived by the Spirit of God, as Rev 11 foretells will happen to the biblical prophets. However, O'Brien does give us one glimpse into the effect of Brother Enoch and Father Elijah fulfilling their mission, through the unlikely character who first helped Father Elijah when he was arrested early in the novel by Israeli security forces: Karin.

Karin was in the audience for the President's speech, and tells Father Elijah what she saw when she visits him after he is held and tortured by the guards who arrested him then. Karin still despairs of her own salvation, saying, "It's too late for me now," but her new-found understanding of Father Elijah's vision has changed her: "At least I know there's something stronger than evil."[59] She explains:

> I'm not sure what I'll feel tomorrow, or where I'll be. I only know that today I'm different. As I watched you and your friend confront the President, I saw the most powerful man in the world become terrified. Never in my life have I seen him afraid of anything. He wasn't afraid of being wounded or killed. He was afraid of you—of your presence.[60]

---

56. O'Brien, *Elijah in Jerusalem*, 251.
57. O'Brien, *Elijah in Jerusalem*, 251.
58. O'Brien, *Elijah in Jerusalem*, 252.
59. O'Brien, *Elijah in Jerusalem*, 274.
60. O'Brien, *Elijah in Jerusalem*, 274.

Karin's words come in the final chapter of the novel, "The Cloak," which, as one could argue of all the novel's chapter titles, has at least a dual meaning. This title could refer to the human inability to see beyond time, a theme repeated throughout the novel, but it also hints towards the mantle of prophecy being thrown on to other humans. The second to last chapter, "Intifada," is, as already noted in the novel, the infamous Palestinian term for "disturbance," or "uprising," but it could also mean "shaking up," the cruel interrogation techniques that Father Elijah is subjected to by the Israeli security forces. Even more shaken, though, is the old Israeli friend who visits Elijah in the aftermath, Lev. A hardened, confirmed atheist, he gives no obvious sign of conversion as Elijah, even while still suffering the wounds of torture, witnesses to him of God's goodness. We don't know exactly what moves Lev, but Karin tells Elijah that Lev is "very shaken. You changed him too." Elijah is not merely being humble in replying, "If that is so, it wasn't I. The truth woke him."[61] This is a key way to understand a prophet's role, O'Brien's fiction, and *Elijah in Jerusalem*. For "the cloak" of the final chapter is the mantle of prophecy that the Old Testament Elijah tosses to his successor, Elisha, but every Christian in baptism becomes "prophet, priest, and king." A true king serves the King of kings, true monarchists understand, and Elijah's words here remind us that a true (as opposed to a false) prophet speaks the truth of the Word of God.

The novel's final chapter shows the cloak of prophecy being taken up by so unlikely a figure as Karin, who can fulfill the role if she is willing to speak the truth. Father Elijah's prophetic mission is completed when he speaks the Word of God to the President, and then to Lev and again in the last chapter to Karin. As he has throughout his life as a priest, Elijah's prophetic word is not gnosis about some unknown future, but rather the crucial truth that should radically affect the daily life of every person who hears it; as he tells Karin, "The One who loves you would have died for you alone."[62] We don't know, ultimately, how this knowledge will affect her, but what we can't know about her is balanced in this final chapter by one further scene which reminds us of the certainty of public revelation.

By this, one cannot mean certainty of interpretation, for this final scene is also shrouded in mystery. Yet there is no question that, as Elijah still recovers from his wounds in bed, he is visited by the actual two

---

61. O'Brien, *Elijah in Jerusalem*, 276.
62. O'Brien, *Elijah in Jerusalem*, 274.

witnesses prophesied in Rev 11. No hint of their identity is given, but Elijah knows it is the two witnesses of Revelation as they begin, "When we two have completed our testimony," and then they complete the prophecy that John foresaw. The two also give us further insight into the meaning of prophecy and "cloak" by recalling how Elijah tossed it to Elisha, affirming that in the time of the New Testament, "dipped in the Blood of the Lamb ... the cloak is now given to all who would follow him in spirit and truth."[63] The scene thus reaffirms the value of private revelation assumed in the prophetic gift of Christian baptism, or even in the human nature of a person like Karin, but like the novel as a whole it points us back towards the unshakable reality of public revelation, however imperfectly we know it.

The importance of Christ's public church is also then reaffirmed through a final priestly word, spoken by another "minor" character from earlier in the novel who reappears in the final chapter. Father David is the young, faithful priest whom Elijah meets just after Karin's party. He comes to Father Elijah at the House of Reconciliation, as the wounds of the interrogation have brought him near the point of death. Father David does give Elijah the real peace that comes with the absolution of the sacrament of reconciliation, or confession, preparing him for it by gently advising: "Just be a very little child. You are in the hands of God. Always in the hands of God. He works everything to the good of those who love Him."[64] Arguably this is also the central theme of *Elijah in Jerusalem*. There are moments of doubt in the final chapter, where the fallen, human element that remains even in a saint like Elijah cries out, "I have failed."[65] Yet by the end of the novel, readers can be sure that this is not God's perspective, and there are much greater truths which Father Elijah has surely succeeded in revealing to us. In the novel's final passage, we could literally say that this novel's Elijah "dies." But memories of the dance with Ibrahim and Katherine's community of witnesses leave no doubt that he ascends to the dance of paradise: "As the light of this world faded from his eyes, the last thing he saw was Ibrahim smiling at him. He saw the Christ of the burned men. 'Now, *Abi*,' said the boy. 'Now you will fly.'"[66]

At 282 pages, *Elijah in Jerusalem* is the second shortest novel in the *Children of the Last Days* series. As with the concise, often paradoxical

63. O'Brien, *Elijah in Jerusalem*, 279.
64. O'Brien, *Elijah in Jerusalem*, 271.
65. O'Brien, *Elijah in Jerusalem*, 270.
66. O'Brien, *Elijah in Jerusalem*, 280.

chapter titles of this novel, this brevity is clearly by design. Modern readers raised on the CBC ideal of style (clarity-brevity-concision) may view O'Brien's late-found brevity as a stylistic advance; though some primitive technique is involved in the 847 pages of *A Cry of Stone*, for me a more ideal length for O'Brien's work is the 488-page *Sophia House*. That length seems to me to allow both the novel of ideas and realistic suspense characteristic of O'Brien's best work. Beyond any stylistic considerations, it is O'Brien's artistic pursuit of the human being that gives his novels such length, for human lives are often long and complex, especially when God becomes involved in them, as he so often does.

In an inverse, paradoxical way, this is the point, as this chapter has tried to show, of the theological aesthetic that O'Brien develops in *Elijah in Jerusalem*. For there are many characters in the novel, such as Victor/Petro, that human art and imagination might wish to develop. If God can lead Father Elijah to him, who knows what else God will do in Petro's life? This question here, though, is not rhetorical. The point is, only God knows.

Elijah in Jerusalem rejects any categorization of O'Brien's art as "private revelation," and instead points us back towards Public Revelation. Exactly the same section of the book of Revelation closes both *Elijah in Jerusalem* as closed *Father Elijah*; it is highly instructive, however, to notice that on finishing the earlier novel we are drawn towards Scripture's account of the miraculous resurrection of the two witnesses, while in the later novel the final words of the quoted section, celebrating "the glory of God," become the place where our heart rests. The Scripture has not changed, only our interest and perception of it. God is God, we are not. God is the Master of Time, and we are not. We will have to wait and see how God unfolds the prophetic symbols revealed to St. John the Divine in the Apocalypse. Our part is to obey Christ's two great commandments. With mind, heart, soul, and strength, to think, love, pray, and stay awake.

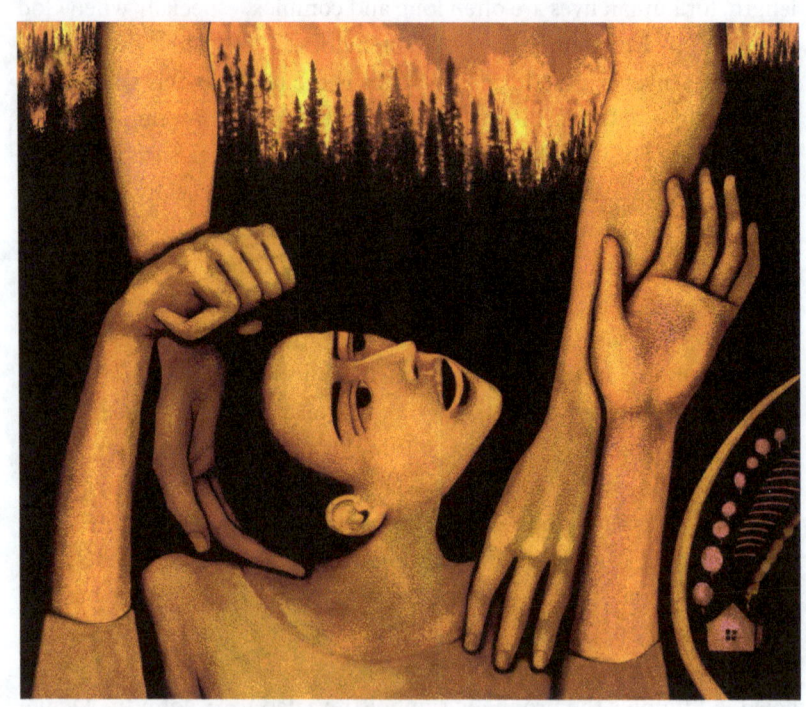

"Birth-Death" from *Letter to the Future*

CONCLUSION

"To Shift the Balance of the World": *Letter to the Future*

> Everything normal, though in my heart I knew that the balance of the universe had radically shifted.
> —Cleve, in O'Brien, *Letter to the Future*, 99

> The story would shift the balance of the world, if it were known. Even if only a little. As does every true word.
> —Esther, in O'Brien, *A Cry of Stone*, 523

> To do the right thing is to speak a word, and to shift, a little, the balance of the world.
> —David Schäfer, in O'Brien, *Sophia House*, 266

By the conclusion of the *Children of the Last Days* series, one should be able to see O'Brien's achievement as definitive proof that art, at least for Catholicism, can be "a bridge to religious experience."[1] My approach to his fiction, theological aesthetics, can be seen first as a way to describe this bridge, to take notice of the materials by which the art has brought us to the point of vision. Beyond that, though, this approach attempts to describe the theological vision thus attained. Though the nature of this vision will (thankfully) vary a little from reader to reader, as God reveals those parts of himself most helpful to the creatures whom he loves, often truly religious vision allows insight into reality which we must affirm as

---

1. John Paul II, "Letter to Artists," §10.

universal, or catholic. To know these truths, as Lubac put it, is to know the "common destiny of man."[2]

To claim this is to willingly become involved in the controversy that seems an inevitable part, at least in this world, of any Christian and every Roman Catholic assertion of reality. Universal claims in the "postmodern" world are often unjustly maligned as intellectual colonialism, but the truly universal allows us to address issues of widespread human concern. Seriously consider just about any major theological-anthropological issue—whether the existence of God, or of the afterlife, or of an eternal soul, or the nature of the human person—and it becomes nearly impossible to assert, in whichever direction one argues, that whatever really is the case will not necessarily affect all of mankind. This is as true in a secular age, or what Reformation historian Brad Gregory calls "the Kingdom of Whatever"[3] as it is in theocratic states of any era. On the whole, I think Gabriel in *Elijah in Jerusalem* is correct: "In reality, nothing is political,"[4] in human life, once we look carefully at both the divine and the human reality involved in any situation.

Just as importantly, it is not only part of the principle of noncontradiction but also essential to historical realism that if something is true, then it remains true beyond its original context. There is an important sense in which O'Brien's work introduces Christianity and Roman Catholicism in the manner of absolute immersion, which for most secular readers would be akin to visiting a foreign country. However, the habits of mind that open us to objective truth outside ourselves—humility, honesty, and curiosity, to name a few—are virtues of arguably universal value for humans of any community.

Moreover, O'Brien's theological aesthetic does not focus solely on the reality of public revelation. There are many elements of his fiction which remind us that the living God speaks to every human being in multiple ways. Perhaps because Sophia House, Pawel's little bookstore in Nazi-occupied Warsaw, offers a quiet space for extended reflection on the nature of language, meaning, culture, and religion, the dialogue between Pawel and David Schäfer extends beyond its cultural moment. In part, this is because it is a dialogue between Christian and Jew in which both recognize that they have much in common, yet also feel both secure and compassionate enough to honestly address the differences between

---

2. See subtitle of Lubac, *Catholicism*.
3. Gregory, *Unintended Reformation*, 112.
4. O'Brien, *Elijah in Jerusalem*, 52.

them. Much of what they have to share comes from a common humanity; as David tells Pawel, "I am human . . . this is a reality common to all men."[5] Pawel touches on a universal problem when he notes, "In reality, other people are as real as me, yet I do not experience them this way," and David asks perhaps the foundational question of human epistemology: "How are we to move beyond the solar system of the self and join in the great dance of the universe?"[6]

The multiple answers of Pawel and David are found in *Sophia House*, as their dialogue progresses. Pawel asks this key question: "The Universe is beautiful. It does not have to be that way. *Why* is it that way?"[7] David helps to articulate the answer so common in O'Brien's fiction, and so central to my approach to O'Brien's art: "Language can give us prayer and poetry, shouts and cursing. . . . But it is not the source. . . . There is the voice of the soul that comes before spoken words."[8] "The soul," of course, is not a concept universally affirmed, but it may be universally true that humans have souls. One can argue ad infinitum about the nature of human interior life, but perhaps Pawel is right when he points David towards divine reality:

> I think the important thing here is that you and I have a scrap of evidence that we are not living in a prison universe. We live in a cosmos that has open doors and windows. Messages from the infinite enter from time to time.[9]

As I have noted, sometimes the "messages" in O'Brien's fiction are italicized, interior voices whose origins must be discerned, tested, yet at times the voice of the Lord is so clear that it cannot be denied. At other times the messages are as objective as those given by angels, papal encyclicals, and Scripture itself. We must not value private over public revelation, as *Elijah in Jerusalem* makes so clear. O'Brien's fiction introduces readers both to the transcendence possible through individual human consciousness and art, while also always affirming and pointing towards the public revelation and providential art that only the divine is capable of. Surely the greatest gift that O'Brien's fiction can give anyone, of any human background, is a rich, full sense of the reality of the living God.

5. O'Brien, *Sophia House*, 265.
6. O'Brien, *Sophia House*, 270.
7. O'Brien, *Sophia House*, 341.
8. O'Brien, *Sophia House*, 268.
9. O'Brien, *Sophia House*, 345.

O'Brien's themes and aesthetic will allow many approaches to his work—and certainly even within theological aesthetics there are many aspects of his novels that space has allowed me to only briefly touch upon—but perhaps it is to the reader already open to theistic meaning that I should address some final words about how to hear the word of O'Brien's fiction. Those reading O'Brien's fiction for the first time are likely to react like many a weary tourist stumbling into a huge cathedral or great panorama of Catholic art, such as the Sistine Chapel. Such a person is often unable to articulate any awareness of this world so clearly beyond their secular horizons. I am reminded of a blogger on *A Cry of Stone*, for example, who admired the novel but did not know what to do with it; what more could she say about it?[10]

In addition to any approach that a critic might bring from outside O'Brien's fiction, we should also be guided by the many portraits given inside his work depicting both inauthentic and fruitful forms of response. As I have noted with each book, the role of interpretation in any response to fiction is foregrounded in O'Brien's work by the iconographic paintings on the covers of his novels. Partly because painting is itself a major topic in his fiction, O'Brien's novels often ask us to reflect on the most fundamental question of criticism: Looking at a work of art, what does one see?

O'Brien's fiction often depicts critical response to art as a form of spiritual discernment. Father Elijah, for example, begins to grasp the nature of the antichrist through the painting he sees when first visiting Don Matteo. Rose Wâbos, in *A Cry of Stone*, does not simply absorb the tradition of great art that she finds in European galleries, but rather hears the word of spiritual conflict in each painting. Pilgrims at the House of Reconciliation, in *Elijah in Jerusalem*, learn to discern the prophetic meaning of the painting entitled *Because He was Faithful*.[11] The painting points to Christ's divinity throughout both the Old and New Testament, for the figures in the painting are "riders on the chariot" because they have faith in the God who is always faithful to them. The spiritual truth of painting can also be true of fiction; consider, for example, how the fiction of Tolkien becomes a guide to reality for Nathaniel Delaney and his children in *Plague Journal*. On a broader but similar level, readers must "see

---

10. McGrew, "What We're Reading."
11. O'Brien, *Elijah in Jerusalem*, 187.

the form" to discern both the rise of totalitarianism and the redemptive acts of providence that comprise the action of *Eclipse of the Sun*.

O'Brien's fiction also gives us some very negative portrayals of how not to respond to works of art. There are general problems: not looking at all, or looking with predetermined commitment to a secular "flatland" devoid of existential reality, or imposing a false, often gnostic, spirituality on a work of art which has little to do with the interpreter's projection. Perhaps the most grievous examples of the latter occur in *A Cry of Stone*, when the sacred art of Rose Wâbos is either dismissed, or reinterpreted as the sublimated expression of some form of natural pantheism. Perhaps even worse, though also common, is the commercial appropriation of art, like that practiced by Dr. Haftmann in *Sophia House*, to secure a comfortable place among the cultural establishment. Hugo Dyson's imagined torture of critics, in *A Cry of Stone*, to see if they can actually create any art of their own, might be a slightly demented reaction to years of unfair criticism. However, it does remind us of the radical difference between the free yet disciplined capacity to create artistic works, and the potential forms of criticism that are nothing other than the expression of a critic's own personal feeling and identity.

Nevertheless, a critic, like any other reader of O'Brien's work, could never be caricatured as a parasite sucking the life out of a work of art. Critics are persons, too, with souls of their own. Art is never, in O'Brien's work, "just culture," some sort of social topping heaped onto materialism to make either capitalism or Communism more palatable. As Pawel Tarnowski tells David in *Sophia House*, for a real writer, fiction "is not merely entertainment"; rather, "it is food."[12] The same novel gives probably the simplest but undeniably authentic response to art when the young Pawel, returning to Warsaw after his sad experience in Paris, weeps in front of an anonymous painting that depicts the loneliness of modern life. The painter himself is present to witness this response, and it means far more to him than any award or financial gain that the painting might accrue. "I have waited fifty years for such a compliment,"[13] his note later tells Pawel, for he recognizes how his art has touched Pawel's soul.

As the worst forms of criticism are applied to Rose Wâbos's painting, *A Cry of Stone* may also give the clearest answer to perhaps the central question raised by O'Brien: What is the purpose of sacred art?

12. O'Brien, *Sophia House*, 410.
13. O'Brien, *Sophia House*, 105.

On her visit to France, Rose goes to see the nuns who had taught her both Catholic doctrine and the techniques of art at the school in Thunder Bay. She tells Sister Jean, the head of these nuns and a woman that Rose regards as a spiritual mother, "For many years I have tried to paint the things of God, and still my work is poor."[14] Mère Jean replies with some key questions:

> Will there be a soul one day, I wonder, who happens to stop before a painting of yours and is struck by a gentle blow in his heart? Will the Holy Spirit then speak to him, because of the word you have made flesh for his eyes to see? Will he perhaps turn to God and consider the impossible question?[15]

"What question," asks Rose, and readers are also now asked to reflect upon which spiritual question is most relevant in any human life. Sister Jean's response is startling in both its simplicity and profundity:

> Is God, after all, what he says he is? If he does ask this, God will answer him. This I believe. You must not doubt it. You may never see it; you may never know for certain; it may occur far from where you live or long after your death. But, because you existed, it will occur. You came into being, and you stood firm in the cold dark places of the world, you continued to walk through the forest in winter even when all bearings seemed lost.[16]

The same could be said of Michael O'Brien, but neither hagiography nor any kind of biographical criticism can replace the sublime spiritual purpose and effect of his art.

In an important sense, this spiritual response is the only kind of "criticism" that really matters for O'Brien's fiction. It is designed to touch our souls, and that effort drove O'Brien's sacrifice and commitment as an artist as clearly as it does Pawel Tarnowski. In *Sophia House*, that writer's journal tells us:

> And who is it for? It does not matter if no one sees, no one hears. The artist's only concern is to bring it into existence. He must speak without listeners. He must do so without thought of reward. This is the path that lies before me. If I were to turn

---

14. O'Brien, *Cry of Stone*, 725.
15. O'Brien, *Cry of Stone*, 725.
16. O'Brien, *Cry of Stone*, 725.

from it, I would surely die. I cling to this with a ferocity that is shocking.[17]

The ferocious realism of O'Brien's most recent novels, particularly *By the Rivers of Babylon* and *Letter to the Future*, extend his legacy.

Letter to the Future, published in 2025, points by its title to the future as clearly as *By the Rivers of Babylon* draws for wisdom on the past, yet like much of O'Brien's work it is an acute analysis of our present culture. The novel opens in an undefined but distant future, with four children tending sheep. In an abandoned cave, they discover some relics of the past, including an old manuscript that a learned priest translates. This is the "Letter to the Future" of Cleve Longworth, who shares the children's surname and is a presumed ancestor. This manuscript makes up the majority of the novel, first telling the story of Cleve's conversion from postmodern nihilism to Catholicism. Like Nathaniel Delaney meeting the "creature" in the cave in *Strangers and Sojourners*, Cleve began to convert because he "met the devil";[18] as for many serious Catholic writers, for O'Brien conversion often comes through either experience of real evil, or the extraordinary grace of supernatural good known by Rose through Jimmy in *A Cry of Stone*. To put it positively, via conversion Cleve discovers not only a "new metaphysic," but "a whole new world... A kingdom actually." Or, to put it another way, Cleve "began to discover what I was intended to be from the beginning."[19] Set in early twenty-first-century Calgary, this realistic and often spiritually insightful story is another prelude to the novel's main narrative: the end of modern Western civilization, as experienced by the key figures in Cleve's life.

This topic, as noted, is what made O'Brien famous, through *Father Elijah*, so some might dismiss this new novel as old paranoia. That is a mistake, however, in my judgment, because *Letter to the Future* is both a realistic update as to how the "end-time" might unfold in the twenty-first century, and an outline of what Catholic families, such as the Longworths, must do to survive into the distant future. So the novel includes a fair bit of the social collapse and rise of technological fascism that many current doomsayers predict. Though most of the social evils that O'Brien portrays are familiar to twenty-first-century Canadians, such as the growth of digital currency, an internet "under total governmental control" and

17. O'Brien, *Sophia House*, 259.
18. O'Brien, *Letter to the Future*, 86.
19. O'Brien, *Letter to the Future*, 81.

"Maid" (medically assisted dying), O'Brien avoids cliché through two key means.[20]

First, realistic characters such as Colleen Lyon, one of many extraordinary wives in the novel, honestly voices the simultaneous attraction and anxiety to modern technology that many feel: "I've always hated these things," she said. "So useful, so efficient, and so always demanding attention. I felt it was starting to own me. I thought I was being irrational about it, but now I'm not so sure."[21] If O'Brien's warnings about technology ring true, perhaps it is because this is an obvious way that fascism could reassert itself in the twenty-first century. O'Brien has thought seriously about the spiritual dangers of anti-culture as a prelude to antichrist, most notably in his 2019 book, *The Family and the New Totalitarianism*. Second, and more importantly, *Letter to the Future* goes beyond sociology by posing the crucial theological question: If Western civilization does self-destruct, how will God preserve a remnant to fulfill Christ's promise that the gates of hell will never overwhelm his church? Unlike many Catholics distraught over the current pontificate, O'Brien does not portray an ecclesial solution.

Rather, this novel depicts providence in action, as dreams inspire many of O'Brien's characters to journey together to an old cabin in the Rocky Mountains. Again, cynics could dismiss this as another "head for the hills" anti-modernist narrative. The novel often reminds us, however, of the numerous biblical precedents in which God used dreams to speak directly to humans living in precarious times, and we are again forced to take theological reality seriously. O'Brien is well aware, as *Elijah in Jerusalem* showed so clearly, that private revelation must not contradict the divine public revelation of Christ to the apostles. *Letter to the Future* reminds us that, whatever "ecclesial confusions" we face, our Father and Good Shepherd will not abandon his sheep.[22]

The novel's narration of its religious dreamers' journey to the cabin is long, sometimes violent, and reminds one of *Eclipse of the Sun*. As in that novel, here technology is smashed, replaced by authentic human characters who gradually reveal divine providence working with souls who cooperate with grace. Along with Cleve, three other characters stand out. First, Rafe Morrow is the primary instrument of Cleve's conversion. Initially giving meaningful employment in a construction company, Rafe

---

20. O'Brien, *Letter to the Future*, 87.
21. O'Brien, *Letter to the Future*, 241.
22. O'Brien, *Letter to the Future*, 106.

befriends Cleve and helps him to understand that Catholicism allows authentic freedom by curtailing sinful liberty. The need for human fathers of this kind in the twenty-first century is obvious, but Rafe's rational and compassionate leadership is also essential to the Catholic civilization that the religious dreamers eventually establish, God helping, in the mountains. Given these two crucial roles, one almost forgets, because it is incidental, that Rafe is a black man whose ethnicity could be appropriated for lesser cultural aims. For O'Brien, Rafe is a leader of the human race, gifted by God with qualities that every human family needs.

A perhaps more relevant racial dynamic, especially in twenty-first-century Canada, is explored through a second key character, Farley Crowshoe. A native of the Blackfoot First Nation common in Alberta and the northwestern US, Farley is an often comical curmudgeon, but both his serious faith and active defense of the native community allow O'Brien to consider issues at the heart of the native-Catholic conflict so much in the news in Canada ever since the scandal of residential schools has become well known. The Canadian government and many other Christian denominations and social agencies bear at least some of the blame for this scandal but, despite mounting evidence that the residential schools' graveyards have been misappropriated,[23] the Catholic Church has most often been blamed, and its churches burned by delinquents, as happens in *Letter to the Future*. O'Brien's *A Cry of Stone* portrays key elements of this scandal, which the novelist himself personally experienced and, in the twenty-first century, testified to at the Truth and Reconciliation Commission set up to explore modes of justice that might address some of the horrors created by the residential schools. O'Brien also, however, had lived experience of the often positive relationship between Catholicism and significant aspects of Canadian Indigenous life.

Farley is a man of deep faith, worthy husband to Kateri (named for Canada's native saint) and uncle to Father Peter Ahanu (whose name combines the leading disciple with a native word meaning "laughing one"). Both relatives play a crucial role in the novel, and at one point O'Brien's narrator reflects on the spiritual ironies of colonialism:

> As the Mass continued, I found it moving to watch this young native celebrating the ancient rite with such profound devotion. A son of the people to whom French missionaries had been sent centuries ago, *he* was now the missionary. I wondered how

---

23. This is still a debatable issue, but see Champion and Flanagan, *Grave Error*.

France was faring? Was it time to send our missionaries to evangelize darkest Europe? Or had the entire world become mission territory?[24]

Letter to the Future often shows the tough but compassionate faith of Farley and his wife Kateri. Ignorance of this faith is satirized by O'Brien, but he also reminds us of figures like Nicholas Black Elk, the Lakota visionary who converted to Catholicism and spent much of his later years witnessing to the gospel. Farley is much more down to earth, but Nicholas Black Elk joins St. Thérèse of Lisieux and other Catholic saints in the dreams by which God gathers the novel's community together. Again, the point is not so much that religion trumps race, but that each human soul is crafted by a loving divine Father who has an eternal plan for his child.

O'Brien's personalist theology is perhaps hardest to see, beyond the distortions of cliché, in the third key character who emerges in the lambs' liberation, Joe Jacobson. A very large, old man who first appears with long white beard and Orwellian T-shirt, "Thought Criminal," Jacobsen appears every inch the crazed survivalist whom liberals demonize. Cleve himself distrusts him instinctively, but again, O'Brien asks us to see him as a person, made with a soul created for the Creator's sublime purposes. Jacobson himself eventually speaks words that reveal the true motivations of his soul:

> Seven fat years and seven lean years is my attitude. Hoarding's not my game, freedom's my aim. A secret stockpile of food just for myself and my pals, and damned be everyone else, is an idea straight from hell.[25]

The Old Testament reference here is one of many surprising connections that one might draw between the ancient Jewish world of *By the Rivers of Babylon* and the modern Canada of *Letter to the Future*. In tents near the modern dreamers' cabin, Rafe describes it as "the tent of meeting." Father Peter Ahanu gets the reference, and "flashed him an appreciative look. 'A name with layers of meaning,' he said."[26] As the faithful dreamers arrive at their cabin, it is Father Peter who draws the most important connection:

> "We have entered the desert," he said in conclusion. "None of us know how short or long our stay here will be, nor what

---

24. O'Brien, *Letter to the Future*, 194.
25. O'Brien, *Letter to the Future*, 277.
26. O'Brien, *Letter to the Future*, 314.

additional trials we may face. But we are not alone. He is with us. We must not let our uncertainty about what lies ahead drag us into fear and despondency. When we begin to fear, we must look up and renew our trust in Him. *Sursum corda*, let us lift up our hearts.[27]

In whatever language, it is the same Lord, the same yesterday, and today, and forever (Heb 13:8), who draws his saints together. O'Brien has Kateri poetically express this most profound link between the ancient and modern world by having her sing:

> Water flows in brooks and rivers,
> It sleeps in pools and roars on seas.
> The Living Water pours not from fractured mountains,
> But from the breast of the Beloved,
> his hidden face I soon will see,
> Aa, Aa, rising, rising, I soon will see!
> Yes, little bird, yes!"[28]

The song here reminds one of the "great song" that Ezekiel was "created for" in *By the Rivers of Babylon*,[29] or "the song of poverty" learned by Nathaniel in *Plague Journal*,[30] or "the fire-song" within Rose in *A Cry of Stone*,[31] or Kahlia's songs in *Sophia House*,[32] or Hannah's song of thanksgiving (1 Sam 2), or Mary's Magnificat (Luke 1: 46–55). These songs are of the same genre: heartfelt cries to the living Lord. In *Letter to the Future*, Farley translates the song from its Blackfoot language, noting that it is impossible to reproduce the song's poetic meter. More important than aesthetics, though, is the clear explanation of the song's meaning given by Cleve's wife, Annie. Cleve had thought that the "bluebird" that he saw in a divinely inspired dream could be the brand of Jacobson's old bus, but after Kateri's song Annie knows the more important truth: "I believe your bluebird represented the Holy Spirit guiding us, bringing together people not united by origins or blood, but by . . . ." Farley completes the thought: "United by the Precious Blood."[33]

27. O'Brien, *Letter to the Future*, 313.
28. O'Brien, *Letter to the Future*, 316.
29. O'Brien, *By the Rivers of Babylon*, 391.
30. O'Brien, *Plague Journal*, 196.
31. O'Brien, *Cry of Stone*, 29.
32. O'Brien, *Sophia House*, 192.
33. O'Brien, *Letter to the Future*, 287–88.

Many other important characters emerge in the novel, though it is interesting that O'Brien does not use the familiar "frame" technique to return to the future of the novel's opening. Instead, Cleve's manuscript has a third major section that outlines the next fifty years of the dreamers' life in the mountains. Here O'Brien draws on the mystical Catholic prophecy of three days of darkness, followed by a universal illumination of conscience and offer of God's mercy.[34] Then a nuclear holocaust seems to follow, which still seems the likeliest way our civilization could end, though O'Brien retains optimism by showing nature recovering and surviving evil. Throughout *Letter to the Future* there is a gritty realism about the practical steps necessary for any humans to survive such a disaster, but perhaps there is another reason for this long third section of the novel. Like Tolkien writing such long appendices to *The Lord of the Rings*, O'Brien seems an author who, having asked us to consider his fictional characters as living persons, now seeks to complete their souls' journeys.

The conclusion of *Letter to the Future*, in which Cleve explains his reasons for writing, sounds like summaries of the motivations that, outside his fiction, O'Brien has suggested of his own art. *Letter to the Future* was written, Cleve tells us, as "my attempt to warn the children of the future about the consequences of self-deification. I wanted to show them *how* we were rescued—and, by implication, *why*."[35]

Yet O'Brien's fiction retains a joy that always reflects the goodness of God. Often this comes through both the trials and joys of marriage, as with Anne and Stephen in *Strangers and Sojourners*, Ezekiel and Leah in *By the Rivers of Babylon*, or Annie and Cleve in *Letter to the Future*. Always there is awareness that Catholic marriage is not just between two persons, but unity in one God; as O'Brien puts it in celebrating marriage in ancient Israel: "Beautiful is she, beautiful is he, beautiful is the Lord who made them!"[36] On marriage in *Letter to the* Future, when O'Brien's narrator Cleve realizes he is in love, he reflects: "Everything normal, though in my heart I knew that the balance of the universe had radically shifted." In the novel's final section, Cleve seems to suggest O'Brien's own long marriage to Sheila, which Cavallin makes clear has been so important to his life as an artist. Cleve says:

---

34. The famous mystics who taught this were Bl. Anna Maria Taigi and Marie-Julie Jahenny.

35. O'Brien, *Letter to the Future*, 334.

36. O'Brien, *By the Rivers of Babylon*, 274.

> Annie and I brought six children into the world, each of them endlessly surprising us with their unique characters and temperaments, their gifts and weaknesses. They made us laugh and they made us cry, but always there was joy.[37]

Yet O'Brien's art usually avoids sentimentality, achieving instead the "contemplative realism" praised by Joshua Hren.[38] Why, however, does his recent fiction not follow the fascinating "faction"[39] of John Paul II and Cardinal Ratzinger in *Father Elijah* by speaking of the current ecclesial crisis that most Catholics today are aware of, involving Pope Francis, Archbishop Vigano, faithful cancelled priests such as Bishop Strickland and Father Altman, the disgraced ex-cardinal McCarrick, and, most disgustingly of all, the anti-art of Marko Rupnik.

Perhaps the answer is the same as the saints living in the mountains unable to explain the nature of the world's nuclear holocaust: "Was the holocaust of supernatural origins, or purely natural, or simply man-made—or was it a combination of all three? No one knew."[40] We can know and condemn the doctrinal errors of modernism and McCarrick's abuses, but can we know that God desires the Catholic Church to have a new hierarchy because Rome is currently corrupt? That is clearly a much more difficult question, and perhaps an artist must remain in the suffering, sacrificial mode which Cleve articulates at the end of *Letter to the Future*:

> We hobble along half blind, ever-repenting, trying to love in all circumstances. Invoking the supernatural grace of Hope, converting fear into trust. Practicing thankfulness for all things, the sweet and the bitter, the soft and the hard. Offering to others our little bits of bread, baked in the kitchen of our weakness.[41]

Cleve further explains in terms central to O'Brien's art: "With the passage of time I have come to believe that there are different ways of imparting truth"; by this he does

> not mean the writing of literature (I long ago abandoned that persona); nor do I mean philosophical arguments to change

---

37. O'Brien, *Letter to the Future*, 334.
38. Hren, *Contemplative Realism*. Hren's manifesto, in fact, quotes O'Brien as an epigraph.
39. Fiction based on factual figures, as in novels such as Malachi Martin's *Vatican*.
40. O'Brien, *Letter to the Future*, 307.
41. O'Brien, *Letter to the Future*, 406.

people's thinking ... nor do I mean historical data and analysis for the informing of mind ... I mean instead our own deepest heart-soul words—living *logos*.[42]

Critical response, to an important extent, must be determined by the kind of art or literature that one is attempting to understand. So many of O'Brien's icons have their eyes closed in his finished paintings. This is true of Christ in the painting *Creation of the Birds*, Oldmary Wâbos in *A Cry of Stone*, Pawel Tarnowski in *Sophia House*, Father Elijah in *Elijah in Jerusalem*, and Ezekiel in *By the Rivers of Babylon*. They are not sleeping, but quietly listening to the still word within them that will well up to allow the life of the divine Word that they will express through human words and actions. Those figures with eyes open—such as Elijah in *Father Elijah*, Stephen and Anne Delaney in *Strangers and Sojourners*, Arrow and Nick in *Eclipse of the Sun*, or Christ lifting Cleve Longworth out of the fire in *Letter to the Future*—have the deep eyes that first catch Pawel Tarnowski's attention when he sees the icons of Rublev. These are the "far-seeing eyes" that Ezekiel sees when first meeting Jeremiah.[43] All of these figures are *living logos*, words spoken by our Father who loves us.

---

42. O'Brien, *Letter to the Future*, 407.
43. O'Brien, *By the Rivers of Babylon*, 43.

"Transcendence"

Bibliography

Augustine. *The Confessions*. Translated by Edward Bouverie Pusey. In *Augustine*, edited by Robert Maynard Hutchins et al., 1–125. Great Books of the Western World 18. Chicago: Encyclopaedia Britannica, 1952.

Avison, Margaret. *Always Now: The Collected Poems of Margaret Avison*. 3 vols. Toronto: Porcupine's Quill, 2003–5.

Balthasar, Hans urs von. "A Résumé of My Thought." Translated by Kelly Hamilton. *Communio* 15 (1988) 468–73. https://www.communio-icr.com/files/1988_Winter_Balthasar_-_a_resume.pdf.

———. *Seeing the Form*. Vol. 1 of *The Glory of the Lord: A Theological Aesthetics*. San Francisco: Ignatius, 1982.

Cavallin, Clemens. *On the Edge of Infinity: A Biography of Michael D. O'Brien*. San Francisco: Ignatius, 2017.

Champion, C. P., and Tom Flanagan. *Grave Error: How the Media Misled Us (and The Truth About Residential Schools)*. Self-published, 2023.

Chesterton, G. K. *The Ballad of the White Horse*. San Francisco: Ignatius, 2001.

Dante. *The Divine Comedy*. Translated by Dorothy L. Sayers. 3 vols. Penguin Classics. London: Penguin, 1962.

Felsenthal, Edward. "The Choice." *Time*, Dec. 24–31, 2018. https://time.com/person-of-the-year-2018-the-guardians-choice/.

Greene, Graham. *The End of the Affair*. London: Heinemann, 1951.

Gregory, Brad S. *The Unintended Reformation: How a Religious Revolution Secularized Society*. Cambridge, MA: Harvard University Press, 2012.

Hopkins, Gerard Manley. *The Poems of Gerard Manley Hopkins*. Edited by W. H. Gardner and N. H. Mackenzie. London: Oxford University Press, 1967.

Hren, Joshua. *Contemplative Realism: A Theological-Aesthetical Manifesto*. San Francisco: Benedict XVI Institute, 2022.

Huxley, Aldous. *"Brave New World" and "Brave New World Revisited."* New York: Vintage, 2007.

Jeffrey, David Lyle, and Gregory Maillet. *Christianity and Literature: Philosophical Foundations and Critical Practice*. Christian Worldview Integration Series. Downers Grove, IL: IVP Academic, 2011.

John Paul II. *Abbà Pater*. Sony Classical 0617052003, 1999, compact disc.

———. *The Acting Person: A Contribution to Phenomenological Anthropology*. Analecta Husserliana 10. New York: Springer, 1979.

———. "Letter of His Holiness Pope John Paul II to Artists." Vatican, Apr. 4, 1999. https://www.vatican.va/content/john-paul-ii/en/letters/1999/documents/hf_jp-ii_let_23041999_artists.html.

———. *Redemptor Hominis*. Ottawa: Canadian Conference of Catholic Bishops, 1979.

Lewis, C. S. *The Abolition of Man*. Complete C. S. Lewis Signature Classics. New York: HarperOne, 2002.

Lubac, Henri de. *Catholicism: Christ and the Common Destiny of Man*. Translated by Lancelot C. Sheppard and Elizabeth Englund. San Francisco: Ignatius, 1988.

Marcel, Gabriel. *The Mystery of Being*. Translated by G. S. Fraser. London: Harvill, 1951.

Maritain, Jacques. *"Art and Scholasticism": With Other Essays*. Translated by J. F. Scanlan. London: Sheed & Ward, 1930.

Martin, Malachi. *Vatican: A Novel*. New York: Harper and Row, 1986.

McGrew, Lydia. "What We're Reading: *A Cry of Stone*." What's Wrong with the World, July 10, 2012. http://www.whatswrongwiththeworld.net/2012/07/what_were_reading_a_cry_of_sto.html.

Nichols, Aiden. *No Bloodless Myth: A Guide Through Balthasar's Dramatics*. Introduction to Hans Urs von Balthasar. Washington, DC: Catholic University of America Press, 2000.

O'Brien, Michael D. *The Art of Michael D. O'Brien*. San Francisco: Ignatius, 2020.

———. *By the Rivers of Babylon*. San Francisco: Ignatius, 2022.

———. *A Cry of Stone*. San Francisco: Ignatius, 2003.

———. *Eclipse of the Sun*. San Francisco: Ignatius, 1998.

———. *Elijah in Jerusalem*. San Francisco: Ignatius, 2015.

———. *The Family & the New Totalitarianism*. Menomonee, WI: Wiseblood—Divine Providence, 2019.

———. *Father Elijah: An Apocalypse*. San Francisco: Ignatius, 1996.

———. *A Father's Tale*. San Francisco: San Francisco: Ignatius, 2011.

———. *The Fool of New York City*. San Francisco: Ignatius, 2016.

———. *Island of the World*. San Francisco: Ignatius, 2007.

———. *A Landscape with Dragons*. San Francisco: Ignatius, 1998.

———. *Letter to the Future: A Novel*. San Francisco: Ignatius, 2025.

———. *The Lighthouse*. San Francisco: Ignatius, 2020.

———. *Plague Journal*. San Francisco: Ignatius, 1999.

———. *The Sabbatical*. San Francisco: Ignatius, 2021.

———. "The Scandals and the Shepherds." In *Abuse of Sexuality in the Catholic Church*, by Gabriele Kuby, 92–124. Belmont, NC: Wiseblood—Divine Providence, 2019.

———. *Sophia House*. San Francisco: Ignatius, 2005.

———. *Strangers and Sojourners*. San Francisco: Ignatius, 1997.

———. *Theophilos*. San Francisco: Ignatius, 2010.

———. *Voyage to Alpha Centauri*. San Francisco: Ignatius, 2013.

"O Canada." Wikipedia, last edited June 13, 2025. https://en.wikipedia.org/wiki/O_Canada.

O'Connor, Flannery. "Letter to A. [Elizabeth Hester]." In *The Habit of Being: Letters of Flannery O'Connor*, edited by Sally Fitzgerald, 97–99. New York: Farrar, Strauss & Giroux, 1979.

Orwell, George. *1984*. San Diego: Harcourt Brace Jovanovich, 1977.

Pearce, Joseph. "A New Catholic Literary Revival?" Benedict XVI Institute, May 30, 2018. https://benedictinstitute.org/2018/05/new-catholic-literary-revival/.

Sarah, Robert Cardinal. *The Power of Silence: Against the Dictatorship of Noise*. With Nicolas Diat. San Francisco: Ignatius, 2017.
Shakespeare, William. *Hamlet*. In *William Shakespeare: The Complete Works*, edited by Stanley Wells and Gary Taylor, 653–90. Oxford: Clarendon, 1988.
———. *A Midsummer Night's Dream*. In *William Shakespeare: The Complete Works*, edited by Stanley Wells and Gary Taylor, 311–34. Oxford: Clarendon, 1988.
———. *Othello*. In *William Shakespeare: The Complete Works*, edited by Stanley Wells and Gary Taylor, 819–54. Oxford: Clarendon, 1988.
Solzhenitsyn, Alexander. "A World Split Apart." In *Finding God at Harvard: Spiritual Journeys of Christian Thinkers*, edited by Kelly Monroe, 95–102. Grand Rapids: Zondervan, 1977.
Tolkien, J. R. R. "Mythopoeia." In *Tree and Leaf: Including "Mythopoeia,"* 97–101. New York: Harper Collins, 1988.
———. *The Letters of J. R. R. Tolkien*. Edited by Humphrey Carpenter and Christopher Tolkien. Rev. ed. London: HarperCollins, 2024.
———. *The Lord of the Rings*. 50th anniv. ed. London: HarperCollins, 2005.
Whitman, Walt. "Out of the Cradle Endlessly Rocking." In *Leaves of Grass*, edited by Harold W. Blodgett and Sculley Bradley, 246–53. New York: Norton, 1965.

www.ingramcontent.com/pod-product-compliance
Lightning Source LLC
Chambersburg PA
CBHW051058230426
43667CB00013B/2352